Winning at the Track

David L. Christopher

First Edition: June, 1983
Second Edition: May, 1985
Third Edition: April, 1987
Fourth Edition: June, 1989
Fifth Edition: May, 1991

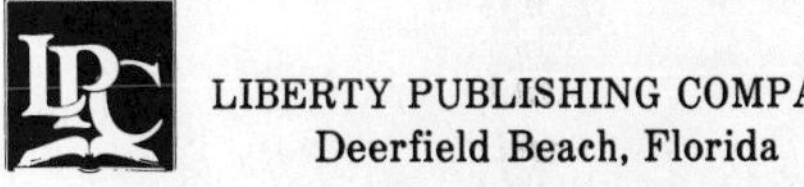

LIBERTY PUBLISHING COMPANY
Deerfield Beach, Florida

Published by:
Liberty Publishing Company, Inc.
440 South Federal Highway
Deerfield Beach, Florida 33441

Library of Congress #83-81134
ISBN 0-89709-195-7

Publisher's Note

Although great care has been taken to present factual and accurate information, both Liberty Publishing Company, Inc. and The Daily Racing Form, Inc. do not assume responsibility for the methodology and/or the accuracy of the material presented herein. Moreover, both publishers and the author will not be responsible for any resulting losses or profits in the past, present or future.

Manufactured USA

Horse Sense is what keeps horses from betting on what people do.

Contents

Preface

Just mention to someone that you have a method to win at the track and watch the reaction. It's doubtful that you will be taken seriously from that moment on. I know. For more than twenty years I've lived with it. But that's okay. I just smile and walk away..."laughing all the way to the bank," as the saying goes.

This book offers a practical and reliable method of handicapping thoroughbreds. I truly believe it to be the best yet devised by Man. The genesis of the system, which I call the "Performance Method," was formulated by a fraternity brother and me during our summer break in 1962. My weekend winnings at the track helped me financially when I was in college and in my early, penny-pinching years of marriage. Handicapping is a hobby that still gives me many hours of great pleasure and a financial reward as well.

As the years have passed, this handicapping method has been revised, refined and retested many times. And now, with a personal computer, many desirable adjustments that were much too time-consuming to be done by hand can be made with just the push of a button. Of course, not everyone has such a machine available, so this book presents the *Performance Method* in two forms. First, is a reliable "shortcut" version for people who do not yet have access to a computer; and then there is a second version presented in greater detail for those who do. The horses' past performances are merely entered into the computer and the selections can be made quickly and easily.

There are two significant advantages the *Performance Method* has over all others that I've seen: (1) it is *trustworthy;* and (2) final selections are based mostly on hard facts and statistics, and less on judgment.

With this method, you cannot win *every* time you go to the track. But, based on many years of personal experience, the probability of returning home with money in your pocket is good. Of course, there is no guarantee that the method will be as successful in the future as it has been in the past. But, in the final analysis, as with any method, you (and your bank account) will be the final judge!

David L. Christopher

Basics to Know

Most readers of this book are acquainted with thoroughbred racing, know how to read the racing tables and are very much "at home" at the track. However, for those readers with less experience, here is a review of some of the basics.

Just as an hour is divided into sixty minutes, in racing, a minute is divided into fifths of a second. This is especially convenient since a horse, running at full speed will cover a 1/4 mile distance (1320 feet) in roughly 25 seconds . . . or about the length of its body in 1/5 of a second. This means that a horse that runs, for example, 4 lengths behind the winner at the finish line, has a time 4/5 of a second slower than the winner. This horse will also have a "Speed Rating" of 4 points lower than the winner (a concept that will be explained later in this chapter).

Another interesting and useful observation: a close look at racing statistics over the years suggests that the weight carried by a horse during a race can affect the horse's speed by as much as 2/5 of a second—and, thus the outcome by as much as two to four lengths. There is a limit to what weight can do, or not do, to a horse's performance, of course. But, in any case, this method assumes that a horse's run can vary by as much as two lengths, or 2/5 of a second, per race when weight is added or deducted from any prior race. For example, if a horse carrying 115 pounds runs 3/4 of a mile (6 furlongs) in 1:11 4/5, the horse's time might be improved by 2/5 of a second, or 1:11 2/5, if the horse carries at least seven pounds less (i.e., not more than 108 pounds). Conversely, if the animal has to carry 122 pounds or more, the time could be 2/5 of a second slower, or 1:12 1/5. It's significant though, since many races can be decided by inches. Most weight changes are modest from one race to the next and some horses are simply stronger and more capable of carrying weight than others. Therefore, it can be said that weight is an important, but not necessarily critical factor . . . but enough so to be taken into consideration before the race begins.

The best source of statistics is the *Daily Racing Form.* It is, for people in this business, what the *Wall Street Journal* is for investors in the stock market. The *Racing Form* tells, among other details, the recent background statistics of each horse in the race. For example, it shows the outcome of the past several races in which each horse ran. It tells which horse won, placed, and showed, as well as how well the other horses in today's race fared in their past races. It also explains past track conditions for those races, how much weight was carried and, of course, how fast the horse ran each time out.

Each issue of the *Daily Racing Form* describes how to read the tables. Therefore, emphasis here will be on extracting, understanding, and making the most of the details that make the *Performance Method* work.

5 HIALEAH — 6 FURLONGS HIALEAH

6 FURLONGS. (1.08⅗) CLAIMING. Purse $7,000. 4-year-olds and upward. Weights, 122 lbs. Non-winners of two races since February 5 allowed 2 lbs. A race since then 4 lbs. A race since January 29, 6 lbs. Claiming Price $16,000 for each $1,000 to $14,000, 2 lbs. (Races where entered for $12,500 or less not considered.) (Red. Florida Breds Preferred.)

Medeiros — Ch. g. 4, by The Big Boss—Cussin' Queen, by Saidam — $16,000 — Br.—Palumbo V A (Md) — Tr.—Steen H Kirk Jr — Own.—Cerulean Farm — 116 — Lifetime 22 3 3 0 $20,765 — 1983 2 0 0 0 $155 — 1982 20 3 3 0 $20,610

30Mar83- 8Hia fst 6f :22⅘ :46⅕ 1:11⅘ Clm 16000 8 5 53½ 43 22 62¾ Rujano M b 116 30.10 82-19 China Village 116hd Clinebell 113½ Deb's Playboy114no Weakened 12
17Feb83-10GP gd 6f :22 :45⅕ 1:11 Clm 15000 8 9 99 1015 911 711 Rujano M b 117 61.00 73-24 Bul Libra 110¾ Governor Bob 117½ Clinebell 117no No speed 10
29Nov82- 7Suf fst 6f :22⅘ :46⅗ 1:13 3+Clm 16000 9 11 87 99 911 75¾ Bush W V b 114 11.00 70-24 China Village 1191 House Odds 114½ Solo Ace 117¾ Outrun 12
5Nov82- 9Suf sly 6f :22⅘ :46⅗ 1:13⅘ Clm 22500 4 2 33 44 46½ 48 Bush W V b 114 4.10 66-31 Wig Gala 1142 Nu Jacques 1192 Power Rig 1194 No rally 5
15Oct82- 9Suf fst 6f :22⅘ :46⅗ 1:13⅘ Clm 22500 2 2 21 22½ 22½ 21½ Gambardella C b 114 4.80 71-31 Power Rig 1141½ Medeiros 114hd Twogun Kenny 114½ Mild rally 5
1Oct82- 9Suf fst 6f :22⅘ :45⅘ 1:12 Clm 22500 8 1 46½ 57 55 45½ Gambardella C b 114 4.20 75-26 Kasha 1193 Power Rig 1142 Hit Parade 114½ No factor 8
17Sep82- 9Suf fst 6f :22⅘ :46⅘ 1:12⅘ 3+Clm c-15000 5 3 34½ 3no 13½ 11½ Penney J C5 b 109 5.10 77-29 Medeiros 1091½ Drink N Think 1143FederalHillStar1101½ Drew off 10
6Sep82-12Suf fst 6f :22⅘ :46⅗ 1:12⅕ 3+Alw 8500 6 5 52¾ 66¾ 68¾ 57¾ Reed J E5 b 106 25.40 72-26 Jolley Charlie 1121½ Sanfoin 114hd Lucrative Way 1141 Tired 7
30Aug82- 9Suf fst 6f :22⅘ :45⅘ 1:12⅘ 3+Alw 8500 5 2 21½ 45 55½ 54¾ Penney J C5 b 106 7.00 73-27 Quiet Monster 116½ Lucrative Way 1142½ B. K.'s Bid 1131¾ Tired 5
12Aug82- 9Suf fst 6f :22⅘ :45⅘ 1:12⅘ 3+Clm 15000 1 3 42½ 33½ 33½ 1½ Penney J C5 b 109 1.90 80-20 Medeiros 109½ Wig Gala 1121½ Trial Judge 1142¾ Driving 6
LATEST WORKOUTS Mar 6 Hia 4f fst :48⅗ h Feb 15 Hia 4f fst :49 b Feb 9 Hia 5f fst 1:02⅗ b

Fiesty Fleet — B. f. 4, by Menocal—Fleet Street, by Fleet Nasrullah — $16,000 — Br.—Marston Lauren S (Fla) — Tr.—Jamtgaard Wayne — Own.—Birchminster Farms — 104[7] — Lifetime 11 1 0 1 $6,020 — 1983 1 0 0 0 $80 — 1982 10 1 0 1 $5,940

19Mar83- 8Hia fst 6f :22⅕ :45⅕ 1:11⅕ ⒻClm 25000 10 6 87½ 89¼ 1112 1012 Gurkas L H7 b 109 10.00 75-14 Her Soir 1162½ Suzy Greene 114¾ Nacunda 1161 Outrun 11
16Dec82- 5Crc fst 6f :22⅘ :47 1:12⅘ 3+Md 20000 1 4 3nk 12 15 19 Gurkas L H10 b 106 7.00 88-18 Fiesty Fleet 1069 Star of Heaven 1191½ComeOnCabin115½ Driving 7
2Dec82- 2Crc fst 6½f :22⅘ :46⅗ 1:20⅘ 3+ⒻMd Sp Wt 4 8 41½ 32 33 38 Gurkas L H10 b 111 33.30 75-21 Made Glorious 1211½ Antic Hay 1224½ Fiesty Fleet 111¾ Evenly 8
28Aug82- 4Mth fst 6f :22⅘ :45 1:11⅕ 3+ⒻMd 35000 8 10 88¾ 910 815 711 Gurkas L H10 b 107 8.40 73-14 Lady Lizzy 1171½ Hex On You 1151½ Come Upstairs 1146 Outrun 10
17Aug82- 4Mth fst 6f :22⅘ :46⅕ 1:11⅘ 3+ⒻMd 40000 6 12 107½ 76 59 411 Gurkas L H10 b 107 15.90 70-22 Classy Nancy 1123½ Insouciance 1107 Acceptor 117¾ Unruly early 12
7Aug82- 4Mth fst 6f :22⅕ :45⅗ 1:12⅕ 3+ⒻMd Sp Wt 7 3 51¾ 44½ 44 63½ Patterson G b 117 65.70 75-15 Petet Gold 117no Raise Rain 1171½ Acceptor 1172 No threat 12
10Jly82- 4Mth fst 6f :22⅘ :45⅘ 1:11⅕ 3+ⒻMd Sp Wt 9 2 21 42½ 47 410 Patterson G b 116 65.60 74-12 Arrived Late 1162 La Reine Noir 116no Pretty Barbie 1162 Tired 11
30Jun82- 9Mth fst 1⅙ :46⅗ 1:11 1:46⅘ 3+ⒻMd Sp Wt 10 1 31½ 411 1020 1019 Patterson G b 114 62.00 54-17 Class Night 1181½ Iceland Spar 114hd Happy Hour Bid 1142 Tired 10
12Jun82- 4Mth fst 6f :22⅕ :45⅘ 1:11⅘ 3+ⒻMd Sp Wt 7 3 51½ 66 811 913 Patterson G b 115 51.40 68-17 Casual 1157 Petet Gold 1151½ Leematt Sue 115½ Tired 12
24Feb82- 6Hia fst 6f :22⅘ :46⅕ 1:12⅕ ⒻMd Sp Wt 3 6 43 54 911 1220 Nemeti W b 120 159.50 62-19 May Day Eighty 1204½ Illiana 1204½ Nettlesome120½ Sp'd for half 12
LATEST WORKOUTS Mar 4 Hia 7f fst 1:31 b

Shortcut To Fame — Gr. h. 5, by On To Glory—Cut It Short, by Nearctic — $15,000 — Br.—Meadowbrook Farm Inc (Fla) — Tr.—Rosas-Canessa Walter — Own.—Rogers Rachel & A S — 118 — Lifetime 58 5 12 5 $57,995 — 1983 7 2 1 0 $11,580 — 1982 19 0 3 3 $10,450 — Turf 7 0 2 0 $4,230

19Mar83-11Hia fst 6f :22⅘ :45 1:10 Clm 19000 10 1 75½ 510 910 1014 Soto S B 114 3.60 79-18 Rufame 116no Gust of Reason 1164½ Jes Tactics 120hd Outrun 11
10Mar83- 8Hia fst 6f :22⅕ :45⅕ 1:10⅘ Clm 14000 11 1 41¾ 43½ 41¾ 1no Soto S B 112 15.60 90-17 Shortcut ToFame112noBulLibra120noFragrantPrince1162½ Driving 12
3Mar83- 2GP fst 6f :22⅘ :46 1:12 Clm 10000 4 2 2hd 1hd 11½ 1½ Soto S B 117 12.90 79-23 Shortcut ToFame117½AngelLike1124½Sadair'sRobler1171½ Driving 12
17Feb83-10GP gd 6f :22 :45⅕ 1:11 Clm 14000 6 2 55½ 69 811 812 Lynch H D5 108 31.00 72-24 Bul Libra 110¾ Governor Bob 117½ Clinebell 117no No speed 10
4Feb83- 5GP fst 6f :22⅘ :45⅘ 1:11⅕ Clm 18000 11 1 89¾ 1113 1013 1012 Solis A5 108 11.00 71-25 Tribal Warrior 1171 Green Path 1171½ Estallido 1141 Outrun 12
29Jan83- 2GP fst 7f :22⅘ :45⅘ 1:24⅘ Clm 19000 6 2 43½ 55½ 57½ 911 Solis A5 110 3.40 71-20 Delta Law 1142½ Erodoto 1191½ Green Path 1171½ Dropped back 11
14Jan83- 5GP fst 6f :22⅘ :45⅘ 1:11 Clm 17000 2 6 64½ 63 41¾ 2no Solis A5 110 7.00 84-20 Pilar'sFlint117noShortcutToFame1101½FstChnge115½ Just missed 12
31Dec82-10Crc fst 6½f :22⅘ :45⅘ 1:18⅘ 3+Clm 17000 5 5 31½ 42¾ 44 86½ Saumell L 115 36.60 84-20 Southern Swing 1161 Fragrant Prince 1152 Rufame 1202 Tired 11
22Dec82- 6Crc fst 6f :22 :45⅘ 1:12 3+Clm 18000 5 2 85¾ 710 811 811 Saumell L 114 23.90 81-17 Rufame 112½ Nocturnal Phantom 1111½ More Dames 1161 Outrun 11
11Sep82- 3Crc fst 7f :22⅕ :45⅘ 1:26 3+Clm 20000 7 1 44 43½ 46 53 Soto S B 112 23.90 83-14 Kentucky Edd 109½ Young Knave 115hd Laughing Kas 113½ Tired 8
LATEST WORKOUTS Feb 26 Crc 5f fst 1:03⅘ h (d)

Big Time Coming — B. g. 5, by Loco Kid—Loey, by Federal Hill — $16,000 — Br.—Johnston E C Jr (Ark) — Tr.—Maziarz Rosemary — Own.—Lucky Clover Fm &Maziarz R — 116 — Lifetime 29 8 4 5 $38,565 — 1983 3 1 0 0 $5,250 — 1982 18 5 2 5 $23,515

10Mar83- 8Hia fst 6f :22⅕ :45⅕ 1:10⅘ Clm 16000 8 3 2hd 2hd 2hd 42¾ MacBeth D 116 7.20 87-17 ShortcutToFame112noBulLibra120noFrgrntPrince1162½ Weakened 12
20Mar83- 4GP fst 6f :22⅘ :46 1:11⅘ Clm 20000 3 3 53¾ 611 68 612 Velez J A Jr 117 10.80 70-24 CapewayCarlo1221RoughDuck115noPleasantDocJ.1151½ No factor 10
3Jan83- 2Crc fst 6f :22 :45⅘ 1:12⅘ Clm c-12500 3 5 1½ 1hd 11½ 1hd Astorga C 120 *1.10 90-16 Big Time Coming120hdPowhatanPrince1164½BulLibra105½ Driving 7
18Dec82- 4Crc fst 6f :22⅕ :46⅕ 1:12 3+Clm 11000 9 1 1½ 11 12 15 Astorga C 118 3.60 92-13 BigTimeComing1185ⒹFriendlyCard108½Dartanin1202½ Ridden out 11
23Nov82-10Crc fst 6f :22⅘ :46⅕ 1:12⅕ 3+Clm 16000 8 2 1hd 2½ 1hd 42¾ Astorga C 120 14.60 89-17 MoreDmes106nkNocturnlPhntom115noJmesPride1161½ Weakened 9
15Nov82- 8Crc fst 6f :22⅕ :46⅕ 1:13⅘ 3+Clm 17000 7 3 3nk 2hd 33½ 65 Astorga C 115 7.90 80-21 SirThomasCutlss115½Rufme1091½NocturnlPhntom1153 Weakened 8
3Nov82- 1Crc fst 6f :22⅕ :46⅕ 1:13 3+Clm 13000 5 4 1½ 1½ 1hd 1hd Acevedo D A5 115 6.10 87-21 Big Time Coming 115hd SplitTiming117noFirstValley1141½ Driving 8
22Oct82- 5Crc fst 6f :22⅘ :46⅕ 1:12⅘ 3+Clm 12500 1 4 11 11 11½ 1no Acevedo D A5 109 4.90 91-16 Big Time Coming 109no Fast Change1181½FirstValley1182 Driving 8
13Oct82- 6Crc fst 6f :22⅕ :45⅘ 1:12⅘ 3+Clm 10000 6 1 2hd 1hd 1hd 21 Acevedo D A5 113 4.70 87-24 Buck'n'Shoe1091BigTimeComing1132LughingRlty116½ Weakened 8
28Sep82-10Crc fst 6f :22⅘ :45⅘ 1:12 3+Clm 14000 4 3 2½ 23 36 65¾ Acevedo D A5 109 6.80 86-15 Sadair's Robler 1092½ First Valley 118½ Appealer 1102 Faltered 7
LATEST WORKOUTS ●Feb 28 Hia 3f sly :36 b Feb 20 Hia 3f fst :37 b Feb 10 Hia 4f fst :51 b

Gold Limit — Dk. b. or br. g. 4, by Limit To Reason—Gold Gala, by Gallant Man — $15,000 — Br.—Marriott P M (Ky) — Tr.—Simms Phillip G — Own.—Golden Acres Inc — 118 — Lifetime 40 10 6 7 $72,310 — 1983 6 1 0 2 $7,210 — 1982 18 1 4 3 $21,790 — Turf 1 0 0 0 $130

Entered 4Apr83- 1 HIA
29Mar83- 5Hia fst 6f :22⅘ :46 1:11⅘ Clm 12500 5 6 44 33½ 21½ 11 Castaneda K 116 3.00 85-18 Gold Limit 1161 Mike Ralph 116hd Twogun Kenny 1161 Driving 10
15Feb83-10GP fst 7f :22⅘ :45⅘ 1:23⅘ Clm 20000 9 4 62¾ 64½ 54 75½ Velez J A Jr 117 3.50 80-23 Limerick 1151 Wooster Sq. 117½ Pleasant Doc J. 1153 No factor 12
7Feb83- 5GP gd 6f :22⅘ :46 1:11⅘ Clm 22500 2 3 2½ 31 21 42¾ Velez J A Jr 115 7.40 81-21 Hot Words 1171 ⒹNocturnal Phantom 117¾ Freedom Lad 113½ 12
7Feb83-Placed third through disqualification
29Jan83- 9GP fst 1⅙ :46⅗ 1:11⅘ 1:45 3+Inv Alw 5 2 21½ 43½ 1013 1013 Castaneda K 117 14.20 63-20 ⒹSouthern Swing 117¾ Kan Reason 122hdCanuck117hd Gave Way 12
25Jan83-10GP fst 6f :23 :46⅗ 1:10⅘ Clm 27500 2 6 73¾ 75½ 55 47 Capodici J 115 19.10 78-21 Intercontinnt115hdIrishSwords1175½Pokr'N'Chips1121½ No factor 11
3Jan83- 8Crc fst 7f :23 :46⅗ 1:25⅘ Clm 25000 1 6 2½ 2hd 1½ 32 Capodici J 116 *1.70 85-16 Tumiga's Flame 1141 The Fugitive 1161 Gold Limit 1164½ Tired 9
24Dec82- 8Crc fst 7f :22⅘ :45⅕ 1:24⅘ 3+Clm 30000 2 5 3nk 21½ 22 34¾ Castaneda K 115 3.60 88-19 Kentucky Edd 1212½ Iron Gladiator1152GoldLimit1154 Weakened 10
20Dec82- 7Crc fst 7f :23 :46⅗ 1:24⅘ 3+Clm 45000 6 1 53¾ 65½ 47 46¾ Castaneda K 116 4.30 86-15 Pokr'N'Chips112hdSomthngWrong1164½RllyFunny1152½ No f ctor 7
11Dec82- 8Crc fst 7f :22⅘ :46⅗ 1:25⅕ 3+Alw 14000 6 1 2hd 2½ 1hd 22½ Castaneda K 115 11.90 88-16 Mr Mar J Mar 1092½ Gold Limit 115hd Sonofagov 1191½ Gamely 8
29Nov82- 7Crc fst 7f :23⅕ :46⅗ 1:24⅘ 3+Clm 30000 2 3 31½ 32 22 24½ Castaneda K 116 2.00 88-17 Kentucky Edd 1104½ Gold Limit 1161 Donna's Boy 1157½ Gamely 5

This is a typical past performance table. **Gold Limit** is a horse that appeared at three different tracks over the past several months:

Gold Limit — Dk. b. or br. g. 4, by Limit To Reason—Gold Gala, by Gallant Man — **118**

Own.—Golden Acres Inc — $15,000 — Br.—Marriott P M (Ky) — Tr.—Simms Phillip G

Lifetime: 40 10 6 7 — $72,310

Year	Starts	1st	2nd	3rd	Earnings
1983	6	1	0	2	$7,210
1982	18	1	4	3	$21,750
Turf	1	0	0	0	$130

Entered 4Apr83- 1 HIA

Date/Race	Track	Dist	Fractions	Class	PP	St	1/4	1/2	Str	Fin	Jockey	Wt	Odds	Speed	Company Line	Comment	Field
25Mar83- 5Hia	fst	6f	:22⅖ :46 1:11⅗	Clm 12500	5	6	4^4	$3^{3\frac{1}{2}}$	$2^{1\frac{1}{2}}$	1^1	Castaneda K	116	3.00	85-18	Gold Limit 116^1 Mike Ralph 116^{hd} Twogun Kenny 116^1	Driving	10
15Feb83-10GP	fst	7f	:22⅖ :45⅖ 1:23⅘	Clm 20000	9	4	$6^{2\frac{3}{4}}$	$6^{4\frac{1}{4}}$	5^4	$7^{5\frac{1}{2}}$	Velez J A Jr	117	3.50	80-23	Limerick 115^1 Wooster Sq. $117^{\frac{1}{2}}$ Pleasant Doc J. 115^3	No factor	12
7Feb83- 5GP	gd	6f	:22⅗ :46 1:11⅕	Clm 22500	2	3	$2^{\frac{1}{2}}$	3^1	2^1	$4^{2\frac{1}{4}}$	Velez J A Jr	115	7.40	81-21	Hot Words 117^1 [D]Nocturnal Phantom $117^{\frac{3}{4}}$ Freedom Lad $113^{\frac{1}{2}}$		12
7Feb83-Placed third through disqualification																	
29Jan83- 9GP	fst	$1\frac{1}{16}$	:46⅖ 1:11⅖ 1:45	3↑ Inv Alw	5	2	$2^{1\frac{1}{2}}$	$4^{3\frac{1}{2}}$	10^{13}	10^{13}	Castaneda K	117	14.20	63-20	[D]Southern Swing $117^{\frac{3}{4}}$ Kan Reason 122^{hd}Canuck117^{hd}	Gave Way	12
25Jan83-10GP	fst	6f	:23 :46⅖ 1:10⅘	Clm 27500	2	6	$7^{3\frac{3}{4}}$	$7^{5\frac{1}{4}}$	5^5	4^7	Capodici J	115	19.10	78-21	Intercontinnt115^{hd}IrishSwords$117^{5\frac{1}{2}}$Pokr'N'Chips$112^{1\frac{1}{2}}$	No factor	11
3Jan83- 8Crc	fst	7f	:23 :46⅗ 1:25⅘	Clm 25000	1	6	$2^{\frac{1}{2}}$	2^{hd}	$1^{\frac{1}{2}}$	3^2	Capodici J	116	*1.70	85-16	Tumiga's Flame 114^1 The Fugitive 116^1 Gold Limit $116^{4\frac{1}{2}}$	Tired	9
24Dec82- 8Crc	fst	7f	:22⅖ :45⅕ 1:24⅗	3↑ Clm 30000	2	5	3^{nk}	$2^{1\frac{1}{2}}$	2^2	$3^{4\frac{1}{2}}$	Castaneda K	115	3.60	88-19	Kentucky Edd $121^{2\frac{1}{2}}$ Iron Gladiator115^2GoldLimit115^6	Weakened	10
20Dec82- 7Crc	fst	7f	:23 :46⅖ 1:24⅗	3↑ Clm 45000	6	1	$5^{3\frac{3}{4}}$	$6^{5\frac{3}{4}}$	4^7	$4^{6\frac{3}{4}}$	Castaneda K	116	4.30	86-15	Pokr'N'Chips112^{hd}SomthngWrong$116^{4\frac{1}{2}}$RllyFunny$115^{2\frac{1}{2}}$	No factor	7
11Dec82- 8Crc	fst	7f	:22⅗ :46⅖ 1:25⅕	3↑ Alw 14000	6	1	2^{hd}	$2^{\frac{1}{2}}$	1^{hd}	$2^{2\frac{1}{2}}$	Castaneda K	115	11.90	88-16	Mr. Mar J. Mar $109^{2\frac{1}{2}}$ Gold Limit 115^{hd} Sonofagov $119^{1\frac{1}{2}}$	Gamely	8
29Nov82- 7Crc	fst	7f	:23⅕ :46⅘ 1:24⅗	3↑ Clm 30000	2	3	$3^{1\frac{1}{2}}$	3^2	2^2	$2^{4\frac{1}{2}}$	Castaneda K	116	2.00	88-17	Kentucky Edd $110^{4\frac{1}{2}}$ Gold Limit 116^1 Donna's Boy $115^{7\frac{1}{2}}$	Gamely	5

The most recent race, which **Gold Limit** won, is highlighted. The race occurred on March 25th. It was the 5th race at Hialeah. That day, the track was rated "fast," and it was a 6 furlongs (3/4 mile) race. The newspaper reported three "splits" (also called "fractional times")— :22 2/5, :46, and 1:11 3/5. The horse (not **Gold Limit**) that led at the quarter pole (2 furlongs) posted a time of 22 2/5 seconds. At the half mile pole (4 furlongs), the leader (again, not **Gold Limit**) had a time of 46 seconds. Our winner, **Gold Limit,** had a final time of 1 minute 11 3/5 seconds. The paper also shows that **Gold Limit** was in post position 5 and was in sixth place after leaving the gate. At the quarter pole, he was fourth, 4 lengths behind the leader. At the half mile pole, he was third, 3 1/2 lengths behind the leader. In the stretch, 1/8 mile from the finish line, **Gold Limit** was second, 1 1/2 lengths behind the leader. He won the race finishing 1 length ahead of the second place horse, Mike Ralph. Using these figures, **Gold Limit**'s time performances at each point in the race can be quickly estimated (:23 1/5 after 2 furlongs, 46 4/5 after four furlongs and 1:11 3/5 at the finish line). **Gold Limit** was carrying 116 pounds on his back that day.

At that time, the track record for 6 furlongs at Hialeah was 1:08 3/5. By running 1:11 3/5, **Gold Limit** was exactly 3 seconds slower than the Hialeah record. Had the horse run 1:08 3/5, he would have had a Speed Rating of "100." For each 1/5 second slower than the record, one point is deducted from 100. Therefore, being 15-fifths below the record, he was awarded a Speed Rating of 85 (100 less 15).

The Track Variant (the number 18 that appears next to the 85 Speed Rating) on the day of that race indicates how much "below par" the winning times of all races were at Hialeah on March 25th. An "18" Track Variant means the average Speed Rating of all the winners that day was 82 (18 points below par). It should be noted that a Track Variant of, say, 30 could be due to a slow or muddy track, or a poor lineup of horses for that day's racing—or both. This point is worth remembering as we move further into the explanation of the *Performance Method.*

Here are a few tidbits of racetrack folklore. Some may be true, some may not. Most are, at least, controversial. Nevertheless, all are worth discussing before continuing.

Many respected trainers believe that every horse has a "best" distance, a distance that can be measured almost in FEET.

This is probably true. Some horses are obviously better suited to sprints, while others run their best in route races. And, as many experienced handicappers know, thoroughbreds' performances can be quite predictable when we measure their ability to adjust from one distance to another or from one track to another. However, this is not, by any means, an exact science!

One old-time saying is: "The pace makes the race."

This is definitely true, but pace is extremely difficult to predict without the *Winning at the Track* software and the new *Pace Analyst* add-on. The pace of the race is often determined by the mix of running styles that comprise the field. As explained in the "Pace" chapter, there are mainly three types of races: 1) One dominant pacesetter; 2) Two pacesetters, one stronger than the other; and 3) Two pacesetters, equal in talent.

It is often said that, in a typical sprint race, the average horse will have only enough energy to run "all out" for about 3/8 of a mile (equal to half of a 6 furlong race, for example).

This is also undoubtedly true, but not very helpful to the handicapper if the horse is not ready to run. The best evidence of the horse's present condition is usually found in the animal's performances within the past sixty or ninety days.

Like chickens, horses have a "pecking order" and already know before they leave the gate which will be the winner.

If this were true, scientists would be working diligently to teach horses to talk. It is true, however, that when a horse "meets its match" during the race, it knows it and frequently gives up more easily than it would otherwise. This is perhaps the most convincing argument in favor of "class" handicapping. But it is not unusual for a horse, well-conditioned and ready to run, to beat a better class horse that is not.

A layoff either means the horse needs a rest or it's hurting.

This saying is usually true and handicappers are forever struggling with this situation. As a general rule, 90 days is a good cutoff time. If the horse is away more than 90 days, the chance is greater there has been an injury – perhaps a serious one. Regarding this subject, and other possible trainer patterns, consider reading *Handicapping Trainers* by John Whitaker.

The horse's age is not an important factor in handicapping.

This is not necessarily true. David Fogel studied more than 3,500 horses in his book *The Mathematics of Horse Racing* and concluded that three-year-olds tend to do less well against older horses, especially early in the third year, and a horse does begin a sharp decline in ability after the age of seven. Fortunately, no one ever told this to the once-great John Henry!

A New Handicapping Method

"It may be that the race is not always to the swift, nor the battle to the strong—but that's the way to bet!"

Damon Runyon

This quotation describes the *Performance Method* almost perfectly! The objective of the method is simply to select the strongest horses that are in the best condition and ready to win or place. That's it! It does not distinguish between a good jockey and a bad one, or the horse's past winnings, "class," or trainer's record. Nor does the prediction vary if the track is muddy or if the horse happens to draw an inside post position at the gate. Many experienced handicappers will argue that each can be important in selecting winners under certain conditions. While this may all be true, these variables need not be studied to select a winner. Again—the object of the *Performance Method* is to select the strongest horses that are in the best condition and ready to win or place.

When a horse is in a tight spot coming into the stretch, most bettors would much rather have a more experienced jockey aboard rather than an apprentice. But most horses will run a race a little faster with a seven pound allowance and an apprentice up than with a much heavier "experienced" jockey just back from winning the Triple Crown.

There are many tracks where an inside post position offers a decided advantage. But I once saw the great horse, **Dr. Fager,** beat all others in the race by five lengths, carrying a ton on his back, after starting from post position eight. Always bet on the *horse*, not on the gate.

Some horses prefer to run—and win—in the mud. However, with the method described in this book, as you will see, selecting a winner is not necessarily made any more difficult by the inclement weather. Most good horses can win on either a muddy or a fast track if they are stronger and in better condition than the competition.

Rating a horse by its "class" is a worthy challenge for any handicapper. The best method seems to be a comparison of the average purse of each horse in the race (see appendix for the calculation). However, by itself, it does not provide a reliable way to make money, in my opinion.

As any good athlete will attest, there are certain times when a person can run and jump like a deer. There are other days when it would have been better just to stay in bed. It seems to be true with horses also. Although it is the trainer's job to make the most of the situation at hand, it is impossible to keep the horse in top form every week. However, it is unusual for a horse to finish last one week, win the following week, and then be last a week later. It can happen, of course, but usually the form cycle is a little more gradual. And, still, much depends on other factors—including the level of competition and the trainer's strategy and objectives for that particular day. Most owners and trainers would like to win every outing; but they can't and they know it. So, they try to keep the horse ready and "go for it" when they think they can win.

In any given race, there is sometimes an identifiable "best" horse. It may, indeed, be the best in the race. But the horse might not have a prayer of winning today—or perhaps on any day for the next two or three weeks. Four weeks from now, though, it could be ready to beat today's winner "going away," as they say.

To summarize the *Performance Method*, each horse in the race is compared with the others in the contest by analyzing four capabilities. They are:

1. The Ability Factor
2. Pure Speed
3. Early Speed
4. Late Speed

To make calculations easier for those who do not have a computer, the four capabilities listed above are simply combined into two factors: THE ABILITY FACTOR and THE CONDITION FACTOR. Each approach is described fully in its respective section of this book.

Regardless of whether or not a computer is used, the *Performance Method* identifies three or four horses *most likely* to win or place second vis a vis today's competition. Knowing this, we must bet accordingly ... a subject to be covered in a later chapter.

Without a Computer

Introduction

This book was written for two readers: one who owns an IBM Personal Computer (or an IBM-Compatible) and one who has no computer at all, nor any access to one. To a growing number of people who already own or have access to a personal computer, there is a general expectation that many, if not most homes will have one before 1995. While this may eventually be true, it is fair to say that most homes today are not yet so equipped. Moreover, since the *Performance Method* was originally developed many years ago without the aid of a computer, the "shortcut" approach explained in this section requires no apologies. This book can be used with or without a computer.

Included in this section is a full description of the "shortcut" version, an explanation of speed rating adjustments and how to calculate them quickly, plus easy instructions for the *Performance Method* Tables which are completed before going to the track.

Once this "shortcut" is mastered, it will take about 10 to 15 minutes to handicap a typical race with a field of eight or nine horses. If you want to enjoy a full day at the races, plan to spend at least an hour the night before. With this effort and a little luck, it could be a very profitable hour!

The Performance Method: A Shortcut

The Speed Rating Adjustment Table

One key ingredient to the *Performance Method* "Shortcut" is the Speed Rating Adjustment Table which eliminates the differences between one track record and another when comparing Speed Ratings. With this adjustment, if a horse runs 1:09 2/5 for 6 furlongs, regardless of where he runs it, he will be awarded the same Speed Rating (88) as another horse also running 1:09 2/5 on another track.

Each of the following speeds should be used as a basis for conversion:

Distance	Time
1/4 mile	:21 1/5
4 f	:44
4 1/2 f	:50
5 f	:56
5 1/2 f	1:02
6 f	1:07
6 1/2 f	1:13 2/5
7 f	1:20
1 mile	1:32
1 mile 70 yds.	1:37
1 1/16	1:39 1/5
1 1/8	1:46
1 3/16	1:52 2/5
1 1/4	1:58 4/5
1 3/8	2:11 3/5
1 1/2	2:24 2/5

When tables similar to those that follow are constructed for each distance to accommodate the various tracks in your section of the country, simply match the tracks' records against the basis times that appear above. *The Performance Method* will work using either *historic* track records or the tracks' best times for the *past three years* (the figures now being used by the *Daily Racing Form*).

The table below, for example, provides most of the 6 furlong adjustments that were needed to complete the examples in this book:

SPEED RATING ADJUSTMENT TABLE
6F (1:07 BASIS)

TRACK	TRACK RECORD	ADJUSTMENT
Aqueduct	1:08*	-5*
Aqueduct (Inner Track)	1:08 4/5	-9
Atlantic City	1:08 1/5	-6
Belmont Park	1:07 4/5	-4
Bowie (now closed)	1:08	-5
Calder	1:10*	-15*
Delaware	1:08 1/5	-6
Fair Grounds	1:09	-10
Finger Lakes	1:09 1/5	-11
Gulfstream Park	1:07 4/5	-4
Hawthorne	1:08 1/5	-6
Hialeah	1:08*	-5*
Keystone (now Phila.)	1:08 1/5	-6
Laurel	1:08 3/5	-8
Meadowlands	1:08 2/5*	-7*
Monmouth	1:08	-5
Penn National	1:08 4/5	-9
Pimlico	1:09 1/5	-11
Saratoga	1:08	-5
Suffolk Downs	1:08 1/5	-6
Tampa Bay	1:09	-10

**Note: When the examples in this book were completed, the following records were in effect: Calder 1:10 2/5; Hialeah 1:08 3/5; Meadowlands 1:08 3/5; Aqueduct 1:08 1/5.*

Remember, a horse runs the length of his body in about 1/5 of a second. Therefore, a horse would have had a Speed Rating of 85 at Pimlico, for instance, if he ran two lengths behind the winning time of 1:11 4/5. The adjusted Speed Rating would, of course, be 74 (85 less 11), which is 5 1/5 seconds slower than 1:07. If another horse at, say, Monmouth, runs an 85 Speed Rating, it can be easily calculated just how much faster the second horse could be if the two should meet. An 85 Speed Rating at Monmouth would be equivalent to an 80 with a 1:07 basis. There is no guarantee that the second horse will beat the first horse by six lengths if they ever meet in head-to-head competition, but the second horse is probably a better bet, nevertheless.

Below is a table for 7 furlongs. A table can and should be constructed for each distance under study to avoid time-consuming calculations later.

SPEED RATING ADJUSTMENT TABLE
7 F (1:20 BASIS)

TRACK	TRACK RECORD	ADJUSTMENT
Aqueduct	1:20 1/5	−1
Belmont Park	1:20 2/5	−2
Bowie (now closed)	1:20 2/5	−2
Calder	1:23 1/5	−16
Charles Town	1:24	−20
Gulfstream Park	1:20 4/5	−4
Hialeah	1:20 3/5	−3
Keeneland	1:21 1/5	−6
Keystone (now Phila.)	1:21 2/5	−7
Laurel	1:22 1/5	−11
Pimlico	1:26	−30
Saratoga	1:20 2/5	−2

Question:

Based solely on the results of these past 6 furlong speed ratings, which horse would you favor to win today's race, disregarding weight?

Horse from:	Speed Rating
Belmont	80
Monmouth	82
Penn National	83
Gulfstream Park	82
Finger Lakes	81
Aqueduct	79

Answer:

Based only on the above information and the Speed Rating Adjustment Table, the horse that ran at Gulfstream Park should be given the edge, followed by the horses from Monmouth and Belmont. The adjusted Speed Ratings would be as follows:

Horse from:	Adj. Rating
Belmont	76
Monmouth	77
Penn National	74
Gulfstream Park	78
Finger Lakes	70
Aqueduct	74

REMEMBER: Constantly check the accuracy of your Speed Rating Adjustment Tables and be aware of the times on which all speed ratings are based.

Beginning in late 1989, the *Daily Racing Form* began the practice of calculating its Speed Ratings by comparing a horse's running time to "the best time for that distance at that track in the past three years." This means that a Speed Rating appearing in the newspaper in, say, February could be based on a different time than one appearing last December.

It is very important that the Speed Ratings being used are reliable and consistent.

The Track Surface

The Track Variant found in the newspaper is usually a good measure of the track's condition... but not always. Most experienced handicappers realize that the Track Variant for a "fast" track can sometimes be greater than the variant for a "muddy" track. Unusual? Yes. Generally, the reverse is true. A fast track will typically have a variant of about 21, or approximately 4 points below the normal 25 of an "off" track. "Good," "slow," "sloppy," "muddy" or "heavy" are very general terms that represent conditions that can vary widely from track to track, or even from one race to the next on the same day. However, on balance, you will find that the two set variants (+21 for a "fast" track and +25 for an "off" track) to be fair measurements of track conditions—at least for our purposes. These two numerical ratings are useful when we want to judge a horse's speed but not be misled by a Track Variant that may not fairly represent the conditions of the track on that particular day.

Let's return to **Gold Limit,** our earlier example, to see how the Speed Ratings and Track Variants are related and how they can be interpreted. Here are **Gold Limit**'s last three 6 furlong races:

Date	Track	Cond.	GL's Time	Place	Weight	Speed Rating	Track Variant
3/25	Hialeah	fast	1:11 3/5	1st	116	85	18
2/7	Gulfstream	good	1:11 3/5	4th (2)	115	81	21
1/25	Gulfstream	fast	1:12 1/5	4th (7)	115	78	21

It appears that **Gold Limit**'s best showing was the March race, particularly given the fact that he won it. However, in terms of effort, the February race was especially noteworthy. Although you can not tell by the Track Variant figures, the 3/5 of a second improvement in the February time was more significant than the figures indicate. The horse carried the same weight under less favorable conditions and still managed to improve his time. By adjusting the Speed Ratings to a 1:07 basis, the horse had a 74 rating in January, a 77 rating in February, and a 77 rating in March. By adding these figures to the 21 or 25 figures described earlier, the horse's overall efforts become: 95 (74 + 21) in January; 102 (77 + 25) in February; and 98 (77 + 21) in March. In January, **Gold Limit** was 5 lengths behind the leader coming into the stretch and fourth by 7 lengths at the wire. In February, he again placed fourth, but the horse was within striking distance throughout the entire race. (Note, too, that in January, the winner's time was 1:10 4/5; in February, the winner's time was 1:11 1/5). The analysis of these three races suggests that if **Gold Limit** has a good day today, with 118 pounds on his back, over a fast track, he could run a 1:12—or maybe a 1:11 4/5. If he were to carry only 115 pounds, his time today could be closer to 1:11 2/5. By applying the same Speed Rating and Track Variant adjustment methods to the most recent 6 furlong races for *each* horse in today's race, we can begin to compare one horse to another.

It also should be noted that **Gold Limit**'s March effort of 98, when compared to January and February, could never be 100% comparable since the races were run on different tracks. Although the surface differences between Hialeah and Gulfstream are obviously not significant, the same cannot be said for many other tracks in North America. Clearly, this is one of the major advantages of the computer program, described in the other section of this book. The computer automatically provides a track variant for every track surface. For people using this "shortcut" approach, it is possible to improve upon the 21 and 25 variants suggested earlier. However, it will be necessary to compare local track results over time and make the adjustments only through trial and error. Remember, today, the horses in this race will *all* be running on the same track and under the same conditions. Which of these horses are the most likely candidates to win or place? THAT is now the question!

A Measure of Condition

When the horse is ready to run, the Condition Factor will very likely tell us. Simply stated, it places the last meaningful race of each horse in today's contest under a microscope, and allows us to make a comparison.

The Condition Factor deals only with the *last* race, equivalent to today's distance. If the race today is 6 furlongs, we would be concerned only with the prior 6 furlong race. If the horse has never run the distance before, examine, instead, the next-closest distance (eg., 6½ furlongs or 7 furlongs). It is far easier for a horse experienced at 7 furlongs to run the shorter distance than for a horse that has never run longer than 5 furlongs to go that extra 1/8 mile. Sometimes a handicapper is without choice and must take only what is available. Remember, fewer reliable statistics represents greater risk!

Let's once again return to **Gold Limit**, our earlier example. Today, he is expected to carry 118 pounds. His last race appears in the paper as follows:

Date	Track	Track Condition	Weight	Speed Rating	Track Variant
3/25	Hialeah	fast	116	85	18

The fact that **Gold Limit** has run within the past thirty days is a good sign. Some horses lose their edge after a layoff of more than four weeks. Another good sign: This is the second time he is running at Hialeah. It is harder coming cold from another track. And finally, it is also worth noting that his most recent race is the same distance that he will be running today. All of this adds to our confidence that his last race is a fair measure of his current condition.

On the basis of 1:07 (see the Speed Rating Adjustment Table), the 85 Speed Rating becomes 77 (85 less 8 points adjustment for the Hialeah track record at that time).

The track on March 25th was rated "fast" by the track foreman.

Therefore, **Gold Limit**'s adjusted Track Variant becomes 21. Had the track been rated anything other than "fast," **Gold Limit** would have been awarded 25 points for his efforts that day.

The 118 pounds **Gold Limit** is expected to carry today is 2 pounds more than he carried on March 25th. This added weight is a negative that we must take into consideration. However, as before, our adjustments for weight (added or subtracted) cannot exceed two points. Had it been a race shorter than 5 1/2 furlongs, no weight adjustments would be made.

Combining these items together, **Gold Limit**'s Condition Factor for today's race is calculated as follows:

Speed Rating	85
Track Variant	+21
Hialeah Track Adjustment	−8
Weight Adjustment	−2
CONDITION FACTOR	96

Just before post time we learned that **Gold Limit** would be carrying 115 pounds, 3 pounds less than we expected. This is a simple adjustment that takes only a minute or two and is made just before the race begins. The explanation for this minor change appears in the next chapter.

The Condition Factor, like the Ability Factor, knows no time limit. If the last race to be used in our calculations occurred six months ago, so be it. However, it can influence how we bet, as you will see later in the chapter, "Learning from Experience." Ideally, all the horses in today's race have run the same distance as today within the past thirty days. Although it *can* happen, it is less likely for a horse to win after having not raced or having no formal workouts within the past 30 to 60 days. It also goes without saying that handicapping Maiden races can be more difficult since many of the horses have a short statistical history. Finally, it is also more difficult to select winners during the first couple weeks of the new racing season when most of the horses have not run on this surface except in workouts.

The Measure of Ability

If you ask a 100 yard dash track star to run a mile race and then expect to use that performance to predict the outcome of his next 100 yard dash, you might be disappointed. Not all good sprinters can run distance. It's also true with horses. Consequently, the best way to measure a horse's ability is to compare apples with apples. If today's race is 6 furlongs, look at past performances involving only 6 furlong races. The past races of distances greater than 7 furlongs might be important to the trainer and his conditioning program, but the results will probably be of little value when we try to handicap today's 6 furlong race without the use of a computer.

The Ability Factor calculation is defined as:

The three most recent races that best represent the horse's current ability to run today's distance.

The Ability Factor is calculated in the following manner . . .

- If today's race is 6 furlongs, add the Speed Ratings and the Track Variants for the *last three* 6 furlong races. In the earlier example, **Gold Limit**'s total would be 304 (85 + 81 + 78 + 18 + 21 + 21).

- Adjust the total (304) by the weight differences between today's expected weight (118) and the weights of each prior race, *but not more than 2 points per race.* Also, *the total adjustment cannot exceed 4 points.* In this case, the adjustment is 4 points, calculated this way:

118 − 116 = 2
118 − 115 = 2 (Max. wt.)
118 − 115 = 2 (Max. wt.)
Total = 6 (Max. wt. − 4 pts.)

The Ability Factor for **Gold Limit**'s race today is, therefore, 300 (304 less 4).

The calculation of the Ability Factor has no time limit. The last three races may have occurred in the past three weeks, or in the past three months (as in the example of **Gold Limit**), or perhaps even a year ago. The more recent, the better. Disregard all other races. You are only interested in the last three 6 furlong races. If today's race is a 7 furlong race, calculate only the last three 7 furlong races and disregard the others.

Sometimes past statistics are not available to the extent needed. For example, if today's race is 6 furlongs and there are only two past races (four figures) to add, make the calculation, and then multiply the total by 1.5. If there is only one race, add the Speed Rating and the Track Variant for that one race, adjust for the weight, and then multiply by 3. In either case, the results are less than satisfactory, but better than nothing. In the prior example, had **Gold Limit** not run in January, the Ability Factor would have been 302, calculated as follows:

March 25	85 + 18 − 2 = 101	
February 7	81 + 21 − 2 = 100	
	201	× 1.5 = 302

Had **Gold Limit** not run either January or February, the Ability Factor would have been 303 (103 less 2 lbs., multiplied by 3).

Once in a while the necessary statistics are not available at all. To make race selections from the newspaper easier, classify races into these categories . . .

Super Sprints	4 furlongs, 4 1/2 furlongs, and 5 furlongs (Do not add or subtract weight to Super Sprint races);
Sprints	5 1/2 furlongs, 6 furlongs, 6 1/2 furlongs, 7 furlongs, and 1 mile;
Routes	1 mile 70 yards, 1 1/16 miles, 1 1/8 miles, and longer.

Try to restrict your newspaper selections for today's race to the appropriate category of today's contest. Favor longer, rather than shorter distances, and the closer the distance, the better. Memorize this rule: Fewer reliable statistics represents greater risk! If you are not comfortable with the numbers available, do not bet the race.

How to Use the P/M Table

The *Performance Method* Table is the heart of this unique handicapping system. Now, all the details explained earlier in this section—the Speed Rating Adjustments, the Surface Adjustments, the Condition Factor, and the Ability Factor—will come together. This table will help the bettor identify the three or four horses from which the winner and second place horses are likely to emerge. The greatest profits will be made by "boxing" these selections in the exactas and quinellas and playing these horses in daily double combinations. See the chapter, "How To Bet."

Once it is mastered, this table will almost certainly become an indispensable tool. Blank worksheet forms may be ordered at a low cost (see order form in the Appendix).

As a general rule, completing the form prior to the race takes about 10 to 15 minutes. The final adjustments and scratches can be noted quickly and easily, but this information is not readily available until just before the race. Except for horses scratched just before post time, your preliminary selections are usually close to your final choices when the betting windows open. Personally, I prefer to calculate the entire racing schedule the day before going to the track (an Advance Edition of the *Racing Form* is often available a day early). Moreover, early calculations allow me to decide whether to bet the race in the first place. Like many who go to the track, I prefer to win.

If there are any questions regarding the following steps, refer back to pages 9 and 10, as well as pages 25 through 35. In addition, there will be several examples in the next chapter which should answer virtually all questions that arise.

Step 1. For each horse, fill in the basics on the table: the horse's name, the date of the last race, and the weight that will be carried today.

In the newspaper, for each horse, place a check next to each of the three races that will be used to calculate the Ability Factor. Remember, the objective here is to select the three most recent races that *most closely* approximate the distance that will be run today. This checking procedure is not absolutely necessary, but these notations will help you calculate more quickly and to easily return to these figures if any questions arise later. Also, for each horse, underline the most recent race of the same distance as today's race. This is the race that will be used to calculate the horse's Condition Factor.

Step 2. In the appropriate column, enter the total of three Speed Ratings and three Track Variants previously checked. Do not adjust these figures; just enter the *total* of the figures that appear in the newspaper.

Step 3. Calculate the weight differences for those three races from today's race (maximum difference 2 pounds per race). Total the numbers, and enter that figure (maximum 4) in the weight adjustment column. The totals from Step 2 and Step 3 are then combined to produce the Ability Factor which is entered in the next column.

Step 4. For each horse, enter the Speed Rating for the most recent race having the same distance as today's contest. Do not adjust the Speed Rating—use the number as it appears in the newspaper. If this Speed Rating occurred on a "fast" track, enter a "21" in the next column. If it was an "off" track (anything other than a fast track), enter a "25" in that column.

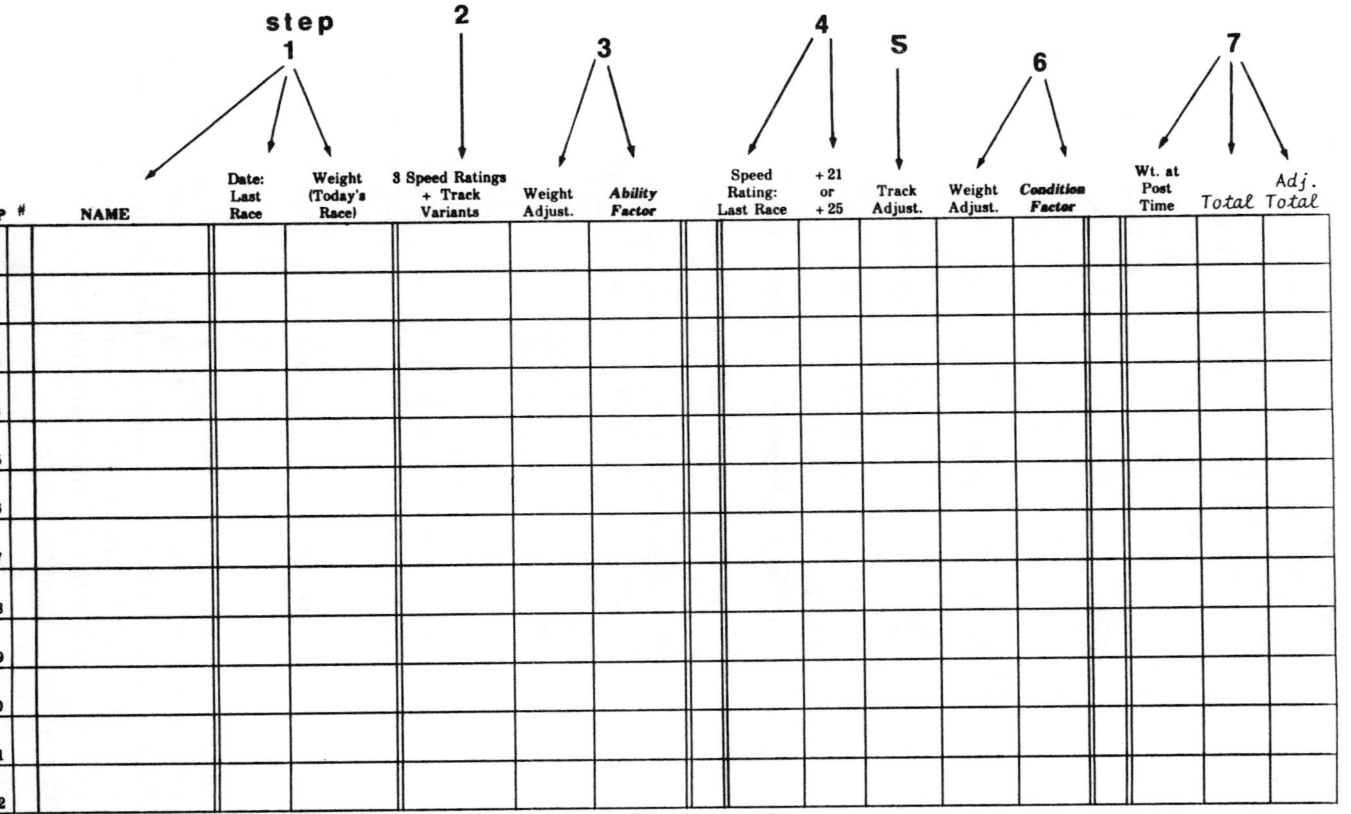

			step 1	step 1	2	3	3		4	4	5	6	6		7	7	7
PP	#	NAME	Date: Last Race	Weight (Today's Race)	3 Speed Ratings + Track Variants	Weight Adjust.	*Ability Factor*		Speed Rating: Last Race	+21 or +25	Track Adjust.	Weight Adjust.	*Condition Factor*		Wt. at Post Time	Total	Adj. Total
1																	
2																	
3																	
4																	
5																	
6																	
7																	
8																	
9																	
10																	
11																	
12																	

Step 5. It is worth the time and effort to construct a Speed Rating Adjustment Table for each distance. A Table should be made for at least each of the following distances: 6 furlongs, 7 furlongs, 1 mile, and 1 1/16 miles. Identify the name of the track on which the Speed Rating in Step 4 was accomplished. Using the appropriate Speed Rating Adjustment Table, enter the track adjustment in the designated column.

Step 6. Note the difference in weight between the amount carried that day and the amount being carried today. Enter the difference (maximum 2 pounds) in the weight adjustment column. Combine the figures of Steps 4, 5, and 6 to arrive at a Condition Factor which is then entered in the appropriate column.

Step 7. Fill in the "Total" column by adding the Ability and Condition factors. Later, at the track, note the horses' post time weights for today's race. If the weights differ from the preliminary weights listed in Step 1, adjust the Totals accordingly. Adjust the weight difference by a maximum of 4 pounds. Finally, circle the two best totals in each category and the three best Totals. Use arrows to note other significant figures for quick and easy reading. If two selected horses have an identical Ability Factor, Condition Factor, or Total, circle both.

Let's return once again to our previous example, **Gold Limit**. Most of the calculations in this illustration appear in the two preceding sections of this book. The only fact that cannot be found in the newspaper is the horse's weight at post time (115 pounds). This information is generally not available until a few minutes before the race. In this case, the last column was completed at the track a few minutes before bets were placed. Rarely do your preliminary conclusions change simply due to post time weight announcements.

Gold Limit — Dk. b. or br. g. 4, by Limit To Reason—Gold Gala, by Gallant Man — **$15,000** — Br.—Marriott P M (Ky) — Tr.—Simms Phillip G — **118**

Own.—Golden Acres Inc

Lifetime				
40	10	6	7	
$72,310				

1983	6	1	0	2	$7,210
1982	18	1	4	3	$21,750
Turf	1	0	0	0	$130

Entered 4Apr83- 1 HIA

25Mar83- 5Hia	fst	6f	:22⅖	:46	1:11⅗		Clm 12500	5	6	4⁴	3³½	2¹½	1¹	Castaneda K	116	3.00 ✓	85-18	Gold Limit 116¹ Mike Ralph 116hd Twogun Kenny 116¹	Driving	10
15Feb83-10GP	fst	7f	:22⅖	:45⅖	1:23⅘		Clm 20000	9	4	6²¾	6⁴¼	5⁴	7⁵¼	Velez J A Jr	117	3.50	80-23	Limerick 115¹ Wooster Sq. 117½ Pleasant Doc J. 115³	No factor	12
7Feb83- 5GP	gd	6f	:22⅗	:46	1:11⅕		Clm 22500	2	3	2½	3¹	2¹	4²¼	Velez J A Jr	115	7.40 ✓	81-21	Hot Words 117¹ [D]Nocturnal Phantom 117¾ Freedom Lad 113½		12

7Feb83-Placed third through disqualification

29Jan83- 9GP	fst	1 1/16	:46⅘	1:11⅗	1:45	3↑	Inv Alw	5	2	2¹½	4³½	10¹³	10¹³	Castaneda K	117	14.20	63-20	[D]Southern Swing 117¾ Kan Reason 122hd Canuck117hd	Gave Way	12
25Jan83-10GP	fst	6f	:23	:46⅖	1:10⅘		Clm 27500	2	6	7³¾	7⁵¼	5⁵	4⁷	Capodici J	115	19.10 ✓	78-21	Intercontinnt115hd IrishSwords1175½Pokr'N'Chips1121½	No factor	11
3Jan83- 8Crc	fst	7f	:23	:46⅗	1:25⅘		Clm 25000	1	6	2½	2hd	1½	3²	Capodici J	116	*1.70	85-16	Tumiga's Flame 114¹ The Fugitive 116¹ Gold Limit 1164½	Tired	9
24Dec82- 8Crc	fst	7f	:22⅖	:45⅕	1:24⅗	3↑	Clm 30000	2	5	3nk	2¹½	2²	3⁴½	Castaneda K	115	3.60	88-19	Kentucky Edd 1212½ Iron Gladiator115²GoldLimit115⁶	Weakened	10
20Dec82- 7Crc	fst	7f	:23	:46⅖	1:24⅗	3↑	Clm 45000	6	1	5³¾	6⁵¾	4⁷	4⁶¾	Castaneda K	116	4.30	86-15	Pokr'N'Chips112hd SomthngWrong1164½RllyFunny1152½	No f ctor	7
11Dec82- 8Crc	fst	7f	:22⅗	:46⅖	1:25⅕	3↑	Alw 14000	6	1	2hd	2½	1hd	2²½	Castaneda K	115	11.90	88-16	Mr. Mar J. Mar 1092½ Gold Limit 115hd Sonofagov 1191½	Gamely	8
29Nov82- 7Crc	fst	7f	:23⅕	:46⅘	1:24⅗	3↑	Clm 30000	2	3	3¹½	3²	2²	2⁴½	Castaneda K	116	2.00	88-17	Kentucky Edd 1104½ Gold Limit 116¹ Donna's Boy 1157½	Gamely	5

PP	#	NAME	Date: Last Race	Weight (Today's Race)	3 Speed Ratings + Track Variants	Weight Adjust.	***Ability Factor***		Speed Rating: Last Race	+21 or +25	Track Adjust.	Weight Adjust.	***Condition Factor***		Wt. at Post Time	*Total*	*Adj. Total*
1		GOLD LIMIT	3/25	118	304	-4	300		85	+21	-8	-2	96		115	396	399
2																	
3																	

Using the *Performance Method* Table: Guidelines to Follow

- From the table, list the best four horses (regardless of whether you intend to bet them) in the order in which you expect them to finish.
- *Always* bet a horse with three circles next to its name (ie., a horse that comes up among the two best Ability Factor choices, among the two best Condition Factor choices *and* among the three best in Totals).
- When betting, favor those horses that rank high in both categories. It is unusual for the winner to rank high in one and not high in the other.
- If your first or second choice horse has not run a race (of *any* distance) within the past 30 days without any workouts, consider the possibility of an upset.
- Do not be discouraged from betting one of your top choices simply because he has not run recently. True, his chances of winning are diminished considerably, but the higher odds will usually make the bet worthwhile (other handicappers see that too.)
- Whenever four horses are selected and not one of them is a clear choice (high in one factor, but low in the other), it is usually a good idea not to bet that race;
- When two horses appear evenly matched on the table and a clear choice is almost impossible, return to the charts to see if they have run any past races head-to-head, or any similar races that may otherwise be compared. This is a good way to break any ties (pay particular attention to track conditions and weight changes). Also, compare "splits" of their last races. See chapter: "In Search of the 'Dark' Horse."
- Be careful when placing your bets. Sometimes the post position and the program numbers are different. You do not want to bet the wrong numbers. Be sure to match the horses' names with the correct numbers for betting.

Learning from Experience

To compile the data for this section, my stuffy publisher insisted on one major restriction: for credibility, I was permitted to use only *one* newspaper—the April 5th issue—rather than allowing me to pick and choose better examples. There *are* definitely better examples. In addition, four of the six races selected were Maiden Claiming contests, which are more difficult to handicap than ordinary claiming, allowance or stakes races.

As most experienced handicappers realize, it is one thing to select the potential winners, and something else to bet the race correctly. It is not impossible to "know" that a horse is going to be "in the money" and still lose by betting incorrectly. This is where self-discipline and experience play a big role. In fact, it can be the difference between success and failure at the track. See the chapter: "How to Bet."

Selecting the best races to play is not always easy. Sometimes the races that seem to have the most promise turn out to be disappointing while others that appear more difficult can surprise you and make good money. Here are a few guidelines to follow:

1. Favor races that have eight, nine or ten horses. A full field of twelve is acceptable, but your first or second choices can be more easily trapped behind the others. However, normally, the odds are greater, making up for the added risk. Fields of four, five or six horses are usually much less profitable.

2. As a general rule, maiden races are not worth the trouble. They can be profitable, however, if most of the horses have run at least three races, have finished within "eyesight" of the winners in those races, and there are no more than two first-time starters.

3. A race becomes more difficult to handicap when the horses in the contest have run a greater variation of distances in the past. The more consistent their past records, the more easily the race can be handicapped (and, probably, with less profit).

4. Most of the time, money can be made betting horses of either sex, but fillies and mares seem to be somewhat less consistent than the males.

5. Higher quality horses are definitely more predictable, and usually less profitable, than the lower-class animals.

6. The outcome of some races can be predicted with greater assurance than others. In the order from the easiest to the most difficult, they are:

   6 furlongs
   6 1/2 furlongs
   7 furlongs
   Route races
   1 mile
   5 1/2 furlongs
   4 1/2 and 5 furlongs

Why the 6 furlong race is the easiest to call is not certain. Perhaps it is due to the fact that it is a difficult sprint race that requires proper conditioning and an all-out effort with a little less pace and strategy than a route race. For those familiar with Track and Field events, it is equivalent to a 1/4 mile sprint race for humans. Shorter races than 6 furlongs are a little more difficult because, sometimes, many entries have little statistical history on which to make a rational judgment. Route races are easier to call with the computer version than with the "short-cut" version (see page 83).

It is important to note whether the horse has ever run the distance of today's race, especially if today's race is over 7 furlongs. If *all* the horses have run today's distance, it would be an easier race to handicap than if, say, three or four are trying the distance for the first time.

This race could be the first half of a promising daily double. It is a 6 furlong race with twelve horses entered. Although only four horses have run on this track previously and three have never run this distance before, it seems to be a worthwhile opportunity. In addition, there will be an exacta.

PIMLICO

6 FURLONGS. (1.09⅗) MAIDEN CLAIMING. Purse $4,500. Fillies. 3- and 4-year-olds. Weights, 3-year-olds, 112 lbs. 4-year-olds, 122 lbs. Claiming price $5,000.

Good N' Intentions
B. f. 3, by Catullus—Gracious Plenty, by Sea O Erin
$5,000 Br.—Sprinkle & Sunnyview Farm (NY)
Tr.—Wallace Roy L
1075
Lifetime 2 0 0 0 $81 — 1983 1 M 0 0 $81 — 1982 1 M 0 0
Own.—Double Bar A Stable
Entered 4Apr83- 2 PEN
9Mar83- 1CT my 4½f :22⅘ :47⅘ :54⅘ Md 5000 8 3 44 57 56 Wallace J L II7 110 4.50 76-14 Safeway Katie 1081 J.C.'s Babe 107½ King Ticket 1201½ Evenly 10
22Jly82- 1Tim fst 4f :24 :48⅕ ⒻMd 10000 5 7 712 711 712 Wallace J L II7 110 4.10 72-11 Vague Chance 1103 Darcy Farrow117nkQuilloStar1171½ Ducked in 9
LATEST WORKOUTS Mar 5 Pim 4f fst :50 hg Feb 24 Pim 3f my :37⅘ hg

Scope Sight
B. f. 3, by Count Brook—I Wont Miss, by Panacean
$5,000 Br.—Armstrong & Vogelman (Md)
Tr.—Vogelman Raymond E
122
Lifetime 1 0 0 0 — 1983 1 M 0 0 — 1982 0 M 0 0
Own.—Vogelman R E Jr
12Jan83- 1Bow gd 6f :23⅕ :47⅕ 1:16 ⒻMd 5000 2 11 1125 1128 1119 79¾ Ford E 120 16.70 50-33 Restless Roman 115nk Gretchen M. 1206 Moon Barbi 1201 Outrun 12
LATEST WORKOUTS Apr 2 Pim 5f fst 1:04 b Mar 27 Pim 4f gd :52 b Mar 23 Pim 3f gd :38 b Mar 17 Pim 4f fst :54⅘ b

Lovran
B. f. 4, by Tatoi—Lido, by The Doge
$5,000 Br.—Wilson O Jr (Va)
Tr.—Tapscott Radcliff C
112
Lifetime 4 0 0 0 — 1983 4 M 0 0 — 1982 0 M 0 0
Own.—Craig B R
23Mar83- 9Pim fst 6f :23⅘ :48⅗ 1:16⅘ 3↑ⒻMd 5000 8 2 45½ 411 68½ 79¾ Pino M G b 122 14.10 52-30 Aggie Sue 1091¼ Snobbish 115¾ Gold Sound 1222 Raced wide 11
9Mar83- 1Bow sly 7f :23⅖ :48 1:29 Md 5000 5 3 2½ 712 719 822 Bracciale V Jr b 115 6.80 38-35 Espionage 120no Sound Hill 1106 Miss Tish's Tudor 1154 Faltered 8
15Feb83- 1Bow fst 7f :23⅕ :46⅘ 1:26⅖ Md 5000 4 7 21 22 57 711 Byrnes D b 115 16.20 62-22 Nolichucky 1152½ Sound Hill 1105 Target Designated 115½ Tired 12
1Feb83- 1Bow fst 6f :23 :47⅕ 1:13 ⒻMd 9500 8 6 911 918 817 715 O'Donnell E E b 118 42.20 60-29 Friendly Hill 120nk This TimeAround120½JessicaLynn1136 Outrun 10
LATEST WORKOUTS Mar 5 Lrl 4f fst :50⅗ b Feb 10 Lrl 4f fst :50⅗ b

Shade of Reason
Gr. f. 4, by Turn to Reason—Troublina, by Star Rover
$5,000 Br.—Lewis Carol S & J W (Md)
Tr.—Leatherbury King T
122
Lifetime 1 0 0 0 — 1983 1 M 0 0 — 1982 0 M 0 0
Own.—Lewis J W
18Mar83- 6Pim sly 6f :24 :47⅘ 1:14 3↑ⒻMd 16500 5 7 76¾ 613 817 819 Passmore W J b 120 4.30 57-26 Lucky Snatch 1154 Miss Verylite 1063 AltitudeSpray1111½ Outrun 8
LATEST WORKOUTS Apr 2 Lrl 3f fst :39 b Mar 11 Lrl 6f my 1:18 b Mar 3 Lrl 5f fst 1:02⅘ bg Feb 26 Lrl 5f fst 1:04⅘ bg

Good Girls Don't
Dk. b. or br. f. 4, by Handsome Boy—Store Bought Woman, by Lucky Debonair
$5,000 Br.—Gaudreau L J (Ind)
Tr.—Gamber Robert
1157
Lifetime 11 0 2 0 $1,134 — 1983 5 M 2 0 $1,134 — 1982 6 M 0 0 — Turf 2 0 0 0
Own.—Gamber R
28Mar83- 1Pen gd 6f :23⅗ :48⅕ 1:15⅖ ⒻMd 3500 8 6 66½ 54½ 33 2hd Santos M H7 b 112 *2.40 67-23 VlentineLove119hdGoodGirlsDon't112½PetitGurr1194 Forced wide 8
19Mar83- 5Pen gd 6f :23 :47⅘ 1:15⅗ ⒻMd 3500 5 6 56½ 53¾ 24 21½ Santos M H5 b 114 26.70 64-24 Coco Tan 1191½ Good Girls Don't 1145MissDancealot1165 Gamely 12
27Feb83- 4CT fst 6½f :24 :48⅖ 1:22 Md 5000 10 7 45½ 68 712 719 Castaneda O b 115 37.00 56-24 Beripity 1081½ Our Chris 1141 Astro View 1148 Outrun 10
19Feb83- 2CT fst 4½f :22⅕ :46⅗ :54⅗ Md 5000 5 4 58½ 714 614 Castaneda O b 115 19.00 67-18 RoughTakeoff1138Marty'sBid1151½Topper'sMouse116¾ No factor 10
29Jan83- 4CT gd 4½f :23 :48⅕ :54⅘ Md 3500 6 9 84½ 74¼ 74½ Delgado H b 115 7.90 75-15 Vogelander 1081½ Viewy 115no Fifi's Girl 115nk No factor 9
31Dec82- 1Lrl fst 6f :23⅕ :48 1:15⅕ 3↑ Md 5000 8 6 1144 1020 1119 1013 Frock C A7 b 113 30.00 54-24 Great Outdoors110hdBrogueRogue1221NauticalSpirit1223¼ Outrun 12
23Dec82- 3Lrl fst 6f :23⅖ :48⅖ 1:14⅕ 3↑ⒻMd 10000 6 11 1115 1113 1011 813 Frock C A7 b 110 60.30 59-23 MrshDncr1204½ThsTmArnd1206MssTsh'sTdr1151 Broke in tangle 11
23Jun82- 4Lrl fst 7f :23 :47 1:28 3↑ⒻMd 12500 5 2 44½ 612 622 619 Kaenel J L b 115 17.20 52-30 My Christy 1183 Bitter Medicine 1151½ Anahauc 111no Tired 6
9Jun82- 5Lrl yl 1 1/16 Ⓣ:46⅘ 1:13⅖ 1:46⅕ 3↑ⒻMd Sp Wt 7 5 614 718 828 828 Pino M G 113 45.00 44-24 Near Hit 113¾ Pirate Princess 1137 My Christy 1221 Tired 8
25May82- 7Lrl fm *1 1/16 Ⓣ:46⅗ 1:12⅕ 1:44⅗ 3↑ⒻMd Sp Wt 7 9 1015 1015 1022 1019 Wright D R 112 76.80 78-03 Countess Elaine 1132½ HitItDarlin113½LengthsAhead1221½ Outrun 10
LATEST WORKOUTS Feb 24 ShD 3f fst :40⅗ b Feb 10 ShD 3f fr :35⅖ h

News Feature
Dk. b. or br. f. 3, by Subpet—Wiscondee, by Wisconsin Boy
$5,000 Br.—Dodson B C (Fla)
Tr.—Donovan L William
112
Lifetime 4 0 0 0 $330 — 1983 4 M 0 0 $330 — 1982 0 M 0 0
Own.—Miranshe Nanbri Stable
4Feb83- 1Bow gd 6f :23⅕ :47⅖ 1:15 ⒻMd 5000 4 10 1014 1115 1014 1020 Duncan G F b 120 14.00 45-36 Ray Ray's Pride1155BonitoWind1203¼SingForMoney1201½ Outrun 12
26Jan83- 1Bow fst 7f :22⅘ :46⅗ 1:27⅘ ⒻMd 8500 5 8 811 819 820 817 Canino E I 120 10.40 49-27 Misky 1152 Marceygo 1208 French Dogwood 1201½ Outrun 10
14Jan83- 4Bow fst 7f :24 :48⅗ 1:29 ⒻMd 11500 8 1 812 1017 1018 1017 Canino E I 120 5.50 43-32 Kitty Dixon 115¾ Condescend 115no Guided Light 1201 Outrun 12
4Jan83- 1Bow fst 6f :23⅗ :48⅕ 1:15⅖ ⒻMd 11500 12 5 43 44¼ 34½ 44½ Canino E I 120 13.20 58-31 Samaura 120no French Dogwood 120½B.J.Baroness1154 Weakened 12
LATEST WORKOUTS Apr 1 Pim 4f fst :52⅗ b

Prom Trotter
B. f. 3, by Medaille D'or—Please Cut In, by Damascus
$5,000 Br.—Jenkins J H (Md)
Tr.—Gaines E Allen
112
Lifetime 2 0 0 0 $190 — 1983 2 M 0 0 $190 — 1982 0 M 0 0
Own.—Jenkins J H Jr
25Feb83- 1CT fst 4½f :22⅖ :46⅖ :53 ⒻMd Sp Wt 6 8 711 616 519 Moreno O 118 13.30 70-14 Nashua Lassie 1187 Ms. Pickup 1183 Rita Z. 1184 No factor 9
28Jan83- 1CT gd 4½f :22⅗ :47 :53⅗ ⒻMd Sp Wt 6 7 816 715 613 Martinez F W 118 2.90 73-13 Favorite Dollar1183MorganaT.1183½DollarDefense1181½ No Factor 9
LATEST WORKOUTS ●Apr 2 CT 3f gd :37⅗ b Mar 19 CT 4f my :51⅕ bg

Beautiful Feeling
B. f. 3, by Tarleton Oak—Bright N Beautiful, by North Flight
$5,000 Br.—Carter Mrs R E III (Va)
Tr.—Tuminelli Joseph M
1075
Lifetime 7 0 0 0 $300 — 1983 4 M 0 0 $300 — 1982 3 M 0 0
Own.—Carter R E
17Mar83- 9Pim fst 6f :23⅘ :47⅘ 1:14⅘ 3↑ⒻMd 8500 10 1 31 47½ 58 77 Young S J5 b 109 22.90 65-25 Sandy Topaz 115¾ Jodel 115nk Princess Blade 112hd Tired 12
18Feb83- 3Bow fst 6f :23⅕ :47⅘ 1:15⅗ ⒻMd 8500 2 4 11½ 1½ 53½ 64 Young S J7 b 112 7.60 58-36 Rubellite 1131 Legendary Gift 115nk PrincessBlade120½ Gave way 8
26Jan83- 1Bow fst 7f :22⅘ :46⅗ 1:27⅘ ⒻMd 8000 8 1 2½ 23 37½ 411 Young S J7 b 112 7.30 55-27 Misky 1152 Marceygo 1208 French Dogwood 1201½ Weakened 10
13Jan83- 2Bow fst 6f :22 :45⅘ 1:13⅗ ⒻMd 7500 3 3 38½ 37 711 66½ Young S J5 b 113 58.80 65-23 Villapath 1152 Mom's Friend 115¾ Rollicking Nel 1131 Tired 12
24Nov82- 1Lrl fst 6f :23 :48⅗ 1:15⅕ ⒻMd 8000 6 8 1½ 53¾ 1012 1117 Leasure W P5 b 112 34.80 50-28 WellResoned1176LittleBoldCotton112½Mom'sFrind117nk Faltered 12
16Nov82- 1Lrl fst 6f :22⅘ :47⅗ 1:15⅕ ⒻMd 10000 6 5 21½ 39 714 1220 Delgado A5 b 112 7.00 47-25 BotingPrty1173¼CountessMurphy1131¼AmberQuote1122¼ Faltered 12
22Oct82- 3Lrl fst 6f :23⅕ :48⅕ 1:15 ⒻMd 16000 2 12 109¼ 1220 1221 1220 Foley D 117 43.40 48-26 Dipped In Ink117nkBoatingParty1173¾PrincessBlade110hd Outrun 12
LATEST WORKOUTS Mar 9 Lrl 5f my 1:06 b Mar 5 Lrl 4f fst :50⅕ b Feb 26 Lrl 5f fst 1:03⅖ b Feb 5 Lrl 4f fst :49 b

Legendary Gift
Dk. b. or br. f. 3, by Gold And Myrrh—Bold Tiny Star, by Bold Bidder
$5,000 Br.—Lerman R S (Ky)
Tr.—Gino Luigi
1075
Lifetime 16 0 1 3 $4,460 — 1983 4 M 1 1 $2,060 — 1982 12 M 0 2 $2,400
Own.—Moore G E
4Mar83- 4Bow fst 7f :23⅗ :48 1:28 ⒻMd 8500 2 6 35 31½ 32 44 McCarthy M J5 b 115 *2.50 61-31 All My Life 120hd Princess Blade 1203 Jodel 1131 Weakened 9
18Feb83- 3Bow fst 6f :23⅕ :47⅘ 1:15⅗ ⒻMd 8500 7 1 67½ 53½ 42½ 21 McCarthy M J5 b 115 3.30 61-36 Rubellite 1131LegendaryGift115nkPrincessBlade120½ Wide, rallied 8
8Feb83- 3Bow fst 7f :23 :46⅕ 1:25⅖ ⒻMd 10500 5 1 53½ 36 311 316 Ryan J S5 b 114 9.30 62-27 Go Rachel1159FriendlyFour1207LegendaryGift1141 Circled horses 9
14Jan83- 4Bow fst 7f :24 :48⅗ 1:29 ⒻMd 10500 9 5 43 42½ 52½ 65 Prough J D5 b 114 3.30 55-32 Kitty Dixon 115¾ Condescend 115no Guided Light 1201 Tired 12
27Dec82- 1Lrl gd 6f :23⅖ :48⅘ 1:14⅘ ⒻMd c-8000 6 3 67 67½ 57½ 58¾ McCarthy M J5 b 110 9.10 60-29 AidAFriend1187Mom'sFriend1091ShesaPenny116hd Unruly pre. st 11
17Dec82- 3Lrl gd 6f :23⅖ :48⅗ 1:14⅘ ⒻMd 10500 11 4 108 912 613 517 McCarthy M J5 b 109 7.20 52-32 MedievalRose1186Dealer'sDouble1183½AidAFriend1181½ No factor 11
3Dec82- 3Lrl sly 7f :23⅕ :48⅕ 1:29⅕ ⒻMd 10000 5 2 66 74½ 34 33½ La Rocca J A5 b 112 3.50 61-23 Amber Quote 1082½ CrossingGuard1171LegendaryGift1122 Rallied 12
23Nov82- 1Lrl fst 7f :23⅖ :47⅗ 1:28⅖ ⒻMd 10500 7 3 2½ 22½ 2½ 41 La Rocca J A5 b 108 9.00 68-27 GallopOnBeddrd117nkAidAFriend117nkNonie'sGirl117½ Weakened 9
2Nov82- 3Lrl fst 6f :23⅕ :48⅕ 1:14⅘ ⒻMd 12500 2 10 87 55½ 55 64 Wright D R b 117 5.50 65-23 Another Laus 1132½ Jodel 117nk Rogue's Pleasure 112hd Even try 12
5Oct82- 5Bow fst 7f :23⅕ :47⅗ 1:27⅖ ⒻMd 20000 8 6 53½ 76¼ 1015 1017 Cooke C 118 17.70 51-23 Cordan 1205 Half Measures 1151½ Altitude Spray 1182 Outrun 12

Miss Nancy M. Dk. b. or br. f. 3, by Provante—Behaving Proper, by Revolutionist Lifetime 1982 4 M 0 0 $296

$5,000 Br.—Vines B H (Pa) 112 4 0 0 0

Own.—Coster P F Tr.—Coster Paul F $296

28Aug82- 1Tim fst *6½f :23⅖ :48⅗ 1:20⅘ ⒻMd 9000 6 1 2^{2} 3^{3} 4^{6} 8^{17} Frock C A^{7} 110 26.60 58-15 BeutifulExchnge$112^{2\frac{1}{2}}$GrtchnM.110^{6}RodToMndly$117^{3\frac{1}{2}}$ Used early 9

20Aug82- 9Tim fst 4f :23⅕ :48 ⒻMd 9000 1 4 3^{5} $3^{5\frac{1}{2}}$ $5^{7\frac{3}{4}}$ Frock C A^{7} 108 17.80 77-14 Ruffincel$117^{4\frac{1}{2}}$GambitsSandlwood$117^{1\frac{1}{2}}$LittleMissBndy115^{nk} Tired 10

6Aug82- 1Tim my 4f :23⅗ :48⅗ ⒻMd 10000 7 4 $6^{5\frac{1}{2}}$ $6^{7\frac{1}{2}}$ 6^{9} Lambert C 118 23.90 73-16 BbyBlossom$118^{3\frac{1}{2}}$I'mforHild118^{1}GmbitsSndlwood$118^{1\frac{1}{2}}$ No factor 8

22Jly82- 1Tim fst 4f :24 :48⅕ ⒻMd 10000 6 4 $6^{5\frac{3}{4}}$ $6^{4\frac{1}{2}}$ $5^{8\frac{3}{4}}$ Lambert C 117 7.30 75-11 Vague Chance 110^{3} Darcy Farrow 117^{nk}QuilloStar$117^{1\frac{1}{2}}$ No factor 9

LATEST WORKOUTS Apr 2 Pim 4f fst :50⅖ bg

Decka Dk. b. or br. f. 3, by Big Brave—Sassy Lark, by Final Ruling Lifetime 1983 1 M 0 0

$5,000 Br.—Keating Penelope A (Md) 112 1 0 0 0 1982 0 M 0 0

Own.—Keating Penelope A Tr.—Shockey Richard W

30Mar83- 9Pim fst 6f :24 :48⅖ 1:14⅖ 3↑ⒻMd 8500 3 10 12^{14} 12^{17} $10^{9\frac{1}{4}}$ $6^{6\frac{1}{2}}$ Runco J C 114 27.10 67-24 DPrincess Blade $112^{\frac{3}{4}}$ Dellis 112^{nk} Mom's Friend $112^{2\frac{1}{2}}$ Outrun 12

LATEST WORKOUTS Mar 24 Lrl 4f fst :50⅘ bg Mar 18 Bow 5f sly 1:02⅘ b Mar 12 Bow 5f fst 1:03⅗ b Feb 26 Bow 5f fst 1:04⅖ bg

Maggy's Edge Ch. f. 3, by Double Edge Sword—Rosie's Queen, by Misty Flight Lifetime 1983 4 M 0 0

$5,000 Br.—Abse Mr-Mrs D I (Md) 107^{5} 8 0 0 0 1982 4 M 0 0 $60

Own.—Scuderi F P Tr.—Ford Richard E $60

16Feb83- 1Bow fst 7f :23⅗ :48 1:29 ⒻMd 5000 12 5 $6^{6\frac{1}{4}}$ $6^{9\frac{3}{4}}$ 9^{16} 11^{23} McCarthy M J^{5} b 115 37.90 37-33 Linda Topaz 120^{8} Road To Mandalay 120^{2} Giger'sGirl120^{1} Outrun 12

4Feb83- 1Bow gd 6f :23⅕ :47⅖ 1:15 ⒻMd 5000 2 11 11^{14} 10^{14} $7^{9\frac{1}{2}}$ 7^{14} Wright D R b 120 46.80 51-36 Ray Ray's Pride115^{5}BonitoWind$120^{3\frac{1}{2}}$SingForMoney$120^{1\frac{1}{2}}$ Outrun 12

25Jan83- 1Bow fst 7f :24 :48⅖ 1:30 ⒻMd 5000 7 4 6^{7} 7^{8} 9^{14} 9^{11} McCarthy M J^{5} 115 35.60 44-36 Excellent Bet $120^{1\frac{1}{2}}$ Road ToMandalay$115^{\frac{3}{4}}$Japonika115^{1} Far back 10

13Jan83- 2Bow fst 6f :22 :45⅘ 1:13⅗ ⒻMd 7500 8 11 9^{25} 9^{25} 9^{18} 9^{11} McCarthy M J^{5} 113 58.00 61-23 Villapath 115^{2} Mom's Friend$115^{\frac{3}{4}}$RollickingNel113^{1} Unruly-pre st. 12

19Nov82- 2CT fst 6½f :23⅘ :48⅘ 1:21⅕ Md 10000 7 3 2^{4} $5^{3\frac{1}{2}}$ 6^{13} 6^{21} Lewis W R Jr 117 32.30 58-25 Wilderbiest 109^{6} Favorite Boy 118^{6} Puppy Balzanna 109^{hd} Tired 10

10Nov82- 1CT fst 4½f :23 :47⅘ :54⅖ ⒻMd Sp Wt 10 1 8^{8} 9^{14} 8^{13} Casey E M 118 35.20 69-16 Shelly's Imp 118^{1} Mito Bandito 118^{1} SingForMoney$118^{1\frac{1}{2}}$ Outrun 10

15Sep82- 3Bow fst 6f :23⅕ :48 1:14⅘ ⒻMd 14500 7 8 8^{11} 10^{11} 10^{21} 10^{22} Wright D R 120 13.00 44-28 Satin Cloud$120^{1\frac{1}{2}}$FrenchDogwood$120^{1\frac{1}{2}}$MedievalRose$120^{1\frac{1}{2}}$ Outrun 10

9Sep82- 5Bow fst 6f :23⅗ :48⅕ 1:14⅘ ⒻMd 23500 12 2 7^{6} 8^{14} 9^{14} 9^{19} Cline V L 120 21.40 47-22 Bold Lily 115^{2} Ligner 120^{3} Aid A Friend 115^{3} Outrun 12

LATEST WORKOUTS Apr 1 Lrl 3f fst :38⅗ bg

Of the twelve horses in this race, four emerge as the best choices. One of them, **Decka,** is clearly the winner, having the highest Ability Factor, the second highest Condition Factor, and the best Total. With three circles next to her name, she is the top pick. The public's first choice is **Legendary Gift** which becomes our second selection. The horse hasn't run for about four weeks but today's shorter distance should compensate for that. It was a difficult decision vs. our third horse, **Beautiful Feeling.** However, on February 18, they ran head-to-head and **Legendary Gift** was three lengths ahead and gaining. Today, both are carrying the same weight. **Good Girls Don't,** with the highest Condition Factor, has little else to offer. she is somewhat reluctantly boxed with our first two selections. Only the first three are bet in the daily double.

Of all the horses outside our top four, **Shade of Reason** offers the greatest upset possibility and is worth an exacta box with **Decka.** It is not unusual for a horse to show good improvement in its second race. This more-mature four-year-old horse has a highly respected trainer who has obviously put her through a serious workout schedule and she appears to be dropping sharply in class.

Our selections for this race are:

1. **Decka**
2. **Legendary Gift**
3. **Beautiful Feeling**
4. **Good Girls Don't**

1st Pimlico 6F (4/5)

PP	#	NAME	Date: Last Race	Weight (Today's Race)	3 Speed Ratings + Track Variants	Weight Adjust.	***Ability Factor***	Speed Rating: Last Race	+21 or +25	Track Adjust.	Weight Adjust.	***Condition Factor***	Wt. at Post Time	Total	Adj. Total
1		Good N' Intentions	3/9	107	270a (4½F)	—	270	N/A	—	—	—	—	110	N/A	N/A
2		Scope Sight	Jan.	122	243a	—	243	50	+25	-5	-2	68	122	311	311
3		Louran	3/23	112	263a	—	263	52	+21	-11	+2	64	112	327	327
4		Shade of Reason	3/18	122	243a	—	243	57	+25	-11	-2	69	122	312	312
5		Good Girls Don't	3/28	115	256	-4	252	67	+25	-9	-2	(81)	115	333	333 ←
6		News Feature	2/4	112	261a	—	261	45	+25	-5	+2	67	113	328	327
7		Prom Trotter	2/25	112	255 (4½F)	—	255	N/A	—	—	—	—	115	N/A	N/A
8		Beautiful Feeling	3/17	107	272	+4	(276)	65	+21	-11	+2	77 ←	109	353	(351)
9		Legendary Gift	3/4	107	270	+4	274 ←	61	+21	-5	+2	(79)	109	353	(351)
10		Miss Nancy M.	Aug.	112	213a (6½F)	—	213	58 (6½F)	+21	-9	-2	68	112	281	281
11		Decka	3/30	112	279	—	(279)	67	+21	-11	+2	(79)	113	358	(357)
12		Maggy's Edge	2/16	107	243	+4	247	51	+25	-5	+2	73	109	320	318
13															
14															
15															
16															

Note: Forty 8 1/2" × 11" blank Performance Method *tables may be ordered by sending* $6.95 plus $1.00 *for shipping and handling to Liberty Publishing Company, Inc. An order form appears in the back of this book.*

FIRST RACE **6 FURLONGS. (1.09⅕) MAIDEN CLAIMING. Purse $4,500. Fillies. 3- and 4-year-olds. Weights, 3-year-olds, 112 lbs. 4-year-olds, 122 lbs. Claiming price $5,000. (18th Day. WEATHER CLOUDY. TEMPERATURE 55 DEGREES.)**

Pimlico

APRIL 5

Value of race $4,500, value to winner $2,700, second $990, third $540, fourth $270. Mutuel pool $29,565. Exacta Pool $41,559.

Last Raced	Horse	Eqt.	A.	Wt	PP	St	¼	½	Str	Fin	Jockey	Cl'g Pr	Odds $1
30Mar83 ^{9}Pim^{6}	Decka		3	113	11	3	5^{hd}	5^{2}	2^{3}	1^{7}	Runco J C	5000	3.40
4Mar83 ^{4}Bow^{4}	Legendary Gift	b	3	109	9	1	$6^{½}$	6^{2}	4^{2}	$2^{¾}$	McCarthy M J^{5}	5000	2.00
18Mar83 ^{6}Pim^{8}	Shade of Reason	b	4	122	4	7	1^{5}	1^{6}	1^{2}	$3^{1¼}$	Passmore W J	5000	5.40
12Jan83 ^{1}Bow^{7}	Scope Sight		3	122	2	11	$9^{½}$	7^{3}	$5^{2½}$	$4^{½}$	Wright D R	5000	25.20
28Mar83 ^{1}Pen^{2}	Good Girls Don't	b	4	115	5	8	10^{2}	$8^{1½}$	7^{5}	$5^{4½}$	Ruch L D^{7}	5000	10.60
16Feb83 ^{1}Bow^{11}	Maggy's Edge	b	3	109	12	4	$4^{1½}$	$4^{½}$	6^{hd}	6^{3}	Young S J^{5}	5000	94.80
28Aug82 ^{1}Tim^{8}	Miss Nancy M.		3	112	10	2	3^{1}	3^{hd}	3^{hd}	$7^{½}$	Smith G P	5000	29.10
25Feb83 ^{1}CT^{5}	Prom Trotter	b	3	115	7	12	12	11^{5}	10^{10}	8^{1}	Moreno O	5000	17.60
4Feb83 ^{1}Bow^{10}	News Feature	b	3	113	6	10	8^{1}	9^{3}	9^{hd}	$9^{½}$	Osani J R Jr	5000	68.10
17Mar83 ^{9}Pim^{7}	Beautiful Feeling	b	3	109	8	9	$2^{½}$	$2^{1½}$	8^{3}	10^{10}	Delgado A^{5}	5000	4.40
9Mar83 ^{1}CT^{5}	Good N' Intentions		3	110	1	5	7^{4}	10^{hd}	11^{5}	11^{7}	Wallace J L II^{5}	5000	35.10
23Mar83 ^{9}Pim^{7}	Lovran	b	4	112	3	6	11^{2}	12	12	12	Grable T C	5000	20.90

OFF AT 1:02 Start good, Won driving. Time, :23⅘, :48⅖, 1:01⅘, 1:14⅘ Track fast.

Official Program Numbers

$2 Mutuel Prices:			
11–DECKA	8.80	4.20	3.00
9–LEGENDARY GIFT		3.20	2.80
4–SHADE OF REASON			4.40

$2 EXACTA 11–9 PAID $30.80.

Dk. b. or br. f, by Big Brave—Sassy Lark, by Final Ruling. Trainer Shockey Richard W. Bred by Keating Penelope A (Md).

DECKA circled and drew off. LEGENDARY GIFT raced between horses and rallied. SHADE OF REASON gave way. SCOPE SIGHT, wide, finished willingly. GOOD GIRLS DON'T had a mile response. MAGGY'S EDGE tired. MISS NANCY M. eakened along the rail. BEAUTIFUL FEELING dropped back.

Owners— 1, Keating Penelope A; 2, Moore G E; 3, Lewis J W; 4, Vogelman R E Jr; 5, Gamber R; 6, Scuderi F P; 7, Coster P F; 8, Jenkins J H Jr; 9, Miranshe Nanbri Stable; 10, Carter R E; 11, Double Bar A Stable; 12, Craig B K.

Trainers— 1, Shockey Richard W; 2, Gino Luigi; 3, Leatherbury King T; 4, Vogelman Raymond E; 5, Gamber Robert; 6, Ford Richard E; 7, Coster Paul F; 8, Gaines E Allen; 9, Donovan L William; 10, Tuminelli Joseph M; 11, Wallace Roy L; 12, Tapscott Radcliff C.

Overweight: Decka 1 pound; Legendary Gift 2; Maggy's Edge 2; Prom Trotter 3; News Feature 1; Beautiful Feeling 2; Good N' Intentions 3.

Decka was claimed by Heil J; trainer, Allen Harold; Prom Trotter was claimed by Ace Stables; trainer, Hayes Donald E.

Scratched—Cree's Royalty; Boys I'm It (23Mar83 ^{9}Pim^{6}); Apparently (28Feb83 ^{2}Bow^{7}); Native Zig (25Mar83 ^{1}Pim^{10}); Bonito Wind (23Mar83 ^{9}Pim^{9}).

In retrospect, the extra $4 box of **Decka** and **Shade of Reason** was unnecessary, but still a wise move. Review the thought process. As it turned out, it was a profitable race and we are now sitting with a few possible daily double win tickets. Just relax and watch the tote board flash the potential values of each ticket. This information helps you bet the second race.

$2 Exacta Wagering	
Bet	$ 34.00
Return	$123.20
Profit	$ 89.20

This race is also a 6 furlong race with twelve horses entered. Unlike the first race, however, more than half of the field has raced at Pimlico recently, and all have run the distance before. In addition to the possible daily double, there will be an exacta.

PIMLICO

6 FURLONGS. (1.09⅕) MAIDEN CLAIMING. Purse $4,500. Fillies. 3- and 4-year-olds. Weights, 3-year-olds, 112 lbs. 4-year-olds, 122 lbs. Claiming price $5,000.

Tuscany's Gem
Ch. f. 4, by Indian Topaz—Evening Flirt, by Tuscany
$5,000 Br.—Alecci J V (Md) Tr.—Shaeffer John A
Own.—Alecci J V
115[7] Lifetime 18 0 0 1 $1,722 | 1983 4 M 0 0 $190 | 1982 11 M 0 1 $1,112

23Mar83- 9Pim fst 6f :23⅘ :48⅗ 1:16⅘ 3+ⒻMd 5000 1 9 812 916 711 57½ Wallace J L II5 b 115 14.60 55-30 Aggie Sue 1091½ Snobbish 115¾ Gold Sound 1222 No factor 11
9Mar83- 1Bow sly 7f :23⅘ :48 1:29 Md 5000 4 1 54 58½ 512 513 Wallace J L II7 b 110 16.00 47-35 Espionage 120no Sound Hill 1106 Miss Tish's Tudor 1154 Evenly 8
19Feb83- 1CT fst 7f :25 :49⅖ 1:29⅘ Md Sp Wt 3 3 32 43 54½ 814 Wallace J L II7 b 110 8.80 59-20 Red White 1203½ Polished 1151½ Full O' Play 1151 Tired 9
30Jan83- 1CT my 4½f :22⅘ :47⅗ :54⅘ ⒻMd Sp Wt 8 2 41½ 44½ 43¾ Wallace J L II7 b 113 12.80 79-11 Another Try 113½ Anniversary Sandi120nkZanibar1203 No Mishap 10
18Jun82- 9Lrl fst 6f :23⅕ :47⅘ 1:13⅕ 3+ⒻMd 7500 1 3 43¾ 53½ 69 510 Kaenel J L b 115 3.70 67-19 Mystification 1151½ Hoot's Missy 1176 Sassy Talk1152¾ No factor 8
9Jun82- 1Lrl fst 6f :23⅕ :47⅘ 1:14 3+ⒻMd 8000 3 1 66½ 66¾ 58¾ 41¾ Conklin WJIII5 b 110 13.90 71-21 Lead Flight 115nk Belmar Summer 110½WhataBadGirl1151 Rallied 8
3Jun82- 2Lrl fst 6f :23⅕ :47⅕ 1:12⅖ 3+ⒻMd 10000 4 8 913 915 920 719 Wallace J L II7 108 53.80 62-18 PioneerBess1124½Cleo'sEvertrue1124¾MissWellington112½ Outrun 9
25May82- 1Lrl fst 6f :23⅖ :48⅖ 1:13⅖ 3+ⒻMd 12500 3 3 54½ 56¾ 514 514 Conklin W J III5 111 22.90 62-21 Ifdadcouldsee 1136 Anahauc 105¾ Miss Wellington107¾ No factor 8
15May82- 4Pen fst 5½f :22⅘ :47⅗ 1:06⅕ Md 10000 6 3 21½ 52½ 42 36¾ Wagner B R5 109 11.40 78-19 A Little Different 1184½ Bill's Gulf1182½Tuscany'sGem1092½ Hung 8
9May82- 1CT fst 4½f :23 :47⅖ :53⅘ ⒻMd Sp Wt 5 2 63½ 65¾ 68¾ Conklin W J III5 115 28.90 76-13 Cute Leslie 1205 Dancing Carpet 113nk Kausha 120hd No factor 10

B. J. Baroness
Gr. f. 3, by What A Rogue—Dot Kiss, by Beau Priam
$5,000 Br.—Piccioni Mr-Mrs J (Md) Tr.—Gino Luigi
Own.—Bar-Jo Farm
107[5] Lifetime 5 0 0 1 $660 | 1983 3 M 0 1 $660 | 1982 2 M 0 0

30Mar83- 9Pim fst 6f :24 :48⅖ 1:14⅕ 3+ⒻMd 8500 6 8 52 63½ 77½1214 McCarthy M J 114 11.70 60-24 ⒹPrincessBlde112¾Dellis112nkMom'sFrind1122½ Bobbled, bumped 12
17Mar83- 9Pim fst 6f :23⅘ :47⅘ 1:14⅘ 3+ⒻMd 8500 11 2 21 2½ 33½1211 McCarthy M J5 109 5.20 61-25 Sandy Topaz 115¾ Jodel 115nk Princess Blade 112hd Faltered 12
4Jan83- 1Bow fst 6f :23⅘ :48⅕ 1:15⅖ ⒻMd 11500 9 3 21½ 2hd 13 3½ Delgado A5 115 8.30 62-31 Samaura 120no French Dogwood 120¾B.J.Baroness1154 Weakened 12
17Dec82- 3Lrl gd 6f :23⅖ :48⅗ 1:14⅘ ⒻMd 12500 5 6 54 47 49½ 921 Feliciano B M Jr5 113 42.60 48-32 MedievlRose1186Deler'sDouble1183½AidAFriend1181½ Drifted out 11
2Nov82- 9Lrl fst 6f :22⅘ :46⅖ 1:12⅘ ⒻMd Sp Wt 10 11 711 9191129 1233 Cooke C 117 28.10 48-23 ThirdDouble1171FlirtingGlance112noMjesticAmber1176 No speed 12
LATEST WORKOUTS Mar 12 Bow 3f fst :36⅘ b Feb 22 Bow 3f fst :38⅖ b

Japonika
Dk. b. or br. f. 3, by Cadet Joe—Dean's Sister, by Telekinesis
$5,000 Br.—Paice D L (Md) Tr.—Delp Richard W
Own.—Delp R W
102[10] Lifetime 13 0 2 3 $4,484 | 1983 5 M 0 1 $840 | 1982 8 M 2 2 $3,644

11Mar83- 9Bow gd 7f :23⅘ :47⅘ 1:29 ⒻMd 5000 3 3 52½ 46½ 56½ 47½ Muino M M10 b 110 6.50 52-33 Bellarus 1151½ Ivegotafeeling 1203BonitoWind1203 Lacked a rally 11
16Feb83- 1Bow fst 7f :23⅘ :48 1:29 ⒻMd 5000 6 1 76½ 59½ 68½ 714 Grable T C b 120 7.70 46-33 Linda Topaz 1208 Road To Mandalay 1202 Giger'sGirl1201 Outrun 12
28Jan83- 2Bow fst 1⅟₁₆ :49⅘ 1:16⅗ 1:52 Md 5000 2 3 52½ 77 10131015 Grable T C5 b 110 2.70 31-35 Sassy Sport1152½JohnnyOneNote1202½LottaJohn1201½ Early foot 12
25Jan83- 1Bow fst 7f :24 :48⅗ 1:30 ⒻMd 5000 2 6 54½ 54½ 44 32½ Grable T C5 b 115 3.80 53-36 Excellent Bet 1201½ Road To Mandalay 115¾Japonika1151 Rallied 10
14Jan83- 3Bow fst 6f :23⅘ :48⅗ 1:14⅗ ⒸClm 5000 6 2 85 88½ 68½ 68½ Pino M G b 113 5.00 59-32 Barbara'sChamp1085Sadie'sTime112½Detectoress1131 Raced wide 8
20Dec82- 3Lrl fst 6f :23 :47⅕ 1:13⅘ ⒻMd 8000 1 2 57 59½ 48 311 Delgado A5 b 113 2.70 63-24 Our Mutual Friend1139GretchenM.1143Japonika1134½ No menace 10
13Dec82- 1Lrl sly 7f :23⅖ :47⅖ 1:26 Md 8000 6 2 1hd 65½ 49 311 Delgado A5 b 107 5.90 70-19 Fast Tale 11310 Star Bucket 118½ Japonika 107nk Weakened 12
24Nov82- 1Lrl fst 6f :23 :48⅗ 1:15⅕ ⒻMd 8000 5 6 75 97½1113 815 FelicianoBMJr7 b 110 5.20 52-28 WllRsond1176LttlBoldCottn112½Mm'sFrnd117nk Bmpd 3/16's pole 12
16Nov82- 1Lrl fst 6f :22⅘ :47⅗ 1:15⅕ ⒻMd 10000 7 7 612 613 511 612 Prough J D5 b 112 7.90 55-25 BotingPrty1173½CountessMurphy1131½AmbrQuot1122½ No factor 12
26Oct82- 3Lrl gd 6f :23⅘ :49⅘ 1:16⅘ ⒻMd 10000 9 1 43½ 31½ 31 2no Prough J D5 b 112 9.30 59-29 Royal Valentine 117no Japonika 1122 Honey 117hd Nosed 12
LATEST WORKOUTS Mar 30 Pim 4f fst :51 b

Smart Shopper
B. f. 3, by Limit to Reason—Boutique II, by Nigromante
$5,000 Br.—Cowles Mr-Mrs R Jr & Goode (Va) Tr.—Daniels Edward J Jr
Own.—Musumeci F
112 Lifetime 4 0 0 0 | 1983 4 M 0 0 | 1982 0 M 0 0

23Mar83- 9Pim fst 6f :23⅘ :48⅗ 1:16⅘ 3+ⒻMd 5000 11 10 1117111810161119 Delgado A5 108 12.80 43-30 Aggie Sue 1091½ Snobbish 115¾ Gold Sound 1222 Raced greenly 11
6Feb83- 2Aqu fst 1⅛ ⊡:50 1:15⅘ 1:56⅕ ⒻMd 20000 10 11 1011 915 814 817 Belmonte J E10 107 79.10 48-22 Vishnacka 1105 Beauty Counts 121½ Hail To Luck 1216 Outrun 11
20Jan83- 2Aqu fst 6f ⊡:23⅘ :48⅖ 1:14⅗ ⒸClm 16000 4 8 819 819 823 828 Belmonte J E10 106 40.80 43-24 Final Stroke 1163MinatoryRose1135IvyLeagueMiss1162¾ Far back 8
10Jan83- 4Aqu fst 6f ⊡:23⅘ :48⅕ 1:14⅘ ⒻMd 13000 3 14 142314211321 1317 Lovato F Jr 117 26.70 53-23 Fast 'N Square 1141½ Angie Plasty1121Maggie'sHaul121nk Outrun 14
LATEST WORKOUTS Apr 2 Lrl 4f fst :51 bg Mar 5 Bow 3f fst :37⅕ bg Feb 18 Bel tr.t 4f gd :53 bg

Lady Swan
Dk. b. or br. f. 3, by Joyful Ruler—Blue Swan, by Winged Step
$5,000 Br.—Penowa Farms (Md) Tr.—Frock Clarence I
Own.—Pestridge Patricia A
112 Lifetime 5 0 0 2 $1,200 | 1983 3 M 0 1 $540 | 1982 2 M 0 1 $660

23Mar83- 9Pim fst 6f :23⅘ :48⅗ 1:16⅘ 3+ⒻMd 5000 5 4 56½ 614 9141015 Nicol P A Jr5 b 108 *2.60 47-30 Aggie Sue 1091½ Snobbish 115¾ Gold Sound 1222 Tired 11
1Mar83- 9Bow sly 6f :23⅘ :47⅘ 1:15⅘ ⒻMd 5000 4 1 11 31 35 35 Nicol P A Jr5 b 115 7.20 56-25 Gretchen M. 1205FrenchDogwood120hdLadySwan115hd Weakened 12
4Feb83- 1Bow gd 6f :23⅕ :47⅖ 1:15 ⒻMd 5000 7 2 3½ 44 8131122 Nicol P A Jr5 b 115 *2.90 43-36 RayRay'sPride1155BonitoWind1203½SingForMoney1201½ Faltered 12
22Oct82- 3Lrl fst 6f :23⅕ :48⅕ 1:15 ⒻMd c-16000 1 1 43 37 610 913 Delgado A5 112 5.00 55-26 DippedInInk117nkBoatingParty1173¾PrincessBlde110hd Gave way 12
8Oct82- 4Bow fst 6f :23⅕ :47⅘ 1:14⅖ ⒻMd 14500 7 3 23 21½ 2½ 32 Delgado A5 115 10.70 66-27 Favorite Medic 1151½ Jim's Miss 119¾ Lady Swan 1151 Hung 12
LATEST WORKOUTS Feb 22 Lrl 4f fst :51⅖ b

Distortion
Ch. f. 3, by Shady Character—Smile Pretty, by No Fear II
$5,000 Br.—Hacker S J (Fla) Tr.—Logan Denis J
Own.—Rodgers Linda S
112 Lifetime 1 0 0 0 | 1983 1 M 0 0 | 1982 0 M 0 0

17Mar83- 9Pim fst 6f :23⅘ :47⅘ 1:14⅘ 3+ⒻMd 8500 7 7 78½ 713 913 87½ Pino M G 113 17.70 65-25 Sandy Topaz 115¾ Jodel 115nk Princess Blade 112hd Drifted wide 12
LATEST WORKOUTS Mar 30 Lrl 5f fst 1:04⅘ b Mar 5 Bow 5f fst 1:04⅕ bg Feb 19 Bow 4f fst :52 b

Nana's Cruise
Gr. f. 3, by Oxford Flight—Nana's Baby, by Run For Nurse
$5,000 Br.—Gordonsdale Farm (Ky) Tr.—Ford Richard E
Own.—Seibel T A
107[5] Lifetime 6 0 0 0 $64 | 1983 3 M 0 0 | 1982 3 M 0 0 $64

9Mar83- 2Bow sly 7f :23⅘ :48⅕ 1:28⅘ ⒸClm 7500 1 5 55½ 55½ 68 612 McCarthy M J5 110 27.50 50-35 U. D. Judge 1163½ Devil Made Me 1121½ Micky 112½ Outrun 7
1Mar83- 9Bow sly 6f :23⅘ :47⅘ 1:15⅘ ⒻMd c-5000 1 11 79½ 69½ 513 610 Young S J7 113 13.30 51-25 GretchenM.1205FrenchDogwood120hdLadySwan115hd Steadied St 12
27Jan83- 4CT gd 4½f :22⅘ :47⅖ :54⅘ Md 10000 1 7 811 69 76 Hansby A E7 b 108 19.30 77-14 Mito Bandito 115½ No Cut Clause 1134 ZipOutCap111hd Steadied 10
20Oct82- 1CT fst 4½f :22⅕ :46⅖ :53 Md Sp Wt 6 3 56 68¾ 610 Figgins O Jr b 115 45.90 79-13 Unique Monique 1152½ Small Paw 118nkKockyKid1184½ No factor 10
23Sep82- 1CT fst 6½f :23⅘ :47⅘ 1:24⅘ Md Sp Wt 9 9 79½ 9181020 927 Figgins O Jr b 115 9.20 35-26 Bibjay 1184½ White Tie 1182 Artic Circle 1183 Outrun 10
11Sep82- 9Bow fst 6f :22⅘ :47 1:13⅘ ⒻMd Sp Wt 11 10 917102311371133 Figgins O Jr 120 17.00 38-24 Northern Sting 1204 Net 120½ Hurley 1206 Outrun 11

Road To Mandalay
Ch. f. 3, by Happy Way—Shining Malissa, by Golden Ruler
$5,000 Br.—Gibson J M (Md) Tr.—Allen Harold
Own.—Queen Ann Stable
107[5] Lifetime 19 0 5 1 $7,099 | 1983 5 M 2 0 $2,166 | 1982 14 M 3 1 $4,933

1Mar83- 9Bow sly 6f :23⅘ :47⅘ 1:15⅘ ⒻMd 5000 8 8 68 812 816 915 Edwards J W b 120 7.40 46-25 Gretchen M. 1205 French Dogwood 120hd LadySwan115hd Outrun 12
25Feb83- 2Pen fst 6f :23⅘ :48⅗ 1:15⅘ ⒻMd 7500 9 5 64 43 32 43¾ Hilburn W J5 b 113 *1.60 62-25 Wine Drop 1101½ Daffy's Sister 118½ Twogunart 1072 Weakened 10
16Feb83- 1Bow fst 7f :23⅘ :48 1:29 ⒻMd 5000 4 2 44 45½ 23 28 Edwards J W b 120 *3.70 52-33 Linda Topaz 1208 Road To Mandalay 1202 Giger's Girl 1201 Wide 12
25Jan83- 1Bow fst 7f :24 :48⅗ 1:30 ⒻMd 5000 8 2 31½ 21½ 11 21½ Delgado A5 b 115 3.90 53-36 Excellent Bet 1201½RoadToMandalay115¾Japonika1151 Weakened 10
13Jan83- 2Bow fst 6f :22 :45⅘ 1:13⅘ ⒻMd 8500 5 9 516 614 410 87¼ Wright D R b 120 9.30 64-23 Villapath 1152 Mom's Friend 115¾ Rollicking Nel 1131 Tired 12
17Dec82- 1Lrl gd 6f :24 :49⅘ 1:17 ⒻMd 8000 1 1 46½ 43½ 52¾ 43½ Hutton G W b 118 4.20 54-32 LittleBoldCotton113½ExcellentBet1081½Flhven1181½ Raced evenly 11
4Dec82- 2Pen gd 6f :23⅕ :46⅘ 1:13⅘ ⒻMd 7500 9 1 86¾ 68½ 23 23 Hutton G W b 116 *2.80 73-18 All Toshed Up 1163 RoadToMandalay1161½MissPrissy1164 Rallied 11
22Nov82- 3Lrl fst 6f :23⅘ :48⅗ 1:14⅖ ⒻMd 10000 10 10 98½ 67 79½ 710 Hutton G W b 117 7.30 61-26 Birdbyrock117½CrossingGurd1171½SwetAspirtions1164½ No factor 12
2Nov82- 9Key fst 6f :22⅘ :46 1:14⅖ ⒻMd 12500 4 12 86¾ 918 917 917 Ruane J b 120 4.00 52-23 Ann's Vibes1164½SassySantee1202¾ChargeTheMost115nk Off slow 12
1Oct82- 3Bow fst 6f :23 :46⅘ 1:14 Md 11500 10 1 44½ 58 33½ 2nk Hutton G W b 117¼ 9.10 70-21 Tameel 112nk ⒹⒽL'Estranger120ⒹⒽRoadToMandalay1174½ Rallied 12
1Oct82-Dead heat

Miss Tish's Tudor — Dk. b. or br. f. 4, by Tudor Gleeman—Bubbling Sue, by Boldnesian
$5,000 Br.—Vaughan T J (NC)
Own.—Vaughan T J — Tr.—Dutrow Richard E — 117⁵
Lifetime 8 0 0 3 $2,010 — 1983 7 M 0 2 $1,350 — 1982 1 M 0 1 $660

25Mar83- 1Pim fst 6f :24⅘ :48⅘ 1:15⅘ 3↑ Md 5000 8 1 2hd 23 46 812 Saumell L b 117 6.10 55-27 John's Rogue 1082½ Intrusive 1071½ Final Way 1096 Tired 10
9Mar83- 1Bow sly 7f :23⅗ :48 1:29 Md 5000 8 5 1½ 14 1hd 36 Miller D A Jr b 115 3.20 54-35 Espionage 120no Sound Hill 1106 Miss Tish'sTudor1154 Gave way 8
28Feb83- 1Bow fst 6f :23⅖ :47⅕ 1:12⅗ Md 5000 4 4 21 2½ 22 48 Miller D A Jr b 115 6.80 69-28 Solitary Prince1155[D]RestlessStuff1203SensablePappa115hd Tired 12
28Feb83-Placed third through disqualification
15Feb83- 1Bow fst 7f :23⅕ :46⅘ 1:26⅖ Md 5000 2 9 11 12 21½ 48 Miller D A Jr b 115 33.90 65-22 Nolichucky 1152½SoundHill1105TargetDesignated115½ Drifted Out 12
3Feb83- 9Bow sly 6f :23⅖ :47⅖ 1:14⅕ Md 5000 9 6 62¾ 53 1016 1016 Miller D A Jr b 115 4.70 53-35 Out Of Trance 1151 Dona Princessa 109¾ Enfant DeFer1151 Wide 11
11Jan83- 2Bow sly 6f :23⅗ :48⅗ 1:15⅖ Md 5000 3 3 21 58 714 720 Miller D A Jr 115 1.50 43-37 Computer 1201 Out Of Trance 1153½ Wake At Sea 1132 Fell back 8
4Jan83- 4Bow fst 6f :23 :47⅕ 1:13 Md Sp Wt 12 4 21½ 26 1223 1233 Pino M G 115 15.50e 42-31 Wild Man 1209 Jay Leiter 115½ Henchman 1203 Tired 12
23Dec82- 3Lrl fst 6f :23⅖ :48⅖ 1:14⅕ 3↑ ⒻMd 13000 4 8 11 1hd 34 311 Delgado A5 115 18.40 61-23 MarshDncer1204½ThisTimeAround1206MissTish'sTudor1151 Tired 11

Issuenique — B. f. 4, by Issue—Satinique, by Stratmat
$5,000 Br.—Just A Farm (Va)
Own.—Clelland Janet H — Tr.—Aguirre Horatio — 122
Lifetime 10 0 2 1 $2,270 — 1983 1 M 0 0 $76 — 1982 9 M 2 1 $2,194

30Jan83- 1CT my 4½f :22⅘ :47⅗ :54⅕ ⒻMd Sp Wt 3 4 53½ 56½ 68½ Marshall E M7 113 5.40 75-11 Another Try 113½ Anniversary Sandi 120nkZanibar1203 No Factor 10
17Dec82- 9Lrl gd 6f :23 :48 1:14⅗ ⒻClm 6250 4 5 88¼ 1016 1118 1123 McMillan K M7 108 62.20 47-32 Sail The Cape 1143 Golden Darter 1093 King's Linn 1151 Outrun 12
10Dec82- 3Lrl fst 6f :23 :47⅘ 1:14 3↑ ⒻMd 7500 3 2 1½ 21½ 31½ 36 McMillan K M5 115 13.10 67-18 Hippodrome 1152½ Dona Princessa 1153½ Issuenique 1151½ Tired 9
23Nov82- 3Lrl fst 6f :23⅕ :48⅖ 1:14 3↑ Md 7500 5 1 1½ 33 48 611 Rujano M 117 10.60 62-27 Susan Blackeyed 1195 Annual Custom1201Nolichucky120nk Tired 7
17Nov82- 3Lrl fst 6f :23 :47⅗ 1:14⅖ 3↑ ⒻMd 10000 5 6 34 49 69¾ 711 Rujano M 120 19.00 60-27 Lady of Lust 1201½ Sandy Topaz 115nkMissWellington1152½ Tired 10
8Nov82- 1Lrl fst 6f :22⅘ :47 1:14⅕ 3↑ Md 10000 9 2 21½ 35½ 55 72½ Hutton G W 117 44.80 69-26 Fast Promoter 120hd Tanxnitan 120hd Dual Prospect 118no Tired 12
27Oct82- 4Lrl fst 6f :23⅘ :49⅕ 1:15⅖ 3↑ ⒻMd 8000 8 7 2hd 22 64½ 67½ Marshall E M10 109 13.40 58-27 Goldies Love 122½ SeeingStars1193½SundownPleasure1151½ Tired 12
12Oct82- 9Bow fst 6f :23⅖ :47⅗ 1:13⅕ 3↑ ⒻMd 5000 4 5 21 23½ 24 28 Marshall E M10 109 5.40 66-24 Eager Nita 1148 Issuenique 1091 Gallant Mitzi 1191 Steadied 12
31Aug82- 9Tim fst *6½f :24 :48⅗ 1:20⅗ 3↑ ⒻMd 5000 10 8 64¾ 46 22½ 21½ Barreira A M 117 10.80 75-20 Willa Wah 1171½ Issuenique 1174½ Smashing Sue 1172 Rallied 10
11Jun82- 2Lrl fst 6f :23⅗ :48⅗ 1:14 3↑ ⒻMd 5000 6 8 816 717 723 724 Hutton G W b 115 3.30 49-24 Stephanie's Dream 1179 OldTimegal1154¾Pippi1172½ Broke slowly 8

LATEST WORKOUTS Mar 11 Bow 4f gd :54 b

Sing For Money — Ro. f. 3, by Rouge Chanteur—Tourn Field, by Top Tourn
$5,000 Br.—Turner D F (Ont-C)
Own.—Rickman W — Tr.—Delloso Anthony J — 107⁵
Lifetime 8 0 0 2 $1,520 — 1983 5 M 0 1 $1,140 — 1982 3 M 0 1 $380

7Mar83- 1Bow fst 6f :23⅕ :47⅘ 1:14⅗ ⒻClm 5000 4 6 79 612 48½ 46½ Bracciale V Jr 116 26.60 60-27 Gretchen M. 117¾ Mandora 1105 Rose Bud Jill 117¾ Lugged in 8
1Mar83- 9Bow sly 6f :23⅗ :47⅘ 1:15⅘ ⒻMd 5000 3 4 47½ 59 716 813 Bracciale V Jr 120 15.20 48-25 Gretchen M. 1205 French Dogwood 120hd Lady Swan 115hd Tired 12
16Feb83- 1Bow fst 7f :23⅗ :48 1:29 ⒻMd 5000 11 6 56 913 1220 1228 Pino M G 120 6.10 32-33 Linda Topaz 1208 Road To Mandalay 1202 Giger's Girl 1201 Wide 12
4Feb83- 1Bow gd 6f :23⅕ :47⅖ 1:15 ⒻMd 5000 3 9 74 65 43 38¼ Bracciale V Jr 120 *2.90 57-36 RyRy'sPrid1155BontoWnd1203½SngForMony1201½ Lacked A Rally 12
14Jan83- 3Bow fst 6f :23⅘ :48⅗ 1:14⅗ ⒻClm 5000 1 3 2hd 2½ 32½ 46½ Ford T L 115 30.30 60-32 Barbara's Champ 1085 Sadie'sTime112½Detectoress1131 Wekened 8
4Dec82- 2Pen gd 6f :23⅕ :46⅘ 1:13⅗ ⒻMd 7500 10 4 65¾ 818 717 716 Lloyd J S 116 3.40 60-18 All Toshed Up 1163 RoadToMandalay1161½MissPrissy1164 Outrun 11
22Nov82- 6Lrl fst 7f :23⅖ :47⅗ 1:28⅘ ⒻMd 16000 11 7 88 918 1014 1013 Moreno O 114 10.00 54-26 ForeverIngenue1173½Rogue'sPlesur1142½AltitudSpry1171½ Outrun 12
10Nov82- 1CT fst 4½f :23 :47⅘ :54⅖ ⒻMd Sp Wt 9 7 42½ 45 32 Moreno O 118 2.30 80-16 Shelly's Imp 1181 Mito Bandito 1181 SingForMoney1181½ Rallied 10

Westminster Seven — Ch. f. 3, by Roanoke Island—Marla Queen, by Jim J
$5,000 Br.—K T Leatherbury Assoc Inc (Md)
Own.—Chaney R — Tr.—Leatherbury King T — 112
Lifetime 8 0 0 0 $825 — 1983 2 M 0 0 $270 — 1982 6 M 0 0 $555

23Mar83- 9Pim fst 6f :23⅘ :48⅗ 1:16⅘ 3↑ ⒻMd 5000 10 3 21½ 22½ 22½ 44 Passmore W J b 113 4.70 58-30 Aggie Sue 1091½ Snobbish 115¾ Gold Sound 1222 Weakened 11
4Feb83- 1Bow gd 6f :23⅕ :47⅖ 1:15 ⒻMd 5000 10 1 5¾ 33 32½ 511 Miller D A Jr b 120 6.40 54-36 RyRy'sPrd1155BontoWnd1203½SngForMny1201½ Wide, Weakened 12
22Nov82- 3Lrl fst 6f :23⅗ :48⅗ 1:14⅖ ⒻMd 9000 6 7 63¾ 78 1118 1121 Passmore W J b 115 3.10e 50-26 Birdabyrock117½CrossingGurd1171½SweetAspirtions1164½ Outrun 12
26Oct82- 3Lrl gd 6f :23⅘ :49⅘ 1:16⅘ ⒻMd 8500 12 2 11½ 2hd 2½ 42 Passmore W J b 114 26.90 57-29 Royal Valentine 117no Japonika 1122 Honey 117hd Weakened 12
8Oct82- 2Bow fst 6f :23⅖ :47⅘ 1:14 ⒻMd 13500 9 8 98¾ 79¾ 911 917 Passmore W J b 118 8.10 53-27 Sawney Lady 1181 Medieval Rose 1206½Ivegotafeeling118nk Wide 11
9Sep82- 5Bow fst 6f :23⅗ :48⅕ 1:14⅘ ⒻMd 23500 4 8 1211 1220 1221 1228 Passmore W J b 120 11.80 38-22 Bold Lily 1152 Ligner 1203 Aid A Friend 1153 Outrun 12
18Aug82- 3Tim fst *6½f :23⅘ :48⅖ 1:20⅕ ⒻMd Sp Wt 3 2 810 714 714 721 Lindberg G b 117 2.80e 57-23 NoBodyElse's1176Phoebe'sPhandango1172¾GalBll1121½ Taken up 9
30Jly82- 3Tim fst 4f :22⅘ :46⅘ ⒻMd Sp Wt 2 7 48½ 48 49½ Lindberg G b 117 7.80 81-10 ScreenGala1171Catherine'sRay117½SearchForSatin1178 No factor 7

LATEST WORKOUTS Mar 19 Lrl 3f my :39⅗ b — Mar 5 Lrl 3f fst :38 b — Feb 25 Lrl 5f gd 1:07 b — Feb 19 Lrl 3f gd :39 b

As in the first race, the *Performance Method* selects one horse, **Distortion**, that appears to be clearly the best choice with the highest Ability Factor, a Condition Factor that merits attention, and the highest Total. **B.J. Baroness** appears to be a good second choice with figures not too much below those of **Distortion.** Do not be misled by **B.J.**'s two most recent races after a two-month layoff. The good early speed in both races is a positive sign. **Japonika** is not to be overlooked, however. She has a good Total despite the big weight shift that occurred at post time. Even for three-year-old fillies, 112 pounds is not an extraordinary burden.

Of the remaining horses, the fourth choice is a tossup between **Sing For Money** and **Westminster Seven**, noting that, despite lower numbers, the latter could be in a more fit condition. Could **Westminster Seven** be the "dark horse" of this race? Much the same could be said for **Miss Tish's Tudor**, but the post time weight of 122 pounds kills that idea.

The four horses to be played in this race are:

1. **Distortion**
2. **B.J. Baroness**
3. **Japonika**
4. **Sing For Money**

Due to a strong first choice in this race, it would be recommended to use a three-horse multiple box in the exacta, plus an additional box of **Distortion** and **Westminster Seven.**

In the daily double, these three top picks should be bet with the top three in the first race. Finally, it appears that a daily double ticket playing the top choice in the first race with **Westminster Seven** would be a worthwhile $2 saver as well.

2ND Pimlico 6F (4/5)

PP	#	NAME	Date: Last Race	Weight (Today's Race)	3 Speed Ratings + Track Variants	Weight Adjust.	*Ability Factor*	Speed Rating: Last Race	+21 or +25	Track Adjust.	Weight Adjust.	*Condition Factor*	Wt. at Post Time	Total	Adj. Total
1		TUSCANY'S GEM	3/23	115	263	-2	261	55	+21	-11	—	65	115	326	326
2		B.J. BARONESS	3/30	107	263	+4	(267)	60	+21	-11	+2	72	109	339	(337)
3		JAPONIKA	3/11	102	258	+4	262	59	+21	-5	+2	(77)	112	339	(335)
4		SMART SHOPPER	3/23	112	216	-2	214	43	+21	-11	-2	51	112	265	265
5		LADY SWAN	3/23	112	237	+2	239	47	+21	-11	-2	55	112	294	294
6		DISTORTION	3/17	112	273 a	—	(273)	65	+21	-11	+1	76 ↙	114	349	(347)
7		NANA'S CRUISE	3/9	107	213 a	—	213	51	+25	-5	+2	73	109	286	284
8		ROAD TO MANDALAY	3/1	107	245	+4	249	46	+25	-5	+2	68	110	317	314
9		MISS TISH'S TUDOR	3/25	117	267	-4	263	55	+21	-11	—	65	122	328	324
10		ISSUENIQUE	JAN.	122	253	-4	249	47	+25	-8	-2	62	122	311	311
11		SING FOR MONEY	3/7	107	253	+4	257	60	+21	-5	+2	(78)	109	335	333 ↙
12		WESTMINSTER SEVEN	3/23	112	254	+4	258	58	+21	-11	+1	69	113	327	326
13															
14															
15															
16															

SECOND RACE **6 FURLONGS. (1.09$\frac{1}{5}$) MAIDEN CLAIMING. Purse $4,500. Fillies. 3- and 4-year-olds. Weights, 3-year-olds, 112 lbs. 4-year-olds, 122 lbs. Claiming price $5,000.**

Pimlico

APRIL 5

Value of race $4,500, value to winner $2,700, second $990, third $540, fourth $270. Mutuel pool $32,070. Exacta Pool $51,242.

Last Raced	Horse	Eqt.	A.	Wt	PP	St	¼	½	Str	Fin	Jockey	Cl'g Pr	Odds $1
17Mar83 ^{9}Pim^{8}	Distortion		3	114	6	7	1^{hd}	2^{5}	1^{2}	1^{6}	Pino M G	5000	2.00
30Mar83 ^{9}Pim^{12}	B. J. Baroness		3	109	2	6	2^{1}	$1^{\frac{1}{2}}$	$2^{1\frac{1}{2}}$	$2^{\frac{3}{4}}$	McCarthy M J^{5}	5000	4.20
11Mar83 ^{9}Bow^{4}	Japonika	b	3	112	3	9	6^{hd}	$5^{2\frac{1}{2}}$	$3^{\frac{1}{2}}$	$3^{2\frac{1}{4}}$	Krone J A†	5000	10.30
23Mar83 ^{9}Pim^{4}	Westminster Seven	b	3	113	12	1	$5^{1\frac{1}{2}}$	4^{hd}	$4^{2\frac{1}{2}}$	4^{2}	Passmore W J	5000	7.50
9Mar83 ^{2}Bow^{6}	Nana's Cruise	b	3	109	7	8	7^{2}	$6^{1\frac{1}{2}}$	$6^{1\frac{1}{2}}$	$5^{1\frac{1}{2}}$	Young S J^{5}	5000	20.60
1Mar83 ^{9}Bow^{9}	Road To Mandalay	b	3	110	8	10	8^{1}	8^{3}	7^{3}	6^{3}	Prough J D^{5}	5000	13.10
25Mar83 ^{1}Pim^{8}	Miss Tish's Tudor	b	4	122	9	3	3^{1}	$3^{1\frac{1}{2}}$	5^{1}	7^{hd}	Hutton G W†	5000	5.70
23Mar83 ^{9}Pim^{5}	Tuscany's Gem	b	4	115	1	5	10^{1}	9^{4}	8^{4}	8^{hd}	Wallace J L II^{7}	5000	37.50
7Mar83 ^{1}Bow^{4}	Sing For Money		3	109	11	11	11^{6}	12	11^{3}	9^{1}	Delgado A^{5}	5000	12.50
23Mar83 ^{9}Pim^{11}	Smart Shopper	b	3	112	4	12	12	11^{1}	$10^{\frac{1}{2}}$	10^{5}	Foley D	5000	42.40
23Mar83 ^{9}Pim^{10}	Lady Swan	b	3	112	5	2	$4^{\frac{1}{2}}$	7^{hd}	9^{hd}	$11^{2\frac{1}{2}}$	Wright D R	5000	15.70
30Jan83 ^{1}CT^{6}	Issuenique		4	122	10	4	$9^{2\frac{1}{2}}$	10^{hd}	12	12	Runco J C	5000	27.10

OFF AT 1:29. Start good, Won driving. Time, :23$\frac{4}{5}$, :47$\frac{4}{5}$, 1:01, 1:14$\frac{2}{5}$ Track fast.

$2 Mutuel Prices:

6–DISTORTION	6.00	3.80	3.00
2–B. J. BARONESS		4.20	3.40
3–JAPONIKA			4.80

$2 EXACTA 6–2 PAID $33.60.

Ch. f, by Shady Character—Smile Pretty, by No Fear II. Trainer Logan Denis J. Bred by Hacker S J (Fla).

DISTORTION disputed the pace and drew off under steady handling. B. J. BARONESS had speed inside but was not good enough. JAPONIKA had a mild rally inside. WESTMINSTER SEVEN lacked a rally outside. NANA'S CRUISE was not a factor. MISS TISH'S TUDOR tired. SING FOR MONEY bore out entering the turn. LADY SWAN had brief speed along the rail.

Owners— 1, Rodgers Linda S; 2, Bar-Jo Farm; 3, Delp R W; 4, Chaney R; 5, Seibel T A; 6, Queen Ann Stable; 7, Vaughan T J; 8, Alecci J V; 9, Rickman W; 10, Musumeci F; 11, Pestridge Patricia A; 12, Clelland Janet H.

Trainers— 1, Logan Denis J; 2, Gino Luigi; 3, Delp Richard W; 4, Leatherbury King T; 5, Ford Richard E; 6, Allen Harold; 7, Dutrow Richard E; 8, Shaeffer John A; 9, Delloso Anthony J; 10, Daniels Edward J Jr; 11, Frock Clarence I; 12, Aguirre Horatio.

† Apprentice allowance waived: Japonika 10 pounds; Miss Tish's Tudor 5. **Overweight:** Distortion 2 pounds; B. J. Baroness 2; Westminster Seven 1; Nana's Cruise 2; Road To Mandalay 3; Sing For Money 2.

Scratched—Snobbish (23Mar83 ^{9}Pim^{2}); Tarnished Silver (16Mar83 ^{4}CT^{7}); Oaklands Porpetta (10Mar83 ^{1}Bow^{10}); Tana Quill; Fredot (11Mar83 ^{9}Bow^{7}).

$2 Daily Double 11–6 Paid $57.20. Daily Double Pool $38,421.

Well, **Distortion** did it! As the horses entered the stretch, the only major question was "Who will be second?"

$2 Exacta Wagering		$2 Daily Double Bets	
Bet	$ 34.00	Bet	$ 30.00
Return	$134.40	Return	$171.60
Profit	$100.40	Profit	$141.60

Once the first race had ended, it would have been possible to "hedge-bet" the three or four logical choices (using straight exactas) that might beat **Distortion** to the wire. In each case, the exacta would pay substantially more than the $2 cost of each ticket, but total profits would be reduced by $8.

This 6 furlong race has a small field after a late scratch. Nevertheless, it might be an opportunity to invest our daily double winnings. An exacta is available.

PIMLICO

6 FURLONGS. (1.09⅕) CLAIMING. Purse $10,000. 3-year-olds. Weight, 122 lbs. Non-winners of two races since February 22, allowed 3 lbs. A race, 5 lbs. A race since February 14, 8 lbs. Claiming price $23,500; for each $2,500 to $18,500, 1 lb. (Races where entered for $16,000 or less not considered.)

Rest

Ch. g. 3, by Good Counsel—Goodnight Irene, by Unconscious
$23,500 Br.—Backer W M (Md) Tr.—Mobberley John C
Own.—Backer W M
117⁵ Lifetime 8 3 0 0 $13,800 | 1983 6 3 0 0 $13,800 | 1982 2 M 0 0

Date	Race	Cond	Dist	Fractions	Class	PP	St	1/4	1/2	Str	Fin	Jockey	Wt	Odds	Comment	Field
29Mar83-	7Pim	fst	6f	:23⅕ :46⅘ 1:13	Clm 30000	7	2	3½	21	23	57¾	Pino M G	b 114	8.50	73-20 PreservationHall1142¼Shekmatyar1142¼Dike'sForecast1081½ Wide	7
19Mar83-	3Pim	sly	6f	:23 :46⅗ 1:12⅖	Clm 18500	1	3	11	13½	13	14½	Pino M G	b 119	5.20	84-16 Rest 1194½ Joe Z. 109nk Pocket's First 112no Driving	6
10Mar83-	3Bow	sly	6f	:23⅕ :47 1:13⅕	Clm 18500	3	5	1hd	1hd	12	1nk	Delgado A5	b 109	2.50	74-24 Rest 109nk Out Of Wedlock 1092 Lou's Image 1142 Driving	5
3Mar83-	7Bow	fst	6f	:22⅖ :45⅗ 1:12⅕	Clm 21000	3	6	58	510	610	510	Delgado A5	b 111	5.40	69-28 Cucuchuchu109½PreservtionHll119½Dike'sForecst1147 Raced wide	7
2Feb83-	7Bow	sly	6f	:22⅘ :46 1:10⅘	Alw 8500	3	7	44	49½	415	620	Pino M G	b 113	14.90	66-29 Unreal Zeal 1128 Warlock's Revenge 120hd Cutter Sark1127 Tired	8
19Jan83-	6Bow	fst	6f	:22⅗ :46⅕ 1:13	Md 25000	4	5	1½	11	13	11	Delgado A5	b 115	5.00e	75-29 Rest 1151 Doajig 1186 J. R.'s Kid 120nk Driving	12
16Dec82-	6Lrl	sly	6f	:22⅗ :47 1:14	Md 25000	11	6	34	21	41¾	58½	Delgado A5	b 113	8.00e	64-34 This Is True 1182¾ Rocket Guitar 118hd Johny Imp1182¾ Faltered	12
26Nov82-	4Lrl	fst	6f	:23⅕ :47⅖ 1:13⅗	Md 25000	2	5	31	22	58½	611	Delgado A5	113	10.20	64-24 BitterWrath1141JohnyImp1165Don'tHurtJane1183½ Raced greenly	9

Out Of Wedlock

B. g. 3, by Sunshine Trail—Cedar Ridge, by Rash Prince
$23,500 Br.—Henderson E E (WVa) Tr.—Berry William S Jr
Own.—Henderson D E
109⁵ Lifetime 15 2 5 0 $15,124 | 1983 10 1 4 0 $9,904 | 1982 5 1 1 0 $5,220

Date	Race	Cond	Dist	Fractions	Class	PP	St	1/4	1/2	Str	Fin	Jockey	Wt	Odds	Comment	Field
21Mar83-	6Pen	sly	6f	:22⅖ :46⅕ 1:12⅗	Alw 4700	4	6	46½	26	24	25¾	McCarthy M J5	b 113	*1.20	75-27 BoToMrket1085¾OutOfWedlock1134¾TwicQuick1134 Reared start	6
10Mar83-	3Bow	sly	6f	:23⅕ :47 1:13⅕	Clm 18500	1	2	52½	58¼	44	2nk	McCarthy M J5	b 109	5.40	74-24 Rest 109nk Out Of Wedlock 1092 Lou's Image 1142 Wide	5
1Mar83-	3Bow	gd	7f	:22⅘ :46⅕ 1:26⅖	Clm 18500	6	5	68	44½	56	68¾	Bracciale V Jr	b 115	3.80	64-24 Islero 1094½ Par Avion 114no Pentastic 1092 Wide, bore in	6
18Feb83-	7Bow	fst	6f	:23⅕ :47⅕ 1:13⅕	Clm 18500	4	1	62½	43	21½	21	McCarthy M J5	b 109	11.70	73-36 MrchngForMrgy1141OtOfWdlck1092Jhn'sMdcn1141 Wide, rallied	7
8Feb83-	5Bow	fst	7f	:22⅘ :45⅘ 1:26⅕	Clm 14500	7	5	56	55¼	3½	21¼	Bracciale V Jr	b 114	7.40	73-27 [D]Roman Fool1091¼OutOfWedlock114nkExcellentWind1141¼ Hung	7
8Feb83-Placed first through disqualification																
27Jan83-	4Bow	fst	6f	:23⅕ :47⅖ 1:13⅗	Clm 14500	3	7	77	710	67	43	Grable T C5	b 109	15.30	70-27 Sir Galaxy 1142¼ MarchingForMargy114nkRomanFool115½ Rallied	7
23Jan83-	10CT	sly	6½f	:24 :48⅕ 1:22⅗	Alw 4800	3	2	32	33	54½	56½	Alexander J P7	b 107	*1.40	65-32 Blue Rogue109hdPeepingPeter1204Cavalry'sRosa1162 Ducked out	7
16Jan83-	10CT	fst	6½f	:23⅘ :47⅖ 1:22⅗	Alw 4500	1	1	1hd	12	13	21½	Alexander J P7	b 111	2.10	70-26 ForgnCommrc1151½OtOfWdlock1111½R.Chrstophr111½ Weakened	6
11Jan83-	7Bow	sly	6f	:23 :46⅘ 1:13	Clm 18500	4	4	45	612	611	613	Hilburn W J5	b 109	23.40	62-37 Dashido 1091¼ Pocket's First 114¾ Gang Racer 1097 Tired	7
1Jan83-	3Lrl	fst	6f	:22⅘ :46⅖ 1:12	Alw 9000	5	3	44	35	59½	612	Delgado A	b 115	16.20	71-19 Illustrious Boat 1157 Tahawas 1151 Martini Break 1151¼ Tired	7

LATEST WORKOUTS ●Mar 28 CT 5f my 1:05⅗ h

Ancient Image

Ch. c. 3, by Plenty Old—Cognition, by Bald Eagle
$23,500 Br.—Audley Farm (Ky) Tr.—Yanofsky Howard
Own.—Chadwick G
114 Lifetime 13 2 3 2 $16,475 | 1983 5 1 2 0 $10,100 | 1982 8 1 1 2 $6,375

Date	Race	Cond	Dist	Fractions	Class	PP	St	1/4	1/2	Str	Fin	Jockey	Wt	Odds	Comment	Field
12Mar83-	5Key	sly	6f	:22⅗ :47⅗ 1:14	Clm 18000	5	2	26	26	2½	21¼	Alligood M A	b 118	4.20	70-31 R. Philip 1161¼AncientImage1181½GamblingTrance111no Game try	6
6Mar83-	7Key	fst	6f	:22⅖ :45⅖ 1:11⅖	Clm 22500	1	6	33½	56	310	410	Alligood M A	b 114	7.90	74-21 HailtoLeader1166TroubleBucks1164You'reAllBd114nk Brief speed	8
2Feb83-	6Key	sly	6f	:22⅖ :45⅘ 1:12⅗	Clm 20000	4	3	44½	46	23	26	Alligood M A	b 112	5.30	72-29 Chief Who 1186 Ancient Image 112¾GrandEvidence1122½ Bumped	7
12Jan83-	4Key	fst	6f	:23⅕ :47⅕ 1:12⅖	Clm 22500	11	3	61¾	77¼	612	58	Alligood M A	b 114	15.60	71-27 Rapid Wing 1151 Heavy Load 1181½ Haps Trance 120nk No factor	11
2Jan83-	5Key	fst	6f	:22⅘ :47⅖ 1:13⅖	Clm 17000	2	3	31½	32	1½	1nk	Alligood M A	b 114	5.70	74-29 Ancient Image 114nk You're All Bad 1163¼ChangHai1202½ Driving	5
27Dec82-	6Key	fst	6½f	:22⅘ :46⅘ 1:19⅘	Clm 17000	2	1	1hd	1hd	34	23½	Alligood M A	b 113	5.40	70-29 Berigorous1173½AncientImge113noDottie'sVlentin1174½ Game try	5
24Nov82-	1Key	fst	6f	:23⅖ :48⅕ 1:14⅘	Md c-12500	5	5	2hd	1½	12	15½	Pizzo P S3	b 117	*1.40	67-33 AncientImage1175½GrandEvidence116noAnDrewAwy110nk Driving	3
12Nov82-	1Key	fst	6f	:22⅗ :46⅗ 1:14⅕	Md 11500	7	8	31½	65½	42½	31½	Pizzo P S3	115	3.90	68-25 AllegedRuler1201Cvlry'sMemories116½AncientImg1151½ Bore out	12
18Oct82-	4Key	fst	6f	:23 :47⅖ 1:14⅕	Md 12500	3	7	72	56½	47½	47½	Pizzo P S3	117	3.00	62-28 Gambling Trance 120no NobleCadet1167DupleArmor120½ Checked	11
3Oct82-	1Key	fst	6f	:23 :47⅖ 1:13⅗	Md 16000	6	8	31	42½	42	56	Pizzo P S3	117	5.80	67-24 NorthernAlantic120½Breckinridge1131¼Intheblck120hd Weakened	11

LATEST WORKOUTS ●Apr 4 Key 3f gd :37⅘ b Mar 28 Key 3f fst :39⅖ b Mar 4 Key 3f fst :36⅖ b

Ineffable Affair

B. g. 3, by Dike—Samantha S, by Francis S
$23,500 Br.—Siegel Jan (Cal) Tr.—Tammaro John III
Own.—Siegel J
114 Lifetime 16 1 0 4 $8,335 | 1983 5 0 0 1 $1,550 | 1982 11 1 0 3 $6,785 | Turf 1 0 0 0

Date	Race	Cond	Dist	Fractions	Class	PP	St	1/4	1/2	Str	Fin	Jockey	Wt	Odds	Comment	Field
18Mar83-	5Pim	sly	6f	:23⅖ :46⅖ 1:11⅖	Clm 30000	2	3	36½	511	516	520	Hutton G W	b 114	7.30	69-26 Cucuchuchu11211PreservationHall115½ChristinRuler114nk Outrun	6
9Mar83-	7Bow	sly	6f	:22⅘ :46⅖ 1:11⅗	Clm 27500	3	1	21½	24	36½	38	Osani J R Jr	b 113	14.20	74-35 MartiniBrek1192PreservtionHll1156IneffbleAffir1133 Drifted wide	7
18Feb83-	6Bow	fst	1⅛	:49 1:14⅖ 1:48⅗	Alw 9000	1	1	11	35½	22½	511	Hutton G W	b 112	10.20	52-36 Canadian Factor 1206Fairsea109noDike'sForecast1134½ Weakened	6
4Feb83-	6Bow	fst	6f	:22⅖ :45⅗ 1:12⅗	Clm 30000	4	2	38	310	38½	47	Hutton G W	b 114	31.60	70-36 Martini Break 1193½Shekmatyar1192Dashido1081¾ Lacked a Rally	7
8Jan83-	3GP	sly	6f	:22⅕ :45 1:10⅘	Clm 22500	6	7	53½	56	912	814	Thornburg B	b 117	16.30	71-17 Devil's Pawn 112nk Proud Johu 1191¼ Speier's Luck 1136 Tired	12
29Dec82-	10Crc	fst	170	:47⅘ 1:14⅖ 1:47	Clm 30000	8	1	11½	1½	54½	98¼	Thornburg B	b 118	32.50	67-17 Game Greek 120nk Squall Warning1141½Mr.Charger1141½ Used up	12
8Dec82-	4Crc	fst	6f	:22⅕ :46⅕ 1:13⅗	Md 20000	9	3	12	14	14	12	Marquez C	b 119	4.90	83-21 Ineffable Affair 1192 Rebrezzed 1191 Ell's BoldLark1191½ Driving	12
15Oct82-	5Med	fst	170	:46⅖ 1:12 1:43⅕	Md Sp Wt	6	1	11	58½	922	931	Thornburg B	b 118	10.40	54-20 Nturlistic1182¾BrightKingdom1185½Dependence1187 Used in pace	9
8Sep82-	4Med	fst	6f	:22⅘ :46⅖ 1:12⅕	Md 25000	5	3	31½	32½	24	36¾	Thornburg B	b 118	4.80	75-18 Admiral's Gin 1163½Bev'sBoy1183½IneffableAffair118nk Weakened	12
18Aug82-	3Atl	fst	5½f	:22⅗ :46⅗ 1:06	Md 25000	1	1	42	32½	32	32½	Feliciano B R	b 116	14.60	86-21 Michael'sBad1202½Mr.ChiefJustice120hdIneffableAffir1167 Evenly	7

LATEST WORKOUTS Mar 29 Pim 3f fst :38 b ●Mar 5 Bow 4f fst :47⅖ b Feb 28 Bow 4f fst :49 b

Cucuchuchu

Ch. c. 3, by Russ Miron—Watcher Run, by Lurullah
$23,500 Br.—Cain Mrs M J (Ohio) Tr.—Nanez R Carlos
Own.—Fischer S G
115⁷ Lifetime 13 3 4 1 $22,280 | 1983 8 2 2 1 $16,310 | 1982 5 1 2 0 $5,970

Date	Race	Cond	Dist	Fractions	Class	PP	St	1/4	1/2	Str	Fin	Jockey	Wt	Odds	Comment	Field
29Mar83-	7Pim	fst	6f	:23⅕ :46⅘ 1:13	Clm 30000	5	4	1hd	31	44	68	Young S J7	b 115	*1.30	73-20 PreservationHall1142½Shekmtyr1142½Dike'sForecst1081½ Faltered	7
18Mar83-	5Pim	sly	6f	:23⅖ :46⅖ 1:11⅖	Clm 30000	5	2	16	110	110	111	Young S J7	b 112	2.70	89-26 Cucuchuchu11211PreservationHall115½ChristinRuler114nk Driving	6
3Mar83-	7Bow	fst	6f	:22⅖ :45⅗ 1:12⅕	Clm 23500	1	3	12	16	15	1½	Young S J7	b 109	9.10	79-28 Cucuchuchu 109½PreservationHall119½Dike'sForecast1147 Driving	7
21Feb83-	7Bow	fst	6f	:22⅖ :46 1:11⅖	Alw 8500	6	5	43½	43½	68½	710	Young S J5	b 109	27.50	73-22 Cutter Sark 117hd A Sip Of Julep 1204 Barter Baron 1202 Tired	8
10Feb83-	6Bow	fst	7f	:23⅕ :46⅘ 1:26⅘	Clm c-18500	1	3	11½	12½	2hd	23¼	Pino M G	b 114	3.30	70-31 PreservtionHll1193¼Cucuchuchu1146NuticlSir1146 Best of others	6
1Feb83-	6Bow	fst	6f	:23⅕ :47 1:13⅕	Clm 18500	6	6	31	2hd	2½	32¼	Pino M G	114	6.00	72-29 Pocket's First 1091½ Bitter Wrath 114¾ Cucuchuchu 114¾ Bore in	7
19Jan83-	7Bow	fst	6f	:22⅖ :45⅘ 1:12⅖	Clm 25000	4	6	54	46½	714	713	Grove P	114	10.40	65-29 Shekmatyar 1132 Dashido 114hd Dike's Forecast 109nk Tired	9
8Jan83-	4Bow	fst	6f	:22⅗ :46⅕ 1:12⅗	Clm 22500	1	4	2hd	2hd	2½	23	Gall D	113	6.70e	74-26 Martini Break 1143 Cucuchuchu 113nk Hardi 115½ Drifted out	8
30Dec82-	5Lrl	fst	6f	:23⅕ :47⅖ 1:13⅗	Clm 16000	6	5	3½	2hd	1hd	2¾	Grove P	116	8.40	74-27 Country General 118¾Cucuchuchu1164GallantGrant1142¼ Bumped	8
21Dec82-	1Key	fst	6f	:23⅕ :47⅗ 1:14⅖	Md 12500	9	1	2hd	15	16	17½	Russo A Jr	120	*3.10	69-27 Cucuchuchu1207½MyRowdyFrnds1201¾MornngFlr115¾ Ridden out	12

Transporter

Dk. b. or br. c. 3, by Son of Bagdad—I'm Trucking, by Dilly Boy II
$23,500 Br.—Harris W R (Md) Tr.—Bailes W Meredith
Own.—Harris W R
114⁵ Lifetime 3 1 1 0 $5,550 | 1983 2 1 0 0 $3,900 | 1982 1 M 1 0 $1,650

Date	Race	Cond	Dist	Fractions	Class	PP	St	1/4	1/2	Str	Fin	Jockey	Wt	Odds	Comment	Field
25Mar83-	3Pim	fst	6f	:24 :47⅖ 1:13⅘	3↑ Md 18500	8	3	2½	2hd	1½	13½	Nicol P A Jr5	b 108	3.30	77-27 Transporter 1083½ A Breezy Spray 110no Denim Guy 1141 Driving	8
14Mar83-	9Bow	fst	6f	:23⅕ :47⅕ 1:12⅘	Md 18500	5	7	53¾	42	54½	76¾	Nicol P A Jr5	b 115	4.70	69-28 Crafty Mate 1154½ Storm Talk 1201 Doajig 120½ Tired	11
28May82-	5Lrl	sly	5f	:23⅗ :47⅘ 1:00⅗	Md Sp Wt	5	6	44½	22½	25	21¾	Nunez A	b 118	10.20	80-23 Informore 1131¾ Transporter 118noKnightOfTheStar118no Gamely	8

LATEST WORKOUTS Apr 2 Lrl 4f fst :50 b Mar 10 Bow 4f sly :50⅖ bg Mar 5 Bow 6f fst 1:15⅕ h Mar 1 Bow 4f gd :50⅕ bg

This is the type of race that you like to see once in a while: a small field with the public betting the wrong horses. The clear choice, **Out of Wedlock,** is being overlooked by the other bettors. As far as your calculations are concerned, there are only three horses in this race:

1. **Out of Wedlock**
2. **Ineffable Affair**
3. **Ancient Image**
4. –

Although you are bothered a little by the fact that **Rest** beat **Out of Wedlock** the last time they met (Bowie, March 10), the weight shift will be in **Out of Wedlock**'s favor. This time, he may be able to catch him.

The difference between our second and third choices and the two remaining horses is not that great. Nevertheless, the three horses should used in a multiple box, along with an additional exacta box featuring **Out of Wedlock** and **Rest.** Assuming your first choice is correct, and if **Rest** does finish second, you will lose little in the process.

3RD PIMLICO 6F (4/5)

PP	#	NAME	Date: Last Race	Weight (Today's Race)	3 Speed Ratings + Track Variants	Weight Adjust.	*Ability Factor*	Speed Rating: Last Race	+21 or +25	Track Adjust.	Weight Adjust.	*Condition Factor*	Wt. at Post Time	Total	Adj. Total
1		REST	3/29	117	291	-2	289	73	+21	-11	-2	81	117	370	370
2		OUT OF WEDLOCK	3/21	109	309	+2	311	75	+25	-9	+2	93	109	404	404
3		ANCIENT IMAGE	3/12	114	297	—	297	70	+25	-6	+2	91	115	388	387
4		INEFFABLE AFFAIR	3/18	114	310	-1	309	69	+25	-11	—	83	114	392	392
5		CUCUCHUCHU	3/29	115	315	-4	311	73	+21	-11	—	83	SCRATCHED		
6		TRANSPORTER	3/25	114	300a	—	300	77	+21	-11	-2	85	119	385	381
7															
8															
9															
10															
11															
12															
13															
14															
15															
16															

THIRD RACE 6 FURLONGS. (1.09⅕) CLAIMING. Purse $10,000. 3-year-olds. Weight, 122 lbs. Non-winners of two races since February 22, allowed 3 lbs. A race, 5 lbs. A race since February 14, 8 lbs. Claiming price $23,500; for each $2,500 to $18,500, 1 lb. (Races where entered for $16,000 or less not considered.)

Pimlico

APRIL 5

Value of race $10,000, value to winner $6,000, second $2,200, third $1,200, fourth $600. Mutuel pool $35,133. Exacta Pool $56,813.

Last Raced	Horse	Eqt.A.Wt	PP	St	¼	½	Str	Fin	Jockey	Cl'g Pr	Odds $1
21Mar83 6Pen2	Out Of Wedlock	b 3 109	2	1	41	3hd	23½	12¾	McCarthy M J5	23500	4.10
18Mar83 5Pim5	Ineffable Affair	b 3 114	4	5	3½	43	41½	2½	Osani J R Jr	23500	5.40
29Mar83 7Pim5	Rest	b 3 117	1	2	23½	14	1hd	32	Delgado A5	23500	1.10
12Mar83 5Key2	Ancient Image	b 3 115	3	4	5	5	5	41¼	Edwards J W	23500	10.30
25Mar83 3Pim1	Transporter	b 3 119	5	3	1hd	21	3hd	5	Byrnes D†	23500	2.20

OFF AT 1:56 Start good, Won ridden out. Time, :23⅕, :46⅕, :59⅘, 1:12⅘ Track fast.

$2 Mutuel Prices:				
	2-OUT OF WEDLOCK	10.20	4.00	2.60
	4-INEFFABLE AFFAIR		7.20	3.40
	1-REST			2.60
	$2 EXACTA 2-4 PAID $52.00.			

B. g, by Sunshine Trail—Cedar Ridge, by Rash Prince. Trainer Berry William S. Bred by Henderson E E (WVa).

OUT OF WEDLOCK drifted out shortly after the start bumping ANCIENT IMAGE, circled, drew off and was hand ridden the final sixteenth. INEFFABLE AFFAIR bumped early had a mild rally. REST gave way. ANCIENT IMAGE bore out leaving the gate and stumbled when bumped soon after the start, TRANSPORTER faltered.

Owners— 1, Henderson E Earle; 2, Siegel J; 3, Backer W M; 4, Chadwick G; 5, Harris W R.

Trainers— 1, Berry William S; 2, Tammaro John III; 3, Mobberley John C; 4, Yanofsky Howard; 5, Bailes W Meredith.

† Apprentice allowance waived: Transporter 5 pounds. Overweight: Ancient Image 1 pound.

Scratched—Cucuchuchu (29Mar83 7Pim6).

After a little concern as they approached the stretch, there were no surprises. It was a good race. It is unusual to find a contest that is as easy to call, with a small field, and provides an exacta payoff of more than $50.

$2 Exacta Wagering	
Bet	$ 22.00
Return	$156.00
Profit	$134.00

Eleven horses are entered in this 6 furlong race. It has the appearance of being a typical race for our needs. An exacta is available.

PIMLICO

6 FURLONGS. (1.09⅗) MAIDEN CLAIMING. Purse $5,500. 3- and 4-year-olds. Weights, 3-year-olds, 112 lbs. 4-year-olds, 122 lbs. Claiming price $8,500; for each $500 to $7,500.

Coupled—Up Bold and Dandy Duc.

Igloo Assessment

Gr. g. 3, by Restless Native—Cold Look, by Nearctic
$8,500 Br.—Christmas Mr-Mrs W G (Md)
Tr.—Murphy James W
Own.—Perrin J K
112
Lifetime 5 0 0 0 | 1983 3 M 0 0 | 1982 2 M 0 0

29Mar83- 3Pim fst 1¹⁄₁₆ :47⅗ 1:13 1:46⅘ 3↑ Md 14500 6 2 21½ 67½ 817 821 Bracciale V Jr b 115 5.70 52-20 Bull HeadBay1243¾AnotherRipple1121½StarPlayboy119no Faltered 8
8Mar83- 9Bow fst 7f :22⅘ :47⅘ 1:26⅘ Md 14500 9 6 11½ 23 36½ 616 Miller D A Jr b 120 8.50 57-24 Little Red Romeo 1208 Denim Guy 120no Flying Cop 1135 Tired 12
19Jan83- 6Bow fst 6f :22⅗ :46⅕ 1:13 Md 20000 6 8 89½ 98¾ 914 58 Bracciale V Jr b 118 *1.80e 67-29 Rest 1151 Doajig 1186 J. R.'s Kid 120nk No threat 12
27Dec82- 9Lrl gd 6f :22⅗ :47⅗ 1:14 Md 20000 3 4 69½ 612 812 58¾ Passmore W J b 118 8.80 64-29 Bowshock 1181 Islero 1184½ My New Toy 1182½ Lacked response 12
16Dec82- 6Lrl sly 6f :22⅗ :47 1:14 Md 25000 8 9 912 816 613 611 Young S J7 b 111 28.20 62-34 This Is True 1182¾ Rocket Guitar 118hd JohnyImp1182¾ No factor 12
LATEST WORKOUTS Mar 26 Lrl 4f fst :50⅗ b Mar 4 Lrl 5f fst 1:06 b Feb 24 Lrl 4f my :52⅖ b Feb 22 Hia 2f fst :24⅕ b

Up Bold

B. g. 3, by Bold Man—Circle Up, by Dedicate
$8,500 Br.—Clelland O (Md)
Tr.—Aguirre Horatio
Own.—Clelland O
112
Lifetime 7 0 0 0 | 1983 5 M 0 0 | 1982 2 M 0 0

31Mar83- 1Pim fst 6f :23⅕ :47⅕ 1:13⅕ 3↑ Md 14500 3 3 47 821 832 — Hutton G W b 112 37.40 — — Doajig 1141½ Bookie's Delight 1081¾ Ratlines 1222 Distanced 8
2Mar83- 2Pen fst 5f :23 :47⅕ 1:00 Md Sp Wt 6 5 3nk 812 816 822 Baker C J b 118 7.30 62-21 Little Tricky 1184¾ Silver Bridge 1181½ Alfarata 1152 Fell back 8
22Feb83- 1Bow fst 6f :23⅗ :47⅘ 1:13⅘ Md 14500 4 3 31 47 79¾ 814 Hutton G W b 120 36.90 57-31 Sum Account 1181½ Bookie's Delight 120nkPoppinJack1133 Tired 8
27Jan83- 5Bow fst 6f :22⅘ :47⅕ 1:13⅘ Md 14500 2 6 57½ 612 1123 1121 Osani J R Jr b 120 15.70 52-27 Nautical Sir 1201 Christian Ruler 1203½Powhattan1202¼ Fell back 12
8Jan83- 9Bow fst 6f :23 :46⅘ 1:12⅘ Md Sp Wt 1 4 43½ 1016 1121 1121 Osani J R Jr 120 59.80 56-26 Wrlock'sRvng120½Xylophon1151½DoblExplsn1153½ Bore out early 12
27Dec82- 9Lrl gd 6f :22⅗ :47⅗ 1:14 Md 20000 4 2 25 49½ 511 811 Hutton G W 118 11.60 62-29 Bowshock 1181 Islero 1184½ My New Toy 1182½ Tired 12
16Dec82- 6Lrl sly 6f :22⅗ :47 1:14 Md 25000 5 2 22 49½ 1016 1219 Hutton G W 118 7.00 54-34 This Is True 1182¾ Rocket Guitar 118hd Johny Imp1182¾ Faltered 12
LATEST WORKOUTS Feb 5 Bow 5f fst 1:00⅗ h

Last Time Out

B. c. 4, by Subpet—Love Chatch, by Missile
$8,500 Br.—Dodson B C (Fla)
Tr.—Donovan L William
Own.—Matheny W H L
122
Lifetime 1 0 0 0 | 1982 1 M 0 0 | 1981 0 M 0 0

4May82- 3Spt fst 6½f :23⅕ :47 1:18⅘ Md Sp Wt 2 2 43 42½ 55 812 Patterson A 120 17.50e 71-19 Twilight's Last 120hd Dreamer Boy 1202½ Cross of Heart 1204½ 9
LATEST WORKOUTS Apr 2 Pim 3f fst :40 b

Carry On Concord

Dk. b. or br. g. 4, by Wardlaw—Back On Top, by Carry Back
$8,500 Br.—Concord Farm (La)
Tr.—Bullock Alec J
Own.—Freed G A
117⁵
Lifetime 4 0 1 0 $1,480 | 1983 3 M 1 0 $1,480 | 1982 1 M 0 0

23Mar83- 1Pim fst 6f :23⅗ :48⅕ 1:14⅘ 3↑ Md 8500 6 5 25 2hd 1hd 2¾ Miller D A Jr b 122 5.20 71-30 Shalm113¾CrryOnConcord1223¾Nitrofrc108no Lugged In,Brushed 9
3Mar83- 5Bow fst 7f :22⅘ :46 1:26 Md 11500 9 4 52 1hd 21 612 Delgado A5 b 114 8.00 63-28 Indian Canoe 1155 Pop The Great 1151½ Big Friendly 111nk Tired 9
3Feb83- 9Bow sly 6f :23⅗ :47⅗ 1:14⅕ Md 5000 11 7 51¾ 2½ 1hd 42¾ Grove P 120 4.90 66-35 Out OfTrance1151DonaPrincessa109¾EnfantDeFer1151 Weakened 11
31Dec82- 1Lrl fst 6f :23⅕ :48 1:15⅕ 3↑ Md 5000 11 7 535 26 26 66 Delgado A5 115 5.10 61-24 GretOutdoors110hdBrogueRogue1221NuticlSpirit1223½ Lugged in 12
LATEST WORKOUTS Apr 2 Pim 3f fst :37 h Mar 22 Pim 3f my :38⅕ h Mar 16 Pim 5f fst 1:03 h ●Mar 12 Pim 5f gd 1:02 h

Dandy Duc

B. g. 3, by Just De Duc—Above Dixie, by Above The Law
$8,500 Br.—Clelland O (SC)
Tr.—Aguirre Horatio
Own.—Schott T J
112
Lifetime 9 0 1 1 $1,919 | 1983 1 M 0 0 | 1982 8 M 1 1 $1,919

25Feb83- 4Bow fst 6f :23⅖ :48 1:14⅘ Md 8500 5 1 63 78½ 85¾ 77½ Osani J R Jr b 120 25.20 58-28 Star Bucket 1131 Sailing Jake 1201½ Flying Cop 1132 No factor 10
30Dec82- 1Lrl fst 6f :23 :47⅘ 1:14⅘ Md 8000 2 12 117½ 916 1014 813 Hutton G W b 118 *2.70 56-27 Victor's Lica 1136 EveningJam1162½JenRac1161½ Broke in tangle 12
15Dec82- 1Lrl my 6f :23⅖ :48⅖ 1:15⅖ Md 8000 9 4 32½ 25 25 27 Hutton G W b 118 4.70 59-29 Noble Thrill 1187DandyDuc118¾MyManMilton1133 Best of others 12
7Dec82- 1Lrl fst 6f :22⅘ :47⅖ 1:14⅕ Md 10500 6 3 34 39 412 58½ Osani J R Jr b 114 25.90 63-25 DrizzlersHste113½ADifferentChoice1181LittleRedRomo1185 Tired 11
24Nov82- 3Lrl fst 6f :23⅕ :48⅖ 1:15⅕ Md 10500 2 8 75 813 813 815 MacKinnon S 114 35.50 52-28 Woody Tucker 1132½ Warrant For Arrest1182½FullIn1182½ Outrun 8
28Oct82- 4Lrl fst 6f :23⅗ :47⅘ 1:13⅘ Md 14000 5 7 75 811 815 815 MacKinnon S 114 13.50e 59-25 Country General 1181 Sir Fieldmont 118hd Johny Imp1163 Outrun 12
1Oct82- 1Bow fst 6f :23¾ :47⅘ 1:13⅕ Md 11500 3 6 41½ 21 31½ 46¼ MacKinnon S 120 6.60 68-21 Orangutan 1202 [D]Diplomatic Pride120½NoWindow1153¾ Impeded 11
1Oct82-Placed third through disqualification
21Sep82- 5Bow fst 6f :23⅕ :46⅘ 1:12⅘ Md 20000 9 10 914 918 715 719 Bracciale V Jr 118 7.80e 58-27 MarchingForMargy1205½Blue'sFriend1203½Shekmtyr118nk Outrun 11
5Sep82- 4Tim fst 4f :23⅕ :47⅗ Md Sp Wt 5 6 69 58½ 46½ MacKinnon S 118 20.30 80-11 Roadmark 1181 Illustrious Boat 1184½ SailingJake1181 Off Slowly 6
LATEST WORKOUTS ●Mar 22 Lrl 4f my :49⅗ b Feb 21 Bow 4f fst :51⅕ b

Annual Custom

B. g. 4, by On the Warpath—Artic Scheme, by Nearctic
$8,500 Br.—Gordonsdale Farm (Va)
Tr.—Carter E Clinton
Own.—Costello Kathleen
122
Lifetime 22 0 8 4 $9,895 | 1983 3 M 3 0 $2,060 | 1982 19 M 5 4 $7,835 | Turf 1 0 0 0

6Mar83- 1CT fst 4½f :22⅘ :46⅕ :52⅘ Md Sp Wt 5 4 21½ 24 23 Palmer R W b 120 4.20 87-09 Double Pacific 1203 Annual Custom 120nk Yeoman 1202 Held 2nd 10
20Feb83- 1CT fst 4½f :23 :47⅗ :54 Md Sp Wt 2 3 2hd 2½ 2¾ Palmer R W b 120 1.80 83-11 Oxford Love 120¾AnnualCustom120noCoolAndRegal1152 Bore out 7
22Jan83- 4CT fst 4½f :22⅘ :47⅗ :53⅘ Md 5000 2 5 21½ 21½ 2no Hansby A E7 b 112 *1.20 85-10 Lil Trader 119no Annual Custom 1122 NuButtons1201 Just missed 9
10Dec82- 9Lrl fst 6f :23 :47 1:13 3↑ Md 10000 12 1 1½ 23 54 86 Wright D R b 117 3.50 72-18 Tanxnitan 113½ Espionage 1131½ Mount Pharos1201 Bore in, tired 12
2Dec82- 3Lrl sly 6f :23⅕ :48 1:14⅖ 3↑ Md 10000 6 1 21 2hd 1hd 3nk Wright D R b 120 4.20 71-24 DonBigShot115nkAngel'sRage116noAnnualCustom1201 Weakened 7
23Nov82- 3Lrl fst 6f :23⅕ :48⅖ 1:14 3↑ Md 7500 7 3 2½ 12 24 25 Wright D R b 120 1.60 68-27 SusanBlackeyed1195AnnualCustom1201Nolichucky120nk Checked 7
8Nov82- 1Lrl fst 6f :22⅘ :47 1:14⅕ 3↑ Md 10000 6 4 31½ 22½ 22½ 4nk Wright D R b 120 10.30 72-26 FastPromoter120hdTanxnitan120hdDulProspect118no Lckd Lt Bid 12
31Oct82- 1CT fst 4½f :22⅘ :47⅗ :53⅘ 3↑ Md Sp Wt 7 4 41¾ 43¼ 41½ Figgins O Jr b 118 5.50 84-13 NtivePukk118½CollosIBlunder118noRussellSprout111¾ No Mishap 10
20Oct82- 4CT fst 4½f :22⅗ :47⅗ :53⅘ 3↑ Md 8000 9 1 2hd 11 2½ Figgins O Jr b 118 2.60 84-13 Saralerno 118½ Annual Custom 1181½ PinballLou118no Just failed 9
6Oct82- 1CT fst 4½f :22⅗ :47 :53⅘ 3↑ Md 10000 3 4 43 44½ 33¾ Figgins O Jr b 118 3.50 81-14 Restless Kind 113¾ Saralerno 1183 Annual Custom 1181½ Evenly 6

Hand Fast

Ro. c. 4, by Master Hand—Gouyave, by Grey Dawn II
$8,500 Br.—Dodderidge R A (Va)
Tr.—Jeffries Robert A
Own.—Dodderidge R A
122
Lifetime 3 0 0 0 | 1982 3 M 0 0 | 1981 0 M 0 0

24Nov82- 2Aqu fst 6f :23⅗ :49 1:14⅗ 3↑ Md 20000 7 10 95½ 67 59½ 59¾ Beitia E b 120 8.90 59-36 NoDrilling1163¾SignalNine1065¾CpitlColonel113¾ P'ssd tired ones 13
14Nov82- 3Aqu fst 6f :22⅘ :46⅖ 1:12⅘ 3↑ Md 20000 8 11 76 77 76½ 77¾ Beitia E b 120 18.90 71-23 LetterPerfect1201½SetTheCharge1111½AngusLane1161½ No factor 12
18Oct82- 4Aqu fst 6f :22⅕ :46⅗ 1:13 3↑ Md 25000 5 13 99½ 1013 108 127½ Sweigert L10 109 56.60 68-23 Oscar My Love 1222½ Andrew Scott 119no Fireman 114hd Outrun 14

Boassionato

Ro. g. 3, by Appassionato—Boog A Do, by Whats Up Doc
$8,500 Br.—Jenkins I E (Md)
Tr.—Horn J Robert
Own.—Jenkins I
112
Lifetime 6 0 0 0 | 1983 6 M 0 0 | 1982 0 M 0 0

22Mar83- 9Pim fst 1¹⁄₁₆ :48 1:14 1:48⅘ 3↑ Md 8500 5 8 98½ 109 913 915 Foley D b 112 10.20 48-22 For All Ages 112hdMuldoon113nkRunAwayJack114nk Hesitated st. 11
11Mar83- 1Bow gd 7f :23⅖ :47⅕ 1:28 Md 8500 5 9 74½ 53 44½ 52½ Foley D b 120 24.90 62-33 Our First Choice 1201 No Hoax 118no SailingJake1201½ No factor 9
25Feb83- 1Bow fst 6f :23 :47⅕ 1:13⅘ Md 8500 4 9 1119 1122 1122 1015 Young S J5 115 14.20 56-28 Oxford Dancer 1205 For All Ages 1151½ CaptainVideo120¾ Outrun 11
9Feb83- 5Bow fst 7f :23⅗ :47 1:26⅘ Md 11500 8 9 77¾ 77¼ 78 78 McCarthy M J5 115 42.10 65-30 Over There 1202½ Latin Illusion 1203 Elude 1151 Outrun 10
28Jan83- 1Bow fst 6f :23⅕ :47 1:13⅘ Md 11500 8 3 74¾ 78 712 712 McCarthy M J5 115 22.60 61-35 ExuberantDve11511CptinVideo120noRunDutchRun120no No factor 9
10Jan83- 1Bow sly 6f :23⅗ :48⅖ 1:15⅗ Md 8500 11 10 88½ 810 79 59½ Feliciano B M Jr7 113 25.60 54-32 Tactition 1133½ Oh Shockalot 115½ Ali Aloof 1151 Wide, Evenly 11
LATEST WORKOUTS Apr 1 Lrl 4f fst :51⅕ b Mar 4 Bow 3f fst :36⅕ b ●Feb 23 Bow 3f fst :35 h

Latin Illusion — Dk. b. or br. c. 3, by Latin Humor—Daughter Of Debt, by Renombre — $7,500 — Br.—Cornett I & Patricia (Md) — Tr.—Castrenze Charles Jr — 110 — Lifetime 16 0 1 1 $3,010 — 1983 8 M 1 0 $1,570 — 1982 8 M 0 1 $1,440
Own.—Cornett I Cecil
28Mar83- 3Pim sly 6f :24 :47⅘ 1:13⅘ Clm 6500 6 4 611 67¾ 65 44 Grable T C 114 12.10 73-21 Paula's Prince1121PamlicoSound1091SpectacularToy1092 Rallied 7
18Mar83- 9Pim sly 1 1/16 :48⅖ 1:14⅘ 1:50⅕ 3↑Md 5000 2 4 713 69½ 57 75¾ Delgado A5 108 *2.10 48-26 Sound Hill 119hd Baldwin Express 1192¾ Oh Shockalot 1091 Tired 12
8Mar83- 9Bow fst 7f :22⅖ :47⅖ 1:26⅖ Md 13500 8 3 87½ 812 714 716 Ryan J S5 113 10.70 57-24 Little Red Romeo 1208DenimGuy120noFlyingCop1135 Raced wide 12
22Feb83- 1Bow fst 6f :23⅗ :47⅘ 1:13⅘ Md 13500 6 2 55½ 58 44½ 54¾ Krone J A 118 2.70 66-31 SmAccont1181½Book'sDlght120nkPppnJck1133 Lacked a response 8
9Feb83- 5Bow fst 7f :23⅖ :47 1:26⅖ Md 11500 2 3 64¼ 32 21 22¼ Krone J A 120 10.80 71-30 Over There 1202¼ Latin Illusion 1203 Elude 1151 Second best 10
4Feb83- 5Bow gd 1 1/16 :49 1:14⅖ 1:49 Md Sp Wt 11 10 919 716 714 822 McMillan K M7 113 58.60 39-36 CanadianFactor1208ProvenWarrior1208RoylFortune1201¾ Outrun 12
21Jan83- 3Bow fst 1 1/16 :49 1:15⅖ 1:50 Md Sp Wt 3 5 45 31½ 56 55¼ McMillan K M7 b 113 18.80 51-39 [D]Diplomatic Pride 115¾ CinnamonBoy115noJohnyImp1203½ Tired 7
10Jan83- 3Bow sly 1 1/16 :48⅕ 1:14⅖ 1:48⅗ Md Sp Wt 5 7 815 720 716 617 Ruch L D7 b 113 20.00 46-32 FourAndSixpence12013DukeOfHrts120½JohnyImp120no No factor 9
23Dec82- 5Lrl fst 6f :23⅕ :47⅖ 1:12⅗ [S]Handicap 5 2 65¾ 57 48½ 39½ McMillan K M b 108 59.70 70-23 King's Corsair 1253½ Just A Friend 1056 LatinIllusion1082 Rallied 6
16Dec82- 3Lrl sly 6f :23 :48⅕ 1:16⅖ Md 10000 9 7 920 1024 913 69 Ruch L D7 b 111 10.40 52-34 Nashold 1154½ Oh Shockalot 118½ Silver Que 118no No factor 12
LATEST WORKOUTS ●Mar 5 Lrl 3f fst :35⅕ h

Solo Again — B. g. 3, by Solo Jim—Issue's Girl, by Issue — $8,500 — Br.—Colvin E J (Md) — Tr.—Leatherbury King T — 107⁵ — Lifetime 1 0 0 0 — 1983 1 M 0 0 — 1982 0 M 0 0
Own.—Colvin E J
26Mar83- 4Pim fst 6f :23⅖ :47 1:13⅘ 3↑Md 11500 10 11 1118 1018 914 86½ Nicol P A Jr5 b 107 14.90 70-20 Mr. Immigrant 112½ Card Party 1122 Ombre Du Nord1221 Outrun 12
LATEST WORKOUTS Apr 2 Pim 4f fst :48⅗ hg Mar 12 Bow 5f fst 1:04⅗ b Mar 5 Bow 4f fst :50⅖ bg Mar 2 Bow 3f sly :39 bg

Also Eligible (Not in Post Position Order):

Nitrofrac — B. g. 3, by Kentucky Gold—Gregora, by Trojan Monarch — $8,500 — Br.—Perkins C D (Ky) — Tr.—Wheeler Robert E — 107⁵ — Lifetime 3 0 0 1 $660 — 1983 2 M 0 1 $660 — 1982 1 M 0 0
Own.—Saroda Stable
23Mar83- 1Pim fst 6f :23⅗ :48⅕ 1:14⅘ 3↑Md 8500 7 1 36½ 59¼ 46¼ 34½ Delgado A5 b 108 13.40 67-30 Shalma 113¾ Carry On Concord 1223¾ Nitrofrac108no Drifted Out 9
15Mar83- 9Bow fst 6f :23 :47⅕ 1:13⅗ Md c-5000 12 7 711 918 922 922 Foley D b 125 38.50 50-25 John P. Bailey 1206 Final Way 1152 LordLapidus1151 Raced wide 12
9Dec82- 1Lrl fst 6f :23⅕ :48⅕ 1:15 Md 8000 11 5 1013 1027 1128 1120 Miller D A Jr 118 9.30 48-25 Mr. GoodParts118¾Flamingo'sMonk114¾LakevilleJet109nk Outrun 12
LATEST WORKOUTS Mar 12 Bow 3f fst :38 b

From a numbers standpoint, there are really only three horses in this race: **Igloo Assessment, Latin Illusion**, and **Carry On Concord**. Now the question is, which are the top two? **Latin Illusion** emerges as the best bet with the highest Total and the highest Condition Factor. On the surface, it appears that **Igloo Assessment** deserves the top spot. However, when this horse is compared more closely with the other two, he should be ranked only third. He has never shown an ability to run 4 furlongs faster than :48. And after that, he fades. Also, his last race was a route with so-so early speed. This is usually not a good omen for a sprint race. **Annual Custom** is the fourth choice. A betting favorite of the public is **Solo Again** for many good reasons, but the numbers are not good enough.

Our betting choices are:

1. **Latin Illusion**
2. **Carry On Concord**
3. **Igloo Assessment**
4. **Annual Custom**

4th Pimlico 6F (4/5)

PP	#	NAME	Date: Last Race	Weight (Today's Race)	3 Speed Ratings + Track Variants	Weight Adjust.	***Ability Factor***	Speed Rating: Last Race	+21 or +25	Track Adjust.	Weight Adjust.	***Condition Factor***	Wt. at Post Time	Total	Adj. Total
1		IGLOO ASSESSMENT	3/29	112	285	+3	(288)	67	+21	-5	+2	(85)	115	373	(370)
2		UP BOLD *	3/31	112	249	+4	253	57	+21	-5	+2	75	113	328	327
3		LAST TIME OUT	MAY	122	264a (6½F)	–	264	71 (6½F)	+21	-10	-2	80	122	344	344
4		CARRY ON CONCORD	3/23	117	287	+2	(289)	71	+21	-11	+2	83↙	122	372	(368)
5		DANDY DUC *	2/25	112	257	+4	261	58	+21	-5	+2	76	112	337	337
6		ANNUAL CUSTOM (4½)	3/6	122	280	-4	276	72	+21	-8	-2	83↙	122	359	359↙
7		HAND FAST	NOV.	122	280	-4	276	59	+21	-6	-2	72	122	348	348
8		BOASSIONATO	3/22	112	266	+4	270	56	+21	-5	+2	74	112	344	344
9		LATIN ILLUSION	3/28	110	284	+2	286↙	73	+25	-11	+2	(89)	110	375	(375)
10		SOLO AGAIN	3/26	107	270a	–	270	70	+21	-11	–	80	109	350	348
11		NITROFRAC	3/23	107	245	+4	249	67	+21	-11	+1	78	107	327	327
12															
13															
14															
15															
16															

FOURTH RACE
Pimlico
APRIL 5

6 FURLONGS. (1.09⅕) MAIDEN CLAIMING. Purse $5,500. 3– and 4–year–olds. Weights, 3–year–olds, 112 lbs. 4–year–olds, 122 lbs. Claiming price $8,500; for each $500 to $7,500.

Value of race $5,500, value to winner $3,300, second $1,210, third $660, fourth $330. Mutuel pool $39,803. Exacta Pool $68,972.

Last Raced	Horse	Eqt.A.Wt	PP	St	¼	½	Str	Fin	Jockey	Cl'g Pr	Odds $1
28Mar83 3Pim^4	Latin Illusion	3 110	9	1	8^1	5^{1½}	2^{1½}	1^½	Krone J A	7500	5.10
23Mar83 1Pim^2	Carry On Concord	b 4 122	4	10	6^{hd}	2^{1½}	1^3	2^5	Miller D A Jr†	8500	2.30
23Mar83 1Pim^3	Nitrofrac	b 3 107	11	5	5^1	4^{1½}	3^{hd}	3^1	Delgado A^5	8500	6.40
6Mar83 1CT^2	Annual Custom	b 4 122	6	6	1^{1½}	1^{hd}	4^{3½}	4^{1¼}	Palmer R W	8500	9.10
24Nov82 2Aqu^5	Hand Fast	b 4 122	7	7	10^{2½}	9^½	5^1	5^1	Passmore W J	8500	8.80
26Mar83 4Pim^8	Solo Again	3 109	10	8	9^3	6^2	6^2	6^{1½}	McCarthy M J^5	8500	4.50
22Mar83 9Pim^9	Boassionato	3 112	8	11	11	11	9^2	7^{nk}	Byrnes D	8500	37.40
29Mar83 3Pim^8	Igloo Assessment	b 3 115	1	4	7^½	8^1	7^1	8^2	Bracciale V Jr	8500	8.40
25Feb83 4Bow^7	Dandy Duc	b 3 112	5	3	3^{hd}	7^1	8^{hd}	9^6	Hutton G W	8500	a-26.30
4May82 3Spt^8	Last Time Out	4 122	3	9	4^1	3^{hd}	10^5	10^8	Osani J R Jr	8500	15.70
31Mar83 1Pim	Up Bold	b 3 113	2	2	2^½	10^1	11	11	Runco J C	8500	a-26.30

a–Coupled: Dandy Duc and Up Bold.

OFF AT 2:24 Start good, Won driving. Time, :23⅗, :47⅘, 1:00⅖, 1:13⅗ Track fast.

$2 Mutuel Prices:				
	9–LATIN ILLUSION	**12.20**	**6.20**	**4.00**
	4–CARRY ON CONCORD		**4.40**	**3.20**
	11–NITROFRAC			**4.40**
	$2 EXACTA 9–4 PAID $50.80.			

Dk. b. or br. c, by Latin Humor—Daughter In Debt, by Renombre. Trainer Castrenze Charles Jr. Bred by Cornett I & Patricia (Md).

LATIN ILLUSION raced between horses then closed determinedly to be along in time. CARRY ON CONCORD split horses around the turn and gave way grudgingly. NITROFRAC raced wide. ANNUAL CUSTOM weakened. HAND FAST circled. SOLO AGAIN was not a factor and lugged in in midstretch. IGLOO ASSEMENT was steadied lacking room, entering the turn, DANDY DUC stopped. LAST TIME OUT faltered. UP BOLD faltered.

Owners— 1, Cornett I Cecil; 2, Freed G A; 3, Saroda Stable; 4, Costello Kathleen; 5, Dodderidge R A; 6, Colvin E J; 7, Jenkins I; 8, Perrin J K; 9, Schott T J; 10, Matheny W H L; 11, Clelland O.

Trainers— 1, Castrenze Charles Jr; 2, Bullock Alec J; 3, Wheeler Robert E; 4, Carter E Clinton; 5, Jeffries Robert A; 6, Leatherbury King T; 7, Horn J Robert; 8, Murphy James W; 9, Aguirre Horacio; 10, Donovan L William; 11, Aguirre Horacio.

† **Apprentice allowance waived:** Carry On Concord 5 pounds. **Overweight:** Solo Again 2 pounds; Igloo Assessment 3; Up Bold 1.

Scratched—Bold Bonus (26Mar83 4CT^3); Peanuckel; Baldwin Express (28Mar83 5Pim^6).

Once the horses entered the stretch, the outcome was never in question. It is always nice to be first at the cashier's window.

$2 Exacta Wagering	
Bet	$ 30.00
Return	$203.20
Profit	$173.20

Note: Had **Igloo Assessment** been selected as one of the two top picks, the profit would have been only $20.80. This is why it is so important to correctly identify the two best horses. The other two horses are merely insurance.

Eight horses are entered in this 6 furlong race. Statistics appear plentiful and promising. A quinella is available.

AQUEDUCT

6 FURLONGS. (1.08⅗) MAIDEN CLAIMING. Purse $12,500. 3-year-olds. Weight, 122 lbs. Claiming price $50,000; for each $2,500 to $45,000, 2 lbs.

Moe Baum

Own.—Rena-Kim Stable
Dk. b. or br. g. 3, by Tarleton Oak—Russian Lullaby, by Cyane
$45,000 Br.—Augustus Peggy (Va)
Tr.—Ferriola Peter
118
Lifetime 5 0 1 0 $2,970 | 1983 3 M 1 0 $2,970 | 1982 2 M 0 0

25Mar83- 5Aqu fst 1⅛ :49 1:17⅖ 1:56 Md Sp Wt 5 1 18 1hd 613 725 Santagata N 122 6.10 30-36 ValDeLaMeuse1221LordHatchet1225½ScrletHobeu12212 Gave way 8
17Mar83- 4Aqu fst 1 :47⅖ 1:12⅘ 1:39⅗ Md 45000 4 1 12 14 16 2½ Santagata N 118 22.20 67-27 Hanover County 1221½ Moe Baum 1186 Slam 118nk Gamely 8
3Feb83- 4Aqu gd 6f ⊡:22⅖ :46 1:11⅘ Md 30000 11 6 105 96½ 1010 1011 Santagata N 118 9.80f 74-18 Native Raid 117hd Plum Numb 1111½ Nalgatic 122¾ Outrun 14
20Dec82- 6Aqu fst 6f ⊡:23⅕ :47⅕ 1:13 Md Sp Wt 6 3 42½ 42½ 67½ 610 Asmussen S M7 111 44.70 69-21 Cutter Sark 1133½ Aztec Red 1182 Fast John 1181 No factor 10
9Sep82- 2Bel fst 7f :22⅘ :46⅕ 1:24⅖ Md 65000 3 5 57 69½ 719 829 Migliore R 118 20.20 51-21 Significantly 11412 Upper Country118¾MyBoyNeal1183¾ Fell back 9
LATEST WORKOUTS Feb 23 Bel tr.t 4f fst :50⅘ b

Piston Lift

Own.—Pambi Stable
B. c. 3, by Shecky Greene—Gray's Choice, by Gray Phantom
$50,000 Br.—Soesbe E (Va)
Tr.—Picou James E
122
Lifetime 3 0 0 0 $750 | 1983 2 M 0 0 $750 | 1982 1 M 0 0

24Mar83- 5Aqu fst 6f :23 :47⅖ 1:12⅘ Md 50000 7 6 83¾ 88 63½ 43½ Asmussen S M5 117 11.10f 73-26 SheathedDgger118nkJohnnyofWinloc122hdSpyGme1183½ Steadied 14
1Jan83- 6Aqu fst 6f ⊡:23⅗ :47⅗ 1:14 Md 50000 5 10 1210 99½ 912 912 Asmussen S M7 115 27.00 62-25 HndsomeDncer111¾PrsonlityCrisis122½SwtAffilition1222¾ Outrun 13
22Dec82- 6Aqu fst 6f ⊡:24 :48⅗ 1:14⅕ Md Sp Wt 3 7 1hd 1hd 56 88¼ Graell A 118 17.50 64-22 Noble Pocket 1113 Spiffy And Cool 118hd NorthGlade1181¼ Tired 10
LATEST WORKOUTS Apr 1 Bel tr.t 5f fst 1:02⅖ b Mar 23 Bel tr.t 3f fst :36⅘ h Mar 14 Bel tr.t 4f fst :48⅕ hg Mar 9 Bel tr.t 6f sly 1:17⅖ b

Spy Game

Own.—Chasrigg Stable
Dk. b. or br. c. 3, by Raja Baba—Konigsalpen, by Priamos
$45,000 Br.—Farish W S III (Ky)
Tr.—DeBonis Robert
118
Lifetime 7 0 2 2 $7,725 | 1983 6 M 2 2 $7,275 | 1982 1 M 0 0 $450

24Mar83- 5Aqu fst 6f :23 :47⅖ 1:12⅘ Md 45000 2 5 105½ 76 3nk 3nk Smith A Jr b 118 *1.80 77-26 SheathedDagger118nkJohnnyofWinloc122hdSpyGame1183½ Rallied 14
17Mar83- 4Aqu fst 1 :47⅖ 1:12⅘ 1:39⅗ Md 45000 6 8 67½ 67½ 511 714 Smith A Jr b 118 *.80 54-27 Hanover County 1221½MoeBaum1186Slam118nk Stmbled,lost iron 8
7Mar83- 4Aqu my 6f ⊡:22⅘ :47 1:12 Md 35000 4 7 65½ 66 52¾ 2nk Davis R G5 b 115 *3.50 84-16 Confirmation 118nk Spy Game 115¾ Purty White 118nk Sharp 14
10Feb83- 4Aqu fst 1⅟₁₆ ⊡:48⅕ 1:14 1:47⅕ Md c-25000 4 4 32 21½ 31½ 21¼ Migliore R b 122 3.70 76-18 Hello Alfred 1131¼ Spy Game 122nk Upper Country 1173 Gamely 12
20Jan83- 2Bow fst 7f :22⅕ :45⅗ 1:25⅕ Md Sp Wt 7 1 59½ 78½ 57½ 59¾ Vigliotti M J 120 5.30 69-28 Disarco's Rib 1201¾ He Can Fly 1202 Laura's Boy 115hd No threat 10
8Jan83- 3Key fst 7f :23⅘ :47⅖ 1:26⅗ Md Sp Wt 4 11 85¾ 69 66¾ 35 Rivera I7 113 5.10 69-25 Classic Steed 1202½ Hagley'sReward1202½SpyGame1131½ Fin. well 12
26Dec82- 1Key fst 6f :23⅕ :47⅗ 1:15 Md Sp Wt 8 4 83 56½ 44½ 44 Rivera I5 115 7.80 62-30 Cogent1203½ClssicSteed120hdRoomWithAView120½ Rallied mildly 9
LATEST WORKOUTS Mar 31 Bel tr.t 4f fst :50 b Mar 15 Bel tr.t 3f fst :38 b Mar 1 Bel tr.t 3f fst :38⅕ b Feb 24 Bel tr.t 4f fst :48⅖ h

Two Dollar Bill

Own.—Minassian H
B. c. 3, by Queen City Lad—Round Key, by Run For Nurse
$45,000 Br.—Parrish T D (Ky)
Tr.—Minassian Harry Jr
118
Lifetime 4 0 0 2 $3,990 | 1983 4 M 0 2 $3,990 | 1982 0 M 0 0

24Mar83- 5Aqu fst 6f :23 :47⅖ 1:12⅘ Md 50000 4 10 63¾ 64½ 74½ 75½ McCarron G b 122 4.30 72-26 SheathedDgger118nkJohnnyofWinloc122hdSpyGme1183½ Steadied 14
14Mar83- 2Aqu fst 6f ⊡:22⅗ :46⅕ 1:11⅗ Md 55000 8 3 32 31½ 42 34 McCarron G b 118 2.60 82-10 Coast Range 1181¾ Let's BeFrank1222½TwoDollarBill118¼ Bore in 9
23Feb83- 4Aqu fst 6f ⊡:23⅕ :47⅖ 1:12⅘ Md 55000 12 2 4¾ 4¾ 52½ 33¾ McCarron G b 118 4.70 76-21 Lutyens 1131 Chaudiere 1182¾ Two Dollar Bill 118½ Rallied 12
30Jan83- 2Aqu fst 6f ⊡:23 :46⅘ 1:13 Md 50000 8 7 52 52¾ 52¾ 42½ McCarron G 122 15.80 76-20 King'sSwn1221¾SweetAffilition122nkLt'sGtPhysicl122½ No threat 10
LATEST WORKOUTS Apr 2 Bel tr.t 4f fst :49⅗ b Mar 11 Bel tr.t 3f sly :36 h (d)

Tina's Double

Own.—Fried A Jr
Dk. b. or br. c. 3, by Nodouble—Elaine, by Round Table
$50,000 Br.—Lasater Farm (Fla)
Tr.—DeStasio Richard T
122
Lifetime 8 0 0 2 $3,720 | 1983 4 M 0 1 $2,400 | 1982 4 M 0 1 $1,320

17Mar83- 4Aqu fst 1 :47⅖ 1:12⅘ 1:39⅗ Md 50000 8 6 57½ 812 713 613 Lovato F Jr b 122 4.20 55-27 Hanover County 1221½ Moe Baum 1186 Slam 118nk Far back 8
23Feb83- 4Aqu fst 6f ⊡:23⅕ :47⅖ 1:12⅘ Md 55000 3 9 98¾ 96½ 77½ 79¾ Beitia E b 118 21.80 71-21 Lutyens 1131 Chaudiere 1182¾ Two Dollar Bill 118½ Outrun 12
14Feb83- 4Aqu fst 6f ⊡:23 :46⅖ 1:11⅗ Md Sp Wt 4 3 41½ 64¾ 78¾ 812 Cordero A Jr 122 19.10 74-13 Quati Gold 122½ Screen Trend 1223½ Atom Smasher 122½ Tired 14
15Jan83- 6Aqu my 170 ⊡:49⅕ 1:15⅕ 1:46⅕ Md Sp Wt 6 3 32 21½ 25 36¾ Beitia E 122 9.50 64-22 Shamrocky1225½ShockWave1151½Tin'sDouble1222½ Lacked a rally 9
29Dec82- 5Med fst 170 :47⅗ 1:12⅘ 1:43⅗ Md pe Wt 4 5 51½ 1hd 32 32 Beitia E 118 14.30 82-18 ⒹMansbray 118hd J. R. Collins 1182 Tina's Double 1185 Bore out 8
10Dec82- 5Aqu fst 1⅟₁₆ ⊡:49⅘ 1:15⅘ 1:49⅗ Md 50000 2 3 52½ 42½ 69½ 812 MacBeth D 118 13.90 53-24 Ghent 1181 Sir Irish Echo 1142½ Handsome Dancer 1115 Tired 9
28Nov82- 6Aqu fst 7f :23⅗ :46⅗ 1:25⅘ Md Sp Wt 8 2 66 67½ 89¾ 811 Asmussen S M7 111 37.60 62-28 GameDncer1182½WildChorus118½KeyToTheOrient1182 No factor 9
11Nov82- 4Aqu fst 6f :22⅘ :46 1:10⅘ Md Sp Wt 2 3 1hd 84¾ 1215 1219 MacBeth D 118 38.80 68-19 Jeff's Companion 1131½ Jungle Dust 1184 Nevado 118¾ Stopped 13
LATEST WORKOUTS Mar 27 Bel tr.t 5f fst 1:02⅖ h Mar 13 Bel tr.t 4f my :50 b (d) Mar 6 Bel tr.t 4f fst :52⅖ b Feb 8 Bel tr.t 4f fst :49⅘ h

First Prez

Own.—Entremont
B. c. 3, by My Dad George—Me Carla, by Gallant Romeo
$45,000 Br.—Bloodstock Partners (Ky)
Tr.—Baeza Braulio
118
Lifetime 3 0 1 0 $1,320 | 1982 3 M 1 0 $1,320

24Oct82- 4Aqu fst 6f :22⅗ :46⅘ 1:12 Md 45000 2 6 33½ 34½ 911 1010 Santiago A b 114 23.60 71-25 Zeb'sHelCat1134EighteenKrt114noBudgetCutter1132½ Tired badly 13
10Oct82- 6Bel fst 1 :47⅘ 1:14⅕ 1:41⅖ Md 50000 5 3 2hd 75 814 820 Santiago A b 118 4.10e 38-28 Iron Sovereign 1161½ Swift Aid 118¾ Advertise 1145 Gaveway 10
14Aug82- 4Del fst 6f :22⅖ :46⅕ 1:13 Md 50000 1 5 32 32½ 31½ 2hd Walford J b 120 10.40e 76-22 Say La Hoy 118hd First Prez 120nk Heavy Load 1202½ Just missed 8
LATEST WORKOUTS Mar 26 Bel tr.t 5f fst 1:01⅗ hg Mar 21 Bel tr.t 4f fst :48⅘ h Mar 15 Bel tr.t 5f fst 1:01⅗ h ●Mar 10 Bel tr.t 1 sly 1:45⅗ b

Laugh With Me

Own.—Blass Patricia
B. c. 3, by Torsion—Fun And Tears, by Hempen
$50,000 Br.—Blass & Davis Mrs D M Jr (Ky)
Tr.—Howe Peter M
122
Lifetime 10 0 0 0 $5,730 | 1983 5 M 0 0 $2,910 | 1982 5 M 0 0 $2,820

7Mar83- 4Aqu my 6f ⊡:22⅘ :47 1:12 Md 30000 5 8 88¾ 76½ 42½ 41½ Santiago A 122 5.20 83-16 Confirmation 118nk Spy Game 115¾ Purty White 118nk Rallied 14
23Feb83- 4Aqu fst 6f ⊡:23⅕ :47⅖ 1:12⅘ Md 55000 6 1 3nk 3nk 31½ 44¾ Santiago A b 118 14.80 76-21 Lutyens 1131 Chaudiere 1182¾ Two Dollar Bill 118½ Weakened 12
3Feb83- 4Aqu gd 6f ⊡:22⅘ :46 1:11⅘ Md 35000 1 14 1412 119½ 97½ 75½ Santiago A b 122 14.50 80-18 Native Raid 117hd Plum Numb 1111½ Nalgatic 122¾ Outrun 14
24Jan83- 6Aqu sly 170 ⊡:48 1:12⅘ 1:43⅖ Md 35000 6 5 43½ 47 416 417 Santiago A b 122 3.40 68-15 TimeForReward1183NativeRid1151½UpperCountry1133½ No factor 7
1Jan83- 6Aqu fst 6f ⊡:23⅗ :47⅗ 1:14 Md 50000 7 1 1hd 1hd 32 44 Vergara O b 122 9.50 70-25 HndsomDncr111¾PrsonlityCrisis122½SwtAffilition1222¾ Weakened 13
18Dec82- 4Aqu fst 6f ⊡:23⅗ :47⅗ 1:13⅘ Md 50000 2 6 54 79 69 47¾ Beitia E b 118 *2.50 69-20 North Junction 114¾ SweetAffiliation1182King'sSwan1185 Rallied 7
8Dec82- 6Aqu fst 6f ⊡:23 :46⅘ 1:12⅘ Md Sp Wt 10 7 52½ 45½ 812 77¾ Maple E b 118 11.80e 74-21 But Who Knows 1181 Unmistaken 1181¼ WhatMommy1131½ Tired 13
11Nov82- 4Aqu fst 6f :22⅘ :46 1:10⅘ Md Sp Wt 10 1 52 43 56 811 Migliore R 118 11.50 76-19 Jeff's Companion 1131½ Jungle Dust 1184 Nevado 118¾ Tired 13
21Oct82- 9Aqu fst 6f :22⅘ :46⅕ 1:11⅕ Md Sp Wt 9 4 24 25 26 47½ Migliore R 118 5.30 78-24 Fibak 1185BoundingBasque118¾StoneyLonesome1181½ Weakened 10
30Sep82- 4Bel fst 6f :22⅘ :46⅕ 1:11⅗ Md Sp Wt 11 10 65½ 35 35 46 Migliore R 118 66.60 78-24 Flip's Little Boy 1183 Write Off 1182½ Sluggard 118½ Weakened 14
LATEST WORKOUTS Apr 2 Bel tr.t 3f fst :37⅘ b Mar 27 Bel tr.t 4f fst :49⅖ b

Got The Hots

Own.—Kimmel C P
Ch. c. 3, by Tom Rolfe—Closing Kick, by Native Charger
$50,000 Br.—Lussky W (Ky)
Tr.—Toner James J
122
Lifetime 4 0 0 0 | 1983 4 M 0 0 | 1982 0 M 0 0

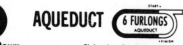

17Mar83- 4Aqu fst 1 :47⅖ 1:12⅘ 1:39⅗ Md 50000 1 2 22 34 815 819 Maple E b 122 7.50 49-27 Hanover County 1221½ Moe Baum 1186 Slam 118nk Early speed 8
5Mar83- 6Aqu fst 170 ⊡:49⅘ 1:14⅕ 1:44 Md Sp Wt 3 10 98¾ 87 58½ 510 Powers T M5 b 117 28.70 72-16 LeadTheWay1222½LordHtchet1223SweetAffilition1222¾ No threat 10
21Feb83- 6Aqu fst 6f ⊡:23 :46⅘ 1:12⅘ Md Sp Wt 3 8 107¾ 1113 811 812 Powers T M5 b 117 10.60f 70-22 North Glade 1223¾ Scarlet Hobeau1222¾Let'sBeFrank1223 Outrun 14
4Feb83- 4Aqu fst 6f ⊡:23⅗ :47⅗ 1:12⅘ Md Sp Wt 2 13 129½ 1215 1124 1023 Velez R I 122 43.30 57-20 PersonalityCrisis117nkAtomSmasher1221¾NorthGlade1222 Outrun 14
LATEST WORKOUTS ●Apr 1 Aqu 3f fst :35⅗ h Mar 14 Aqu 5f fst 1:03⅖ b ●Feb 28 Aqu ⊡ 1 fst 1:43⅕ b ●Feb 18 Aqu ⊡ 5f fst 1:02⅖ h

Here is another example of the importance of careful handicapping once the best three or four horses are selected. Based solely on the numbers, **Laugh With Me** would be the first choice. The horse has the highest figures in all three areas. However, this horse has been out of action for nearly a month, finished behind **Two Dollar Bill** on February 23rd, and is gaining weight from that matchup. Moreover, **Spy Game** has beaten them both recently, first on March 7th and then later on March 24th.

Spy Game should win this race, but second place is less clear. Since the likely winner is also the heavy favorite, we will not add a fourth horse to the betting scheme. If you must play one more quinella, use only **Spy Game** with that selection.

The betting choices are:

1. **Spy Game**
2. **Two Dollar Bill**
3. **Laugh With Me**
4. —

6th AQUEDUCT 6F (4/5)

PP	#	NAME	Date: Last Race	Weight (Today's Race)	3 Speed Ratings + Track Variants	Weight Adjust.	**Ability Factor**	Speed Rating: Last Race	+21 or +25	Track Adjust.	Weight Adjust.	**Condition Factor**	Wt. at Post Time	Total	Adj. Total
1		MOE BAUM	3/25	118	270a	—	270	74	+25	-9	—	90	118	360	360
2		PISTON LIFT	3/24	122	272	-4	268	73	+21	-6	-2	86	122	354	354
3		SPY GAME	3/24	118	295	-4	291	77	+21	-6	—	92	118	383	383
4		TWO DOLLAR BILL	3/24	118	287	+2	289	72	+21	-6	+2	89	118	378	378
5		TINA'S DOUBLE	3/17	122	266	-4	262	71	+21	-9	-2	81	122	343	343
6		FIRST PREZ	OCT.	118	291a	—	291	71	+21	-6	-2	84	118	375	375
7		LAUGH WITH ME	3/7	122	294	-2	292	83	+25	-9	—	99	122	391	391
8		GOT THE HOTS	3/17	122	254a	-2	252	70	+21	-9	-2	80	122	332	332
9															
10															
11															
12															
13															
14															
15															
16															

SIXTH RACE **6 FURLONGS. (1.08⅕) MAIDEN CLAIMING. Purse $12,500. 3–year–olds. Weight, 122 lbs. Claiming price $50,000; for each $2,500 to $45,000, 2 lbs.**

Aqueduct

APRIL 5

Value of race $12,500, value to winner $7,500, second $2,750, third $1,500, fourth $750. Mutuel pool $120,948, OTB pool $115,482. Track Quinella Pool $157,489. OTB Quinella Pool $155,596.

Last Raced	Horse	Eqt.	A.	Wt	PP	St	¼	½	Str	Fin	Jockey	Cl'g Pr	Odds $1
24Mar83 ^{5}Aqu^{3}	Spy Game		3	118	3	3	$6^{2\frac{1}{2}}$	3^{2}	$1^{\frac{1}{2}}$	1^{4}	Cordero A Jr	45000	.90
24Mar83 ^{5}Aqu^{7}	Two Dollar Bill	b	3	118	4	6	$3^{\frac{1}{2}}$	$1^{\frac{1}{2}}$	2^{hd}	2^{nk}	Gomez E R	45000	6.80
24Mar83 ^{5}Aqu^{4}	Piston Lift	b	3	122	2	5	$1^{\frac{1}{2}}$	$2^{\frac{1}{2}}$	$3^{2\frac{1}{2}}$	$3^{1\frac{3}{4}}$	McCarron G	50000	8.10
7Mar83 ^{4}Aqu^{4}	Laugh With Me		3	122	7	7	7^{hd}	$6^{\frac{1}{2}}$	$4^{1\frac{1}{2}}$	$4^{1\frac{1}{2}}$	Gonzalez A	50000	5.40
24Oct82 ^{4}Aqu^{10}	First Prez	b	3	118	6	1	5^{1}	8	$7^{1\frac{1}{2}}$	$5^{\frac{3}{4}}$	Santiago A	45000	22.20
17Mar83 ^{4}Aqu^{8}	Got The Hots	b	3	122	8	8	8	7^{2}	$5^{\frac{1}{2}}$	6^{2}	Maple E	50000	23.90
25Mar83 ^{5}Aqu^{7}	Moe Baum		3	118	1	2	2^{hd}	$5^{\frac{1}{2}}$	$6^{1\frac{1}{2}}$	7^{3}	Santagata N	45000	4.90
17Mar83 ^{4}Aqu^{6}	Tina's Double	b	3	122	5	4	$4^{\frac{1}{2}}$	$4^{\frac{1}{2}}$	8	8	Lovato F Jr	50000	32.50

OFF AT 3:28 Start good, Won ridden out. Time, :23, :47, 1:12 Track fast.

$2 Mutuel Prices:

3–(C)–SPY GAME	**3.80**	**2.80**	**2.40**
4–(D)–TWO DOLLAR BILL		**5.20**	**2.80**
2–(B)–PISTON LIFT			**3.60**

$2 QUINELLA 3–4 PAID $11.80.

Dk. b. or br. c, by Raja Baba—Konigsalpen, by Priamos. Trainer DeBonis Robert. Bred by Farish W S III (Ky).

SPY GAME made a run from the outside leaving the turn and drew away under intermittent urging. TWO DOLLAR BILL sent into contention between horses early, took over nearing the stretch but was no match for the winner. PISTON LIFT showed speed to midstretch and weakened. LAUGH WITH ME rallied approaching the final furlong but failed to sustain his bid. FIRST PREZ showed some early foot. MOE BAUM had brief speed. TINAS DOUBLE gave way leaving the turn.

Owners— 1, Chasrigg Stable; 2, Minassian H; 3, Pambi Stable; 4, Blass Patricia; 5, Entremont; 6, Kimmel C P; 7, Rena-Kim Stable; 8, Fried A Jr.

Trainers— 1, DeBonis Robert; 2, Minassian Harry Jr; 3, Picou James E; 4, Howe Peter M; 5, Baeza Braulio; 6, Toner James J; 7, Ferriola Peter; 8, DeStasio Richard T.

It's nice to be right (and maybe a little lucky), but not much money was made here. Furthermore, it is easy to see how money could have been lost on this contest.

$2 Quinella Wagering	
Bet	$ 8.00
Return	$23.60
Profit	$15.60

This race, the 5th at Hialeah, has a great deal of promise. Most of the nine horses entered have raced the distance many times and most have run at Hialeah recently. In addition, among the horses entered, is our old friend Gold Limit. A perfecta is available.

HIALEAH

6 FURLONGS. (1.08⅗) CLAIMING. Purse $7,000. 4-year-olds and upward. Weights, 122 lbs. Non-winners of two races since February 5 allowed 2 lbs. A race since then 4 lbs. A race since January 29, 6 lbs. Claiming Price $16,000 for each $1,000 to $14,000, 2 lbs. (Races where entered for $12,500 or less not considered.) (Red. Florida Breds Preferred.)

Medeiros

Ch. g. 4, by The Big Boss—Cussin' Queen, by Saidam
$16,000 Br.—Palumbo V A (Md) Tr.—Steen H Kirk Jr
Own.—Cerulean Farm
116 Lifetime 22 3 3 0 $20,765 | 1983 2 0 0 0 $155 | 1982 20 3 3 0 $20,610

Race	Cond	Dist	Times	Class	Running line	Jockey	Wt	Odds	Speed	Finishers	Comment
18Mar83- 8Hia	fst	6f	:22⅗ :46⅖ 1:11⅗	Clm 16000	8 5 53½ 43 22 62½	Rujano M	b 116	130.10	82-19	China Village 116hd Clinebell 113½ Deb's Playboy114nk	Weakened 12
17Feb83-10GP	gd	6f	:22 :45⅕ 1:11	Clm 15000	8 9 99 1015 911 711	Rujano M	b 117	61.00	73-24	Bul Libra 1104½ Governor Bob 117½ Clinebell 117nk	No speed 10
20Nov82- 7Suf	fst	6f	:22⅗ :46⅖ 1:13	3↑Clm 16000	9 11 87 99 911 75¾	Bush W V	b 114	11.00	70-24	China Village 1191 House Odds 114½ Solo Ace 117¾	Outrun 12
5Nov82- 9Suf	sly	6f	:22⅘ :46⅗ 1:13⅖	Clm 22500	4 2 33 44 46½ 48	Bush W V	b 114	4.10	66-31	Wig Gala 1142 Nu Jacques 1192 Power Rig 1194	No rally 5
15Oct82- 9Suf	fst	6f	:22⅘ :46⅗ 1:13⅗	Clm 22500	2 2 21 22½ 22½ 21½	Gambardella C	b 114	4.80	71-31	Power Rig 1141½ Medeiros 114hd Twogun Kenny 114½	Mild rally 5
1Oct82- 9Suf	fst	6f	:22⅗ :45⅘ 1:12	Clm 22500	8 1 46½ 57 55 45½	Gambardella C	b 114	4.20	75-26	Kasha 1193 Power Rig 1142 Hit Parade 114½	No factor 8
17Sep82- 9Suf	fst	6f	:22⅗ :46⅘ 1:12⅘	3↑Clm c-15000	5 3 34½ 3nk 13½ 11½	Penney J C5	b 109	5.10	77-29	Medeiros 1091½ Drink N Think 1143FederalHillStar1101½	Drew off 10
6Sep82-12Suf	fst	6f	:22⅘ :46⅖ 1:12⅕	3↑Alw 8500	6 5 52¾ 66¾ 68¾ 57¾	Reed J E5	b 106	25.40	72-26	Jolley Charlie 1121¾ Sanfoin 114hd Lucrative Way 1141	Tired 7
30Aug82- 9Suf	fst	6f	:22⅖ :45⅘ 1:12⅖	3↑Alw 8500	5 2 21½ 45 55½ 56½	Penney J C5	b 106	7.00	73-27	Quiet Monster 116½ Lucrative Way 1143½ B. K.'s Bid 1131¾	Tired 5
12Aug82- 9Suf	fst	6f	:22⅖ :45⅘ 1:12⅕	3↑Clm 15000	1 3 42½ 33½ 33½ 1½	Penney J C5	b 109	1.90	80-20	Medeiros 109½ Wig Gala 1121½ Trial Judge 1142¾	Driving 6

LATEST WORKOUTS Mar 6 Hia 4f fst :48⅗ h Feb 15 Hia 4f fst :49 b Feb 9 Hia 5f fst 1:02⅗ b

Fiesty Fleet

B. f. 4, by Menocal—Fleet Street, by Fleet Nasrullah
$16,000 Br.—Marston Lauren S (Fla) Tr.—Jamtgaard Wayne
Own.—Birchminster Farms
104⁷ Lifetime 11 1 0 1 $6,020 | 1983 1 0 0 0 $80 | 1982 10 1 0 1 $5,940

Race	Cond	Dist	Times	Class	Running line	Jockey	Wt	Odds	Speed	Finishers	Comment
15Mar83- 8Hia	fst	6f	:22⅕ :45⅕ 1:11⅕	ⒻClm 25000	10 6 87¼ 89¾ 1112 1012	Gurkas L H7	b 109	10.00	75-14	Her Soir 1162½ Suzy Greene 114¾ Nacunda 1161	Outrun 11
16Dec82- 5Crc	fst	6f	:22⅘ :47 1:12⅘	3↑Md 20000	1 4 3nk 12 15 19	Gurkas L H10	b 106	7.00	88-18	Fiesty Fleet 1069 Star of Heaven 1191½ComeOnCabin115½	Driving 7
2Dec82- 2Crc	fst	6½f	:22⅗ :46⅘ 1:20⅖	3↑ⒻMd Sp Wt	4 8 41½ 32 33 38	Gurkas L H10	b 111	33.30	75-21	Made Glorious 1213½ Antic Hay 1224½ Fiesty Fleet 111¾	Evenly 8
28Aug82- 4Mth	fst	6f	:22⅗ :45 1:11⅕	3↑ⒻMd 35000	8 10 88½ 918 815 711	Gurkas L H10	b 107	8.40	73-14	Lady Lizzy 1171½ Hex On You 1151½ Come Upstairs 1146	Outrun 10
17Aug82- 4Mth	fst	6f	:22⅘ :46⅕ 1:11⅘	3↑ⒻMd 40000	6 12 107½ 76 59 411	Gurkas L H10	b 107	15.90	70-22	Classy Nancy 1123½ Insouciance 1107 Acceptor 117¾	Unruly early 12
7Aug82- 4Mth	fst	6f	:22⅕ :45⅖ 1:12⅕	3↑ⒻMd Sp Wt	7 3 51¾ 44½ 44 63½	Patterson G	b 117	65.70	75-15	Petet Gold 117nk Raise Rain 1171¼ Acceptor 1172	No threat 12
10Jly82- 4Mth	fst	6f	:22⅗ :45⅘ 1:11⅕	3↑ⒻMd Sp Wt	9 2 21 42½ 47 410	Patterson G	b 116	65.60	74-12	Arrived Late 1162 La Reine Noir 116no Pretty Barbie 1168	Tired 11
30Jun82- 9Mth	fst	1$\frac{1}{16}$	:46⅖ 1:11 1:46⅖	3↑ⒻMd Sp Wt	10 1 31½ 411 1020 1019	Patterson G	b 114	62.00	54-17	Class Night 1181½ Iceland Spar 114hd Happy Hour Bid 1142	Tired 10
12Jun82- 4Mth	fst	6f	:22⅕ :45⅗ 1:11⅘	3↑ⒻMd Sp Wt	7 3 51¾ 66 811 913	Patterson G	b 115	91.40	68-17	Casual 1157 Petet Gold 1151¼ Leematt Sue 115½	Tired 12
24Feb82- 6Hia	fst	6f	:22⅖ :46⅕ 1:12⅕	ⒻMd Sp Wt	3 6 43 54 911 1220	Nemeti W	b 120	159.50	62-19	May Day Eighty 1202½ Illiana 1203½ Nettlesome120½	Sp'd for half 12

LATEST WORKOUTS Mar 4 Hia 7f fst 1:31 b

Shortcut To Fame

Gr. h. 5, by On To Glory—Cut It Short, by Nearctic
$15,000 Br.—Meadowbrook Farm Inc (Fla) Tr.—Rosas-Canessa Walter
Own.—Rogers Rachel & A S
118 Lifetime 58 5 12 5 $57,995 | 1983 7 2 1 0 $11,580 | 1982 19 0 3 3 $10,450 | Turf 7 0 2 0 $4,230

Race	Cond	Dist	Times	Class	Running line	Jockey	Wt	Odds	Speed	Finishers	Comment
19Mar83-11Hia	fst	6f	:22⅕ :45 1:10	Clm 19000	10 1 75½ 510 918 1014	Soto S B	114	3.60	79-18	Rufame 116no Gust of Reason 1164½ Jes Tactics 120hd	Outrun 11
10Mar83- 8Hia	fst	6f	:22⅕ :45⅕ 1:10⅗	Clm 14000	11 1 41¾ 43¼ 41¾ 1nk	Soto S B	112	15.60	90-17	Shortcut ToFame112nkBulLibra120nkFragrantPrince1162¼	Driving 12
3Mar83- 2GP	fst	6f	:22⅘ :46 1:12	Clm 10000	4 2 2hd 1hd 11½ 1½	Soto S B	117	12.90	79-23	Shortcut ToFame117½AngelLike1122½Sadair'sRobler1171½	Driving 12
17Feb83-10GP	gd	6f	:22 :45⅕ 1:11	Clm 14000	6 2 55½ 69 811 812	Lynch H D5	108	31.00	72-24	Bul Libra 1104½ Governor Bob 117½ Clinebell 117nk	No speed 10
4Feb83- 5GP	fst	6f	:22⅗ :45⅘ 1:11⅕	Clm 18000	11 1 88½ 1113 1013 1012	Solis A5	108	11.00	71-25	Tribal Warrior 1171 Green Path 1171½ Estallido 1141	Outrun 12
29Jan83- 2GP	fst	7f	:22⅗ :45⅖ 1:24⅖	Clm 19000	6 2 43½ 55¼ 57½ 911	Solis A5	110	3.40	71-20	Delta Law 1142½ Erodoto 1191½ Green Path 1171½	Dropped back 11
14Jan83- 5GP	fst	6f	:22⅗ :45⅘ 1:11	Clm 17000	2 6 64½ 63 41¼ 2no	Solis A5	110	7.00	84-20	Pilar'sFlint117noShortcutToFame1101½FstChnge115½	Just missed 12
31Dec82-10Crc	fst	6½f	:22⅗ :45⅘ 1:18⅘	3↑Clm 17000	5 5 31½ 42¾ 44 86½	Saumell L	115	36.60	84-20	Southern Swing 1161 Fragrant Prince 1152 Rufame 1202	Tired 11
22Dec82- 6Crc	fst	6f	:22 :45⅗ 1:12	3↑Clm 18000	5 2 85¾ 710 811 811	Saumell L	114	23.90	81-17	Rufame 112½ Nocturnal Phantom 1111½ More Dames 1161	Outrun 11
11Sep82- 3Crc	fst	7f	:22⅕ :45⅘ 1:26	3↑Clm 20000	7 1 44 43½ 46 53	Soto S B	112	23.90	83-14	Kentucky Edd 109½ Young Knave 115hd Laughing Kas 113½	Tired 8

LATEST WORKOUTS Feb 26 Crc 5f fst 1:03⅘ h (d)

Spaghetti Tree *

B. g. 7, by Bay Detty—Ollie B B, by Mr Brick
$16,000 Br.—Bruder G A III (Ill) Tr.—Wesbrook Chet
Own.—Kuhn Gwenn
116 Lifetime 61 9 6 12 $45,807 | 1983 1 0 0 0 $250 | 1982 17 2 2 4 $14,030 | Turf 5 0 0 0 $927

Race	Cond	Dist	Times	Class	Running line	Jockey	Wt	Odds	Speed	Finishers	Comment
28Mar83- 9Tam	fst	5f	:22⅖ :46⅘ 1:00⅕	3↑Alw 5000	1 1 22 23 31½ 43½	Seabo G E	115	5.20	81-27	SilverDollrBoy116¾CroziersAce122nkProspctKitty1172½	Weakened 8
19Aug82- 4Atl	fm	*5½f	Ⓣ:22⅖ :46⅗ 1:05⅕	3↑Clm 15500	2 2 21½ 31½ 42½ 43½	Feliciano B R	122	5.90	83-13	Gardener 1072½BroadwayDirector113hdNeverRome1201	Weakened 10
4Aug82- 7Atl	fm	5½f	Ⓣ:21⅘ :45⅗ 1:03⅘	3↑Clm 22500	9 1 2hd 21 52½ 63¾	Feliciano B R	120	15.40	90-11	Barrister Sib 1141¼ Raven Delight 1181 Searchin Lou 116hd	Tired 9
9Jly82- 6Atl	fst	6f	:22⅕ :45⅗ 1:11⅗	3↑Clm 20000	3 2 11 1½ 11 1nk	Feliciano B R	116	22.70	85-20	Spaghetti Tree 116nk Proofs Hed 116hd Untamed 120¾	Driving 9
30Jun82- 8Atl	gd	6f	:21⅘ :45⅘ 1:12⅗	3↑Clm 15500	5 1 1hd 22 1hd 11	Feliciano B R	116	5.90	79-23	Spaghetti Tree1161Jayne'sGent1123½GallantWhimsey120½	Driving 6
21Jun82- 5Atl	fst	6f	:22⅕ :45⅖ 1:11⅘	Clm 15500	5 2 11 32½ 34½ 33½	Feliciano B R	116	7.50	79-27	Joe Montage 116½ Jesterson's Quest1163SpaghettiTree1162	Tired 6
12Jun82- 3Atl	fst	6f	:22⅖ :45⅘ 1:10⅘	Clm 15500	1 3 11 21½ 33½ 35½	Hilburn K D	116	13.60	82-20	Raven Delight 1162½ Eddie Dibbs 1183 Spaghetti Tree 1162	Tired 6
4Jun82- 6Atl	fst	6f	:22⅕ :46⅖ 1:11⅘	Clm 14500	2 2 21 3½ 36 36¾	Feliciano B R	114	6.50	76-28	Eddie Dibbs 1133¾OspreySpirit1203SpaghettiTree1142½	Weakened 6
15May82- 5GP	fm	1	Ⓣ:46 1:10⅘ 1:35⅖	Clm 15000	2 1 11½ 32 711 713	Feliciano B R	113	11.90	80-12	Iron Clarion 1151½ Sublime 117½ Voukefalos 113no	Bore Out 7
8May82- 4GP	fst	6f	:22⅖ :45 1:10⅖	Clm 15000	3 1 1½ 1½ 32 34¼	Feliciano B R	117	24.30	83-14	Nuit EtJour1174LordOfTheSea117nkSpaghettiTree1172	Weakened 9

LATEST WORKOUTS ●Mar 26 Tam 3f fst :35 b ●Mar 22 Tam 3f fst :35⅗ b

Big Time Coming

B. g. 5, by Loco Kid—Loey, by Federal Hill
$16,000 Br.—Johnston E C Jr (Ark) Tr.—Maziarz Rosemary
Own.—Lucky Clover Fm &Maziarz R
116 Lifetime 29 8 4 5 $38,565 | 1983 3 1 0 0 $5,250 | 1982 18 5 2 5 $23,515

Race	Cond	Dist	Times	Class	Running line	Jockey	Wt	Odds	Speed	Finishers	Comment
10Mar83- 8Hia	fst	6f	:22⅕ :45⅕ 1:10⅗	Clm 16000	8 3 2hd 2hd 2hd 42¾	MacBeth D	116	7.20	87-17	ShortcutToFame112nkBulLibra120nkFrgrntPrince1162¼	Weakened 12
2Mar83- 4GP	fst	6f	:22⅘ :46 1:11⅗	Clm 20000	3 3 53¾ 611 68 612	Velez J A Jr	117	10.80	70-24	CapewayCarlo1221RoughDuck115nkPleasantDocJ.1151½	No factor 10
3Jan83- 2Crc	fst	6f	:22 :45⅘ 1:12⅖	Clm c-12500	3 5 1½ 1hd 11½ 1hd	Astorga C	120	*1.10	90-16	Big Time Coming120hdPowhatanPrince1162½BulLibra109½	Driving 7
18Dec82- 4Crc	fst	6f	:22⅕ :46⅕ 1:12	3↑Clm 11000	9 1 1½ 11 12 15	Astorga C	118	3.60	92-13	BigTimeComing1185ⒹFriendlyCard108½Dartanin1202¼	Ridden out 11
23Nov82-10Crc	fst	6f	:22⅖ :46⅕ 1:12⅕	3↑Clm 16000	8 2 1hd 2½ 1hd 42¼	Astorga C	120	14.60	89-17	MoreDmes106nkNocturnlPhntom115nkJmesPride1161¾	Weakened 9
15Nov82- 8Crc	fst	6f	:22⅕ :46⅕ 1:13⅖	3↑Clm 17000	7 3 3nk 2hd 33½ 65	Astorga C	115	7.90	80-21	SirThomasCutlss115½Rufme1091½NocturnlPhntom1153	Weakened 8
3Nov82- 1Crc	fst	6f	:22⅕ :46⅕ 1:13	3↑Clm 13000	5 4 1½ 1½ 1hd 1hd	Acevedo D A5	115	6.10	87-21	Big Time Coming 115hd SplitTiming117nkFirstValley1141½	Driving 8
22Oct82- 5Crc	fst	6f	:22⅖ :46⅕ 1:12⅕	3↑Clm 12500	1 4 11 11 11½ 1no	Acevedo D A5	109	4.90	91-16	Big Time Coming 109no Fast Change1181½FirstValley1182	Driving 8
13Oct82- 6Crc	fst	6f	:22⅕ :45⅘ 1:12⅘	3↑Clm 10000	6 1 2hd 1hd 1hd 21	Acevedo D A5	113	4.70	87-24	Buckn'Shoe1091BigTimeComing1133LughingRlity116¾	Weakened 8
28Sep82-10Crc	fst	6f	:22⅖ :45⅘ 1:12	3↑Clm 14000	4 3 2½ 23 36 65¾	Acevedo D A5	109	6.80	86-15	Sadair's Robler 1092¼ First Valley 118½ Appealer 1102	Faltered 7

LATEST WORKOUTS ●Feb 28 Hia 3f sly :36 b Feb 20 Hia 3f fst :37 b Feb 10 Hia 4f fst :51 b

Gold Limit

Dk. b. or br. g. 4, by Limit To Reason—Gold Gala, by Gallant Man
$15,000 Br.—Marriott P M (Ky) Tr.—Simms Phillip G
Own.—Golden Acres Inc
118 Lifetime 40 10 6 7 $72,310 | 1983 6 1 0 2 $7,210 | 1982 18 1 4 3 $21,790 | Turf 1 0 0 0 $130

Entered 4Apr83- 1 HIA

Race	Cond	Dist	Times	Class	Running line	Jockey	Wt	Odds	Speed	Finishers	Comment
25Mar83- 5Hia	fst	6f	:22⅖ :46 1:11⅗	Clm 12500	5 6 44 33½ 21½ 11	Castaneda K	116	3.00	85-18	Gold Limit 1161 Mike Ralph 116hd Twogun Kenny 1161	Driving 10
15Feb83-10GP	fst	7f	:22⅖ :45⅖ 1:23⅘	Clm 20000	9 4 62¾ 64¼ 54 75¼	Velez J A Jr	117	3.50	80-23	Limerick 1151 Wooster Sq. 117½ Pleasant Doc J. 1153	No factor 12
7Feb83- 5GP	gd	6f	:22⅗ :46 1:11⅕	Clm 22500	2 3 2½ 31 21 42¼	Velez J A Jr	115	7.40	81-21	Hot Words 1171 ⒹNocturnal Phantom 117¾ Freedom Lad 113½	12
7Feb83-Placed third through disqualification											
29Jan83- 9GP	fst	1$\frac{1}{16}$	:46⅖ 1:11⅗ 1:45	3↑Inv Alw	5 2 21½ 43½ 1013 1013	Castaneda K	117	14.20	63-20	ⒹSouthern Swing 117¾ Kan Reason 122hdCanuck117hd	Gave Way 12
25Jan83-10GP	fst	6f	:23 :46⅖ 1:10⅘	Clm 27500	2 6 73¾ 75¼ 55 47	Capodici J	115	19.10	78-21	Intercontinnt115hdIrishSwords1175½Pokr'N'Chips1121½	No factor 11
3Jan83- 8Crc	fst	7f	:23 :46⅗ 1:25⅘	Clm 25000	1 6 2½ 2hd 1½ 32	Capodici J	116	*1.70	85-16	Tumiga's Flame 1141 The Fugitive 1161 Gold Limit 1164½	Tired 9
24Dec82- 8Crc	fst	7f	:22⅖ :45⅕ 1:24⅗	3↑Clm 30000	2 5 3nk 21½ 22 34½	Castaneda K	115	3.60	88-19	Kentucky Edd 1212½ Iron Gladiator1152GoldLimit1156	Weakened 10
20Dec82- 7Crc	fst	7f	:23 :46⅖ 1:24⅗	3↑Clm 45000	6 1 53¾ 65¾ 47 46¾	Castaneda K	116	4.30	86-15	Pokr'N'Chips112hdSomthngWrong1164½RllyFunny1152¼	No f ctor 7
11Dec82- 8Crc	fst	7f	:22⅗ :46⅖ 1:25⅕	3↑Alw 14000	6 1 2hd 2½ 1hd 22¼	Castaneda K	115	11.90	88-16	Mr. Mar J. Mar 1092½ Gold Limit 115hd Sonofagov 1191½	Gamely 8
29Nov82- 7Crc	fst	7f	:23⅕ :46⅘ 1:24⅗	3↑Clm 30000	2 3 31½ 32 22 24½	Castaneda K	116	2.00	88-17	Kentucky Edd 1104½ Gold Limit 1161 Donna's Boy 1157½	Gamely 5

House Odds — B. g. 5, by A Gambler—Private Screening, by Silent Screen
$16,000 Br.—Lotsoc Farm (NJ)
Own.—Provost J — Tr.—Provost Joseph
116 — Lifetime 54 3 4 7 $36,705 — 1983 6 0 0 2 $2,580 — 1982 21 0 3 2 $11,730

18Mar83- 8Hia fst 6f :22⅗ :46⅖ 1:11⅗ Clm 16000 4 8 88 88¼ 74¼ 4¾ Hernandez C 116 8.00 84-19 China Village 116hd Clinebell 113¾ Deb's Playboy 114nk Rallied 12
28Feb83- 4GP fst 7f :22⅕ :45⅖ 1:24 Clm 16000 8 2 62¾ 75 53 31½ Lopez C C 117 8.80 82-24 Governor Bob 117no Mike Ralph 1171½ House Odds 117hd Gamely 12
21Feb83- 2GP fst 6f :22 :45 1:10⅘ Clm 18000 5 11 1012 816 813 610 Lopez C C 117 14.20 75-24 Capeway Carlo 1221 On the Helm 1173 Rufame 1171 No Factor 12
7Feb83- 3GP gd 7f :22⅗ :45⅘ 1:24⅗ Clm 15000 11 2 33 31½ 1hd 3¾ Lopez C C 117 20.80 80-21 PleasantDocJ.117¾Greers'Leader117nkHouseOdds117nk Weakened 12
28Jan83- 5GP fst 7f :22⅘ :46⅕ 1:25⅖ Clm 20000 1 9 74¼ 63¾1113 1111 Lopez C C 113 113.20 66-27 Bishops Pride 113no Nocturnal Phantom1121Ye-Ye1171 Fell back 12
17Jan83- 4GP fst 6f :22⅗ :45⅘ 1:11 Clm 18000 10 1 96¾ 79½ 58 59½ Lopez C C 113 35.30 74-22 Southern Swing 1194 Rufame 1151 Green Path 117hd No factor 12
27Nov82-10Suf fst 1 1/16 :48 1:13⅕ 1:48 3↑Clm c-16000 9 5 58 54½ 43½ 55¼ Baez R 114 4.80 64-33 Olympic Dash 114¾ Snappy Delivery 1141GoldenProfit1122 Evenly 10
20Nov82- 7Suf fst 6f :22⅗ :46⅖ 1:13 3↑Clm 16000 4 8 107¼ 87½ 58 21 Baez R 114 14.10 75-24 China Village 1191 House Odds 114½ Solo Ace 117¾ Clipped heels 12
6Nov82- 9Suf gd 1 :47⅗ 1:12 1:38⅖ 3↑Alw 10000 1 3 33 34 45½ 412 Petro N J5 109 6.80 73-26 Pat Sprat 114hd Sue's Destroyer 1094½ Tested Leader 1127 Tired 7
31Oct82- 8Suf fst 170 :47⅕ 1:12⅕ 1:43⅘ 3↑Clm 35000 4 4 56 54¾ 64 69¾ Luhr R D 113 97.00 71-23 Foolish Move 114no Waterloc 1121¾ Josiah W. 1174 Steadied 7
LATEST WORKOUTS Mar 12 Hia 5f fst 1:00⅖ h

Twogun Kenny — Ch. g. 4, by Twogundan—Flying Royal, by Royal Union
$16,000 Br.—Smith Theodore (Ont-C)
Own.—Mongeon Kathy — Tr.—Mongeon Kathy
116 — Lifetime 32 5 3 8 $37,144 — 1983 2 0 0 1 $752 — 1982 23 3 2 6 $26,510

25Mar83- 5Hia fst 6f :22⅖ :46 1:11⅗ Clm 12500 4 8 87¼ 912 65¼ 31 Cruguet J 116 41.40 84-18 Gold Limit 1161 Mike Ralph 116hd Twogun Kenny 1161 Rallied 10
18Mar83- 8Hia fst 6f :22⅗ :46⅖ 1:11⅗ Clm 16000 7 10 99½1116 1115 1013 Iannelli F 116 60.20 72-19 China Village116hdClinebell113¾Deb'sPlayboy114nk Unruly pre-st. 12
22Oct82- 8Suf fst 6f :22⅘ :46⅖ 1:12 Clm 15000 8 9 106½ 87¼ 610 69 Ernst P 114 3.90 72-29 Wig Gala 1226 Ackuation 109hd My Father's Son 119hd Outrun 10
15Oct82- 9Suf fst 6f :22⅘ :46⅗ 1:13⅗ Clm 22500 3 1 42½ 44½ 46 31½ Ernst P 114 4.80 71-31 Power Rig 1141½ Medeiros 114hd Twogun Kenny 114½ Rallied 5
8Oct82- 9Suf sly 6f :22⅘ :47 1:14 3↑Clm 15000 7 1 78¾ 59½ 56½ 34½ Johnson L 114 2.20 66-33 Wig Gala 1221½ Koranarga 1193 Twogun Kenny 1141½ Mild rally 8
19Sep82- 8Suf fst 6f :22⅗ :46⅖ 1:12⅗ Clm 20000 6 1 57¼ 68¾ 59 57¾ Johnson L 114 4.50 70-27 HoggBackMountain1142¾PowerRig1123¾HitParde114nk No threat 6
10Sep82- 9Suf fst 6f :22⅗ :45⅘ 1:12 3↑Alw 9000 1 6 77¼ 716 714 713 Johnson L 109 10.90 68-25 Delightful Dancer 1141¼ Daring Reb 1142 OldGrayFox119¾ Trailed 7
25Aug82- 3Sar sly 6f :22⅕ :45⅗ 1:11⅗ Clm 30000 5 2 32 33½ 33½ 21¾ Ernst P 114 18.10 80-17 Private Sun 1171¾ Twogun Kenny 114hd Hello Federal1104½ Wide 7
18Aug82- 2Sar fst 6½f :22⅘ :46⅕ 1:17⅕ Clm 20000 11 8 106¼108¼ 57½ 47½ Lapensee M 113 34.90 78-15 Whale's Eye 1171 Duck Call 1194½ Itsabore 1172½ Rallied 13
6Aug82- 9Suf fst 6f :22⅖ :44⅘ 1:09⅖ Clm 22500 6 7 76½ 79 610 511 Skelton R A 114 10.70 83-16 Hit Parade1147SevenKarats109nkHoggBackMountain114½ Outrun 7
LATEST WORKOUTS Mar 15 Hia 4f fst :48 h Feb 20 Hia 4f fst :49 b

Lo The Dutchman — Dk. b. or br. h. 6, by Bushido—Dutch Maid, by Piet
$16,000 Br.—Fisher Susan B (Md)
Own.—Weston E L — Tr.—Mulnix Henry
116 — Lifetime 39 6 5 8 $39,541 — 1983 3 0 0 0 $275 — 1982 12 2 0 ? $8,824

28Mar83- 9Tam fst 5f :22⅖ :46⅘ 1:00⅕ 3↑Alw 5000 8 6 87½ 87¾ 810 812 Buisson R 116 7.70 73-27 Silver DollarBoy116¾CroziersAce122nkProspectKitty1172½ Outrun 8
15Jan83- 8Tam fst 5f :22⅕ :45⅘ :59 Alw 4500 1 2 1hd 2hd 23 44 Buisson R b 116 9.20 87-24 Cross His Heart1131½TrafficBreaker119½FirstValley1132 Steadied 8
8Jan83- 9Tam fst 6f :22⅕ :45⅗ 1:11⅕ 3↑Chryslr Spnt 11 2 41¼ 21 46 913 Buisson R 115 10.70 76-23 TrafficBreaker1206SilverDollarBoy116nkBigMav121no Brief speed 11
9Dec82- 9Tam fst 6f :22⅗ :45⅗ 1:11⅘ 3↑Alw 4000 4 3 1½ 12 11½ 13 Buisson R 115 2.10 86-25 Lo The Dutchman 1153 Cregan's Cap 1223Mr.CeeBee1139 Driving 8
4Dec82- 8Tam fst 5f :22 :45⅘ :59⅕ 3↑Alw 4500 4 4 55 53¼ 42½ 32¼ Buisson R b 115 21.80 88-20 RonnyTurcotte113nkOleWindBag1142LoTheDutchman1152 Rallied 9
23Jly82- 7Atl sly 6f :21⅗ :44⅗ 1:10⅗ 3↑Alw 10000 8 5 55½ 713 824 828 Melendez J H b 114 28.30 61-23 Flashy Wings 1141 Megalopolis 1143 Music Time 1172 Tired 8
7Jly82- 3Crc fst 6f :22 :45⅘ 1:12⅘ Clm 25000 6 2 2hd 2½ 714 722 Salinas P L b 116 13.30 66-17 Appealer 116½ Galactico 1185¾ Solo Heritage 116½ Tired 7
14Jun82- 7Crc fst 6f :21⅘ :45⅖ 1:12⅘ Clm 32500 5 2 21 34 520 624 Salinas P L b 114 10.80 64-16 Galactico 112½ Sunshine Prince 1162½ Jazz Pop 1139½ Tired 7
26May82- 8Crc sly 6f :22 :45⅗ 1:13 Clm 25000 7 1 11½ 15 14 1¾ Salinas P L b 116 11.30 87-19 Lo The Dutchman 116¾ Limbo Limited1111½FlipFlip116hd Driving 7
4May82- 8GP sly 6f :22 :45⅗ 1:11⅕ Clm 30000 7 5 12 11½ 31½ 77 Salinas P L b 117 10.40 76-25 Motinero 114½ Sunshine Prince 117½ Harmonella 1151 Tired 8
LATEST WORKOUTS Mar 23 Tam 4f fst :49⅗ b Mar 19 Tam 3f fst :37⅕ b

This could be a good race to bet and to watch. There are three clear choices with **Big Time Coming** the most logical play. Even though **Shortcut to Fame** beat **Big Time Coming** on March 10, the numbers suggest that things will be different this time out. **Gold Limit**'s weight, being revised down just before post time, is a definite plus. **Spaghetti Tree** has the ability, but hasn't run this distance since last July and may not be ready.

The choices in this race are:

1. **Big Time Coming**
2. **Gold Limit**
3. **Shortcut to Fame**
4. **Spaghetti Tree**

5th HIALEAH 6F (4/5)

PP	#	NAME	Date: Last Race	Weight (Today's Race)	3 Speed Ratings + Track Variants	Weight Adjust.	***Ability Factor***	Speed Rating: Last Race	+21 or +25	Track Adjust.	Weight Adjust.	***Condition Factor***	Wt. at Post Time	Total	Adj. Total
1		MEDEIROS	3/18	116	292	−1	291	82	+21	−8	—	95	116	386	386
2		FIESTY FLEET	3/15	104	282	+4	286	75	+21	−8	+2	90	104	376	376
3		SHORTCUT TO FAME	3/19	118	306	−4	302 ↙	79	+21	−8	−2	90	118	392	392 ↙
4		SPAGHETTI TREE (5F)	3/28	116	313	—	(313)	85	+21	−7	—	(99)	116	412	(412)
5		BIG TIME COMING	3/10	116	304	+3	(307)	87	+21	−8	—	(100)	116	407	(407)
6		GOLD LIMIT	3/25	118	304	−4	300 ↙	85	+21	−8	−2	96	115	396	(399)
7		HOUSE ODDS	3/18	116	298	−1	297	84	+21	−8	—	97	116	394	394 ↙
8		TWOGUN KENNY	3/25	116	294	−2	292	84	+21	−8	—	97	116	389	389
9		LO THE DUTCHMAN (5F)	3/28	116	294	−4	290	76	+21	−10	−1	86	116	376	376
10															
11															
12															
13															
14															
15															
16															

FIFTH RACE
Hialeah Park
APRIL 5

6 FURLONGS. (1.08⅗) CLAIMING. Purse $7,000. 4-year-olds and upward. Weights, 122 lbs. Non-winners of two races since February 5 allowed 2 lbs. A race since then 4 lbs. A race since January 29, 6 lbs. Claiming Price $16,000 for each $1,000 to $14,000, 2 lbs. (Races where entered for $12,500 or less not considered.) (Red. Florida Breds Preferred.)

Value of race $7,000, value to winner $4,200, second $1,260, third $840, fourth $350, balance of starters $70 each. Mutuel pool $49,723. Perfecta Pool $57,329.

Last Raced	Horse	Eqt.	A.	Wt	PP	St	¼	½	Str	Fin	Jockey	Cl'g Pr	Odds $1
10Mar83 8Hia4	Big Time Coming		5	116	5	1	2^5	2^1½	1½	1^hd	Velez J A Jr	16000	4.30
25Mar83 5Hia1	Gold Limit		4	115	6	4	4^2	4^6	2^hd	2^4	Castaneda K	15000	2.60
19Mar83 11Hia10	Shortcut To Fame		5	118	3	3	3^hd	3^1½	3^4	3^nk	Soto S B	15000	4.60
18Mar83 8Hia6	Medeiros	b	4	116	1	8	8^hd	6½	5^1½	4^3½	Rujano M	16000	23.30
15Mar83 8Hia10	Fiesty Fleet	b	4	104	2	7	5^hd	5^2	6^2½	5^1	Gurkas L H7	16000	37.20
18Mar83 8Hia4	House Odds		5	116	7	9	9	8^2	7^1½	6½	Mayorga W	16000	6.80
25Mar83 5Hia3	Twogun Kenny		4	116	8	6	7½	9	9	7^1½	Cruguet J	16000	5.30
28Mar83 9Tam8	Lo The Dutchman	b	6	116	9	2	1^3	1^1	4^1	8^1½	Buisson R	16000	15.70
28Mar83 9Tam4	Spaghetti Tree		7	116	4	5	6^2	7½	8^hd	9	Seabo G E	16000	4.80

OFF AT 3:00 Start good, Won driving. Time, :22⅕, :45⅘, 1:11⅕ Track fast.

$2 Mutuel Prices:				
	5-BIG TIME COMING	**10.60**	**4.20**	**2.80**
	6-GOLD LIMIT		**3.60**	**3.00**
	3-SHORTCUT TO FAME			**3.40**
	$2 PERFECTA 5-6 PAID $40.00.			

B. g, by Loco Kid—Loey, by Federal Hill. Trainer Maziarz Rosemary. Bred by Johnston E C Jr (Ark).

BIG TIME COMING pressed the pace from the outset, gained the advantage in midstretch, then held off GOLD LIMIT through the final eighth while being brushed by that one inside the final sixteenth. GOLD LIMIT raced forwardly, joined the winner in midstretch, bore in to brush that one inside the final sixteenth and just missed. The rider of GOLD LIMIT claimed foul against the winner charging interference inside the final sixteenth. The claim of foul was disallowed. SHORTCUT TO FAME well-placed, reached sharp contention in midstretch, but had little left. MEDEIROS was outrun. LOTHE DUTCHMAN quickly opened a clear lead but was finished in early stretch. SPAGHETTI TREE showed little.

Owners— 1, Lucky Clover Fm & Maziarz R; 2, Golden Acres Inc; 3, Rogers Rachel & A S; 4, Cerulean Farm; 5, Birchminster Farms; 6, Provost J; 7, Mongeon Kathy; 8, Weston E L; 9, Kuhn Gwenn.

Trainers— 1, Maziarz Rosemary; 2, Simms Phillip G; 3, Rosas-Canessa Walter; 4, Steen H Kirk Jr; 5, Jamtgaard Wayne; 6, Provost Joseph; 7, Mongeon Kathy; 8, Mulnix Henry; 9, Wesbrook Chet.

Corrected weight: Gold Limit 114 pounds. **Overweight:** Gold Limit 1 pound.

Big Time Coming was claimed by Sirola B; trainer, Paradise Jerry; Gold Limit was claimed by Deno Stable; trainer, Loring B Dean; Twogun Kenny was claimed by Barely Able Stable; trainer, Young Steven W.

This is an ideal race and a perfect example in almost every way. The top three horses were clear choices and the race unfolded exactly as expected.

Of the three horses with early speed, only **Lo The Dutchman** and **Big Time Coming** showed the way. In the stretch, only two horses could finish with authority.

$2 Perfecta Wagering	
Bet	$ 30.00
Return	$160.00
Profit	$130.00

With
a
Computer

Editor's Note

The *Winning at the Track* computer software program is designed for the IBM personal computer and all IBM-compatibles with minimum memory capacities of 256K.

As time passes and track records change, you will want the program updated, perhaps every year or two. For a small fee, you may purchase a program update. Write to the publisher for details.

How to Begin

1. Before all else, make a backup copy of the program, either onto another formatted disc or onto a hard disc. If there are any questions, type the following line at the DOS prompt: type install . The instructions for making a backup copy and how to start the program will appear on your screen. Once the backup has been made, put the original away in a safe place and use the second copy.
2. Read pages 83 to 138 of this book thoroughly before proceeding.
3. Enter the program by typing the word HANDICAP.
4. Review again the diagram on page 91 as you read the HELP screens. When you know exactly where you are in the program, moving in and out is accomplished quickly and easily.
5. For first-time users who would like a step-by-step tutorial, begin by typing: TYPE README

Introduction

You are about to use the most advanced thoroughbred handicapping method available anywhere!

The "shortcut" version of the *Performance Method*, explained earlier, is an excellent tool for those who do not have access to a computer. But, sadly, there are several important time-consuming variables that have to be ignored when calculations are made without one.

For example, not all tracks have the same racing surface. Some are fast, others are not. The computer automatically adjusts each horse's statistics to accommodate the surface differences of more than 100 racetrack courses throughout North America.

Also, horses do not always run the same distance from one week to the next. The racing histories of the horses in each contest can differ substantially. Some may have raced only in sprints, some only in route races, some in turf races, and others may have raced in all three. The computer knows, for example, that a horse clocked at 1:12 in a 6 furlong race on a fast dirt track could also be capable of running 1 1/16 miles in 1:46 2/5 over the same surface. If the horse runs the same distance on a softer dirt track, the time could be closer to 1:47. These necessary time-adjustments are made automatically by the computer program, using what is commonly referred to as a "parallel speed table." And different calculations are made for horses with different capabilities.

Is this approach infallible? No, not at all! But many key variables are taken into consideration, thus allowing the handicapper a better chance to compare "apples with apples" rather then "apples with oranges."

The capability of the *Winning at the Track* program can be enhanced dramatically with the application of *The Pace Analyst*, a new software package introduced recently. This program add-on, which can be purchased directly from the publisher, reads a completed *Winning at the Track* file. It identifies the likely pacesetters and the horses capable of running with the pace. *The Pace Analyst*, in effect, adds a totally new dimension to *Winning at the Track* with very little additional work. See the chapter, "Pace Handicapping."

Finally, the computer can calculate an entire race card with lightning speed. With this new tool, we can now avoid spending hours of valuable time pouring over the past performances of horses that have little or no chance of being "in the money."

The Performance Method: In Detail

The Computer Keys

The "Arrow" keys on the number pad will move the cursor up and down on the Race Card, on the P/M Table, on the HELP menu, and in all directions on the History Worksheets. Menu choices at the bottom of each screen can be made by either moving the cursor with the Right or Left Arrow keys, or by simply hitting the first letter of each menu selection.

The Num Lock key, when "on," will allow the user to enter the figures with the number pad. This will save a great deal of time entering data. No longer will it be necessary to reach for the numbers at the top of the keyboard. It is not necessary to turn the Num Lock key "off" to move the cursor. Instead, simply use the Shift key simultaneously with the Arrow keys.

The + and – keys to the right of the number pad will move the cursor to the right or to the left when the Num Lock key is "on." This feature allows the user to backspace quickly when data is being entered onto the History Worksheet.

The "Enter" or "Return" key will move the cursor to the next cell in the program, or allow you to proceed in the program as indicated by the cursor.

The "Esc" (Escape) key will call up the menu at the bottom of the screen.

The "Q" (Quit) key will return you to the previous screen or allow you to quit the program from the Race Card.

The "Alt" key hit simultaneously with the "H" key will produce the HELP menu.

Always be sure to SAVE the data after completing each History Worksheet for each horse.

From the Newspaper

Entering data into the computer and handicapping the final selections will be the only major effort required. The information, readily available, needs only to be typed onto the program's "History Worksheet" for each horse. The race selection process for one of the components, the Ability Factor, will require some judgment. Otherwise, the computer will do all the work and "number-crunching" for you.

The *Performance Method* Rating

Four separate calculations comprise the *P/M Rating.* They are: the Ability Factor, the Pure Speed, the Early Speed, and the Late Speed.

The **Ability Factor** total tells us which horses in this race should be best suited to this distance and "class" of company. The Ability Factor is also, to some extent, a measure of each horse's "form cycle," designed to tell us whether the horse is ready to run today.

The **Pure Speed** calculation will show us exactly how fast each horse has run today's distance (or its equivalent) from all of the historical figures available.

The **Early Speed** total expresses each horse's capability to lead the other horses in the first part of this race. In a sprint, it measures the speed of each horse to the 1/2 mile pole (4 furlongs). In a route race, it measures the normal speed of each horse from the gate to the 3/4 mile pole (6 furlongs).

The **Late Speed** calculation tells us which horses are capable of running the last part of this race and which animals could have more difficulty. In a sprint race, Late Speed refers to each horse's best past performance between the 1/2 mile pole and the finish line; and, in route races, its best showing between the 3/4 mile pole and the finish line. Comprising this calculation is a measure of each horse's "Speed" (or "Pole Speed") to the 1/2 mile pole, or 3/4 mile pole, and also a measure of its endurance to the finish line (the "Last Quarter").

The P/M Rating is a weighted value of these four components. They are totalled and displayed automatically on the *Performance Method* Table.

The Measure of Ability

Of the four components to this handicapping method, this is the only one that requires some personal attention. The other three are simply the best figures available and the computer can find them easily. For the Ability Factor, the computer is given three recent performances of each horse. It extracts the Speed Ratings and Track Variants of these three selected races, adjusts the figures, and automatically enters this total into the P/M table.

The Ability Factor calculation is, again, defined as:

> **The three most recent races that best represent the horse's current ability to run today's distance.**

In an earlier chapter, the Ability Factor was described in its simplest form by the mere addition of the Speed Ratings and Track Variants for the last three races of today's distance. On balance, this rather uncomplicated method works well and is easily calculated. However, its accuracy is often diminished by special (albeit not out-of-the-ordinary) circumstances. Perhaps the horse is returning after a long layoff, or the animal is recovering from an injury. Maybe he has a new owner and trainer, or has never before run today's distance.

While it is easy to use the last three races, there are a few alterations that can improve the performance of the method, leaving all the necessary adjustments to the computer. For example, now the Ability Factor need not be comprised of only races of the same *distance*. With the computer, it can be races of the same *category* (i.e., Super Sprints, Sprints, or Route Races).

Also, it is worth noting whether the horse made an effort in the race or was just being entered for conditioning purposes. Here, the "5/5 Rule" can be useful.

> **The 5/5 Rule.** A horse is within the 5/5 Rule whenever it finishes no worse than 5th place *and* no worse than 5 lengths behind the winner. Use this rule to judge whether the horse made a concerted effort to win purse money.

The three races that are used to calculate the Ability Factor can be entered into the computer in two ways. First, by marking the three races in the newspaper before all else and then simply entering those figures onto the first three lines of the program's History Worksheet. Or secondly, the statistics can be typed onto the worksheet and then, later, the three races are chosen by using a special selection feature. Either way, some judgment is required.

The most common problem that arises when entering the Ability Factor is the horse's "form cycle." If the Ability Factor is comprised of three races, all run within the past four to six weeks, the total can be considered a fair measure of today's performance. On the other hand, if the most recent race occurred ten days ago, after a two or three month layoff, the horse might need one or two more races before he is back in form. In this instance, the Ability Factor could be overstating today's potential. Use a little judgment. The computer's output will be no better than the numbers that are entered into it.

Once the figures have been entered into the machine, and you notice that none of the three races were run within the past two months, beware! For this reason, it is a good idea to also enter a personal note or date next to the horse's name when it is first typed into the program. This helps with the selection and betting process later.

The most effective way to overcome the problem of the form cycle is to establish a rule whereby the most recent past performance line is ALWAYS entered except in dire circumstances (the jockey fell off, etc.), along with two good efforts within the past 60 days. If the last race was out of the ordinary, omit it, and make a note next to the horse's name for your benefit later. In most cases, the three Ability Factor races will consist of the best three of the last four races run in the past 60 days or so.

Here is a perfect example. The underlined races are those that were used as the Ability Factor for this February 16 sprint. If all of **Baked Alaska**'s last four races were entered onto the History Worksheet, then a quick visit to the Ability Factor screen would enable you to change the computer's automatic selection. This is sometimes faster than thinking about which race to enter when sitting at the keyboard.

Baked Alaska — B. f. 3(Apr), by Yukon—Cumberland Island, by Kirtling
Own.—Franks John — $50,000 — Br.—Parrish Hill Farm (Ky) — Tr.—Johnson Philip G — 1145
Lifetime 8 2 2 1 $39,940

Date/Race	Trk	Cond	Dist		Fractions			Class							Jockey	Wt	Odds	Speed	Top finishers
3Feb91- 4Aqu		fst	6f	⊡	:224	:47	1:132	ⒻClm 60000	2	1	2hd	1hd	2½	3¾	Vasquez M 05	109	*.90	73-19	Mezzanotte116¾ Starsawhir'
23Jan91- 5Aqu		fst	6f	⊡	:22	:45	1:112	ⒻClm 60000	6	2	2hd	1½	12	12	Vasquez M 05	107	*1.60	86-10	BakedAlaska1072D…
20Dec90- 5Aqu		fst	170	⊡	:48	1:131	1:42	ⒻClm 75000	4	1	1½	2½	46½	616¾	Chavez J F	116	9.80	78-12	SthnSnds1146½SprtCh…
6Dec90- 5Aqu		fst	6f	⊡	:222	:461	1:124	ⒻMd 75000	7	2	1½	1½	1½	11	Chavez J F	117	*1.10e	82-12	Baked Alaska1171 Sweet Ab…
23Nov90- 3Aqu		fst	7f		:223	:46	1:252	ⒻMd 75000	6	3	2hd	1hd	11½	21¾	Chavez J F	117	2.80	73-21	QuickGlance1131¾BakedA…
16Nov90- 5Aqu		fst	6f		:214	:452	1:122	ⒻMd Sp Wt	8	4	33½	34	511	66¾	Chavez J F	117	3.40	71-20	Slick Delivery1173 …
24Oct90- 5Bel		fst	6f		:222	:46	1:104	ⒻMd Sp Wt	8	6	32½	31	44½	48	Chavez J F	117	*1.20	77-14	MissRichardE.1173Slick…
12Oct90- 5Bel		fst	6f		:222	:461	1:114	ⒻMd Sp Wt	4	1	11½	1½	1hd	21½	Chavez J F	117	6.50	78-19	HeyHeyPul1171½BkedAl…

Speed Index: Last Race: –8.0 3–Race Avg.: –6.0 7–Race Avg.: –6.4 O…

LATEST WORKOUTS Jan 20 Bel tr.t 3f fst :36 H Jan 15 Bel tr.t 4f fst :484 H Jan 3 Bel tr.t 4f fst :473 H

Actually, in this example, the Ability Factor was almost unaffected by the change, although it would not have been apparent by glancing at the results of each race.

To summarize, in deciding which three races to enter, use the following guidelines: (1) Enter the most recent race on the top line of the History Worksheet unless it is a race that has to be thrown out based on the trouble line. (2) It is usually good to have the best race the horse has run in the past 60 days included in the Ability Factor. (3) Favor those races run in the past 90 days over those that are older. (4) Be absolutely sure to make a note next to the horse's name if the horse has been away – especially more than three months.

The Ability Factor is most accurate when it includes the most recent race, along with two others showing a level of competence, preferably at today's distance, all within the past 60-90 days.

If there are, say, only one or two races available, such as in a typical maiden claiming race, you can find the Ability Factor by using a 6/6 Rule, or a 7/7 Rule. Do not go beyond a 6/6 Rule unless you must. Unfortunately, there are many races in which a 5/5 Rule is simply not possible. Again, favor only those races that are consistent with the category of today's race. You can use distances outside the proper category. The computer will automatically adjust every race to today's distance. However, the calculation then becomes a little less reliable.

The Computer "Menus"

The *Winning at the Track* computer program includes twelve menus or screens. Here is a diagram of the entire program:

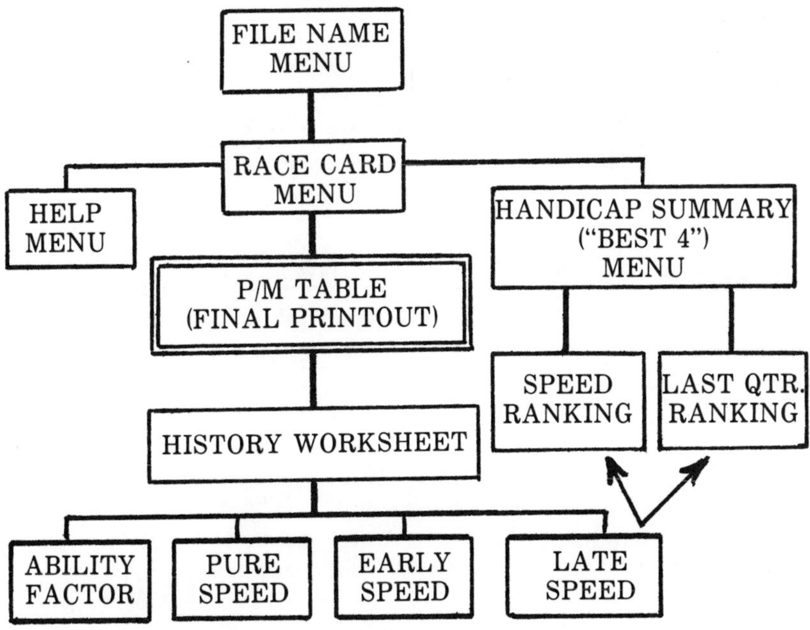

1. The File Name Menu

   Upon entering the program you will be asked to name the new file. For ease of use and rapid recall, the following procedure is recommended: use the *date of the race* (not the date of the newspaper) and the *track abbreviation* as the file name. For example, if you plan to travel to Maryland to attend Laurel Race Course on August 2, 1992, the file name **8-2-92.lrl** would be inserted in the designated space. You should also enter the track of today's races in the other designated space. Next, hit the "return" key to go directly to the Race Card Menu.

```
WINNING at the Track

David L. Christopher

Copyright (C) 1985  - All Rights Reserved




Enter Race File Name:              [4-5-88.hia]

Enter Racetrack for Today's Races:      [hia]
```

2. The Race Card Menu

   Now you are in the program. Move the cursor to the cell designated "Distance," hit the return key, and one by one, fill out the entire day's racing card, from the first race to the last. Move down the line, using the letters shown to set the appropriate distance (eg., hit "e" for a 6 furlong race, hit "j" for a 1 1/16 mile race, and so on). From the Race Card, it is also possible to go to the Handicap Summary Menu, or to go directly to the "Help" Menu. Once the Race Card is complete, continue on to the P/M Table.

Hialeah Park April 5, 198-
Race Card

Race	Distance
1st	7 f
2nd	6 f
3rd	6 f
4th	6 f
5th	6 f
6th	7 f
7th	1 1/8
8th	6 f
9th	6 f
10th	1 1/16

Horse	Ability	P/S	Early Speed	Late Speed	P/M Rating
Medeiros	483	93	288	782	3372
Fiesty Fleet	469	101	293	789	3410
Shortcut to Fame	490	99	295	784	3415
Spaghetti Tree -5f	483	97	303	775	3380
Big Time Coming	494	105	306	794	3481
Gold Limit	484	100	303	786	3424
House Odds	486	94	290	776	3364
Twogun Kenny	480	96	286	786	3390
Lo the Dutchman -5f	482	100	308	789	3434

P/M Table Distance Race Date Best 4 Capsule Help Quit

3. The Handicap Summary ("Best 4") Menu

   Later, after all the race data has been entered, you will return to the Race Card. From there, go to the Handicap Summary ("Best 4") Menu. Here, the computer lists the four horses with the highest P/M Ratings in each race. The Handicap Summary can be printed on an 8 1/2″ × 11″ sheet for your convenience. The four listed are the computer's selections based solely on the numbers from the P/M Table. These are not your final selections, however. Instead, it is used merely as a guide once you have finished entering all the data and complete the final selection process.

```
5 - Big Time Coming           5:1   3481
9 - Lo the Dutchman    -5f  15:1   3434
6 - Gold Limit                3:1   3424
3 - Shortcut to Fame          5:1   3415

Best 4     Speed     Last Qtr      Quit
Display Best 4 P/M Ratings
```

Based on years of experience, it can be said there is a high probability that one or both of the first two horses to cross the finish line will be among these four.

When using the Handicap Summary, you will notice that two additional tools are available. The first is called the *Pole Speed Ranking*, derived from the statistics used to calculate the Late Speed. Listed are the four horses having the fastest splits within the Late Speed calculation. This tool will be particularly useful when making your final selections for sprint races and races on hard, fast tracks.

```
4 - Spaghetti Tree      -5f   5:1    92
9 - Lo the Dutchman     -5f  15:1    92
3 - Shortcut to Fame          5:1    91
5 - Big Time Coming           5:1    89

Best 4    Speed    Last Qtr    Quit
Display Best 4 Speed Rankings
```

The second screen available is called the *Last Quarter Ranking*, which is also derived from the Late Speed figures. Listed are the four horses having the best "last quarter" numbers. This tool will be especially useful when making your final selections for route races and sprint races on muddy and/or soft tracks.

```
2 - Fiesty Fleet            30:1    192
5 - Big Time Coming          5:1    192
6 - Gold Limit               3:1    192
7 - House Odds               7:1    191

Best 4    Speed    Last Qtr    Quit
Display Best 4 Quarter Rankings
```

4. The *Performance Method* Table

   The P/M Table is the final product (one table for each race). Once all the information and data are entered, a table is printed on an 8 1/2″ × 11″ sheet. If you handicap eight races, you will be going to the track with nine sheets of paper: a P/M Table for each race, plus one copy of the Handicap Summary.

Hialeah Park April 5, 198–
5th Race 6 f

PP	Horse Name	Morn. Line	Ability Factor	Pure Speed	Early Speed	Late Speed	Max. Form	P/M RATING
1	Medeiros	20:1	483	93	288	782	1070	3372
2	Fiesty Fleet	30:1	469	101	293	789	1082	3410
3	Shortcut to Fame	5:1	490	99	295	784	1079	3415
4	Spaghetti Tree -5f	5:1	483	97	303	775	1078	3380
5	Big Time Coming	5:1	494	105	306	794	1100	3481
6	Gold Limit	3:1	484	100	303	786	1089	3424
7	House Odds	7:1	486	94	290	776	1066	3364
8	Twogun Kenny	6:1	480	96	286	786	1072	3390
9	Lo the Dutchman -5f	15:1	482	100	308	789	1097	3434

Times: 2 f ---------
4 f ---------
Finish ---------

Selections:

--- ---------------------
--- ---------------------
--- ---------------------
--- ---------------------

Results:

--- ---------------------
--- ---------------------
--- ---------------------
--- ---------------------

Paid:

5. The History Worksheet

   This is the worksheet onto which all newspaper data is entered and it is the source of date for the four individual components of the *Performance Methods*. All final calculations for the Ability Factor, the Pure Speed, the Early Speed, and the Late Speed for each horse are automatically sent to their respective screens and to the P/M Tables from this worksheet. See page 102 for a more complete description of this screen.

6. The Ability Factor Screen

   Displayed on this screen are all the statistics that are used, and those that can be used, to calculate an Ability Factor.

484...ABILITY FACTOR Gold Limit

	From the Worksheet					Adjustments			Ability Rating
	Track	Dist.	Weight	SR	TV	Track	Dist.	Wt.	
1	HIA	6 f	116	85	18	60	0	0	161
2	GP	6 f	115	81	21	61	0	0	163
3	CRC	7 f	116	85	16	61	-2	0	160
4	GP	7 f	117	80	23	61	-2	0	162
5	GP	1 1/16	117	63	20	60	13	0	156
6	CRC	7 f	115	88	19	61	-2	0	166
7	CRC	7 f	115	88	16	61	-2	0	163
8	CRC	7 f	116	88	17	61	-2	0	164

Selections: 2 1 3 Computer Selected

7. The Pure Speed Screen

On this screen are all the numbers that were examined by the computer to arrive at the best Pure Speed. The data sources for this calculation are the speed ratings that were entered onto the History Worksheet.

100...PURE SPEED Gold Limit

	From the Worksheet			Adjustments			
	Track	Dist.	SR	Track Record	Dist. Adj.	Surf. Adj.	Pure Speed
1	HIA	6 f	85	-5	0	16	94
2	GP	6 f	81	-4	0	18	95
3	CRC	7 f	85	-16	-2	30	97
4	GP	7 f	80	-4	-2	18	92
5	GP	1 1/16	63	-5	13	18	89
6	CRC	7 f	88	-16	-2	30	100
7	CRC	7 f	88	-16	-2	30	100
8	CRC	7 f	88	-16	-2	30	100

Selection: 6 Computer Selected

The Pure Speed calculation is simply the horse's fastest time (or equivalent) found within the data available. The Speed Rating of that race is related to the base time of today's distance and a surface adjustment is added.

8. The Early Speed Screen

This screen displays the data used to calculate each horse's Early Speed. The data sources for this calculation are the time splits that were typed onto the History Worksheet.

303...EARLY SPEED Gold Limit

			1/4 Mile				1/2 Mile					
	Track	Dist.	Time	Out	Speed	Adj	Time	Out	Speed	Adj	SR	SR
1	HIA	6 f	0:22.2	4	90	5	0:46.0	4	86	5	95	91
2	GP	6 f	0:22.3	1	92	6	0:46.0	1	89	6	98	95
3	CRC	7 f	0:23.0	1	90	8	0:46.3	0	87	8	98	95
4	GP	7 f	0:22.2	3	91	6	0:45.2	4	89	6	97	95
5	GP	1 1/16	0:46.2	2	86	6	0:46.2	2	86	6	97	92
6	CRC	7 f	0:22.2	0	94	8	0:45.1	2	92	8	102	100
7	CRC	7 f	0:22.3	0	93	8	0:46.2	1	87	8	101	95
8	CRC	7 f	0:23.1	2	88	8	0:46.4	2	84	8	96	92

Selections: 6 7 6 Computer Selected

For a sprint race, the Early Speed is defined as the rating of the horse's two fastest 1/4-mile splits plus its fastest 1/2-mile split. For a mile race, it is the two fastest 1/2-mile splits plus its fastest 3/4-mile split. And for a route race, it is the horse's fastest 3/4-mile splits.

9. The Late Speed Screen

Displayed on this screen are all the figures from which the best Late Speed calculation was derived.

786...LATE SPEED Gold Limit

	Track	Dist.	Time	Out	Time	Out	TV	Pole Speed	Last Qtr.	Late Speed
1	HIA	6 f	0:46.0	4	1:11.3	0	18	86	186	774
2	GP	6 f	0:46.0	1	1:11.1	2	21	89	183	775
3	CRC	7 f	0:46.3	0	1:25.4	2	16	87	186	774
4	GP	7 f	0:45.2	4	1:23.4	5	23	89	180	768
5	GP	1 1/16	1:11.2	4	1:45.0	13	20	88	179	759
6	CRC	7 f	0:45.1	2	1:24.3	5	19	92	184	783
7	CRC	7 f	0:46.2	1	1:25.1	2	16	87	189	783
8	CRC	7 f	0:46.4	2	1:24.3	5	17	84	192	786

Selection: 8 Computer Selected

Of the four components to the P/M Rating, the Late Speed is the most helpful and the most complex. It is comprised of several elements, including Pole Speed (a measure of speed to the 1/2-mile pole in sprints, or 3/4-mile in routes), a measure of speed between either of these poles and the finish line (the Last Quarter), and adjustments for the surface and the distance.

10. The "Help" Menu

The user of this program can obtain assistance in one of two ways: (1) By going to the Help Menu from the Race Card Menu; or, (2) By hitting the "Alt" and "H" keys simultaneously whenever a question arises while statistics are being entered into the program. After the question is answered, you will be returned to the exact spot that you left.

```
HELP TOPICS (Select by letter)
------------------------------
A...... The Race Card

B...... The P/M Table

C...... The History Worksheet

D...... The Ability Factor

E...... The Pure Speed

F...... The Early Speed

G...... The Late Speed

H...... General Information

I...... List of Tracks in the Program
```

It is impossible to become "lost" in this computer program. To exit from anywhere in the program, simply hit the keys marked "escape" and "Q" ("quit").

The History Worksheet

Below is the History Worksheet as it will be presented initially on your monitor. The cursor will immediately appear top-right. Here, you enter today's jockey weight. Hit the "return" key and the cursor will move left to the first open cell on the first line. If the track and the distance need to be changed, backspace, and make the change before continuing. The illustrations to follow show how the numbers are typed into their respective cells. Simply type the figures as they appear in the *Daily Racing Form* into the appropriate cells on the worksheet.

royal reviewer 1st Race Aqueduct (Main) NY December 15, 199-

{ HISTORY } Split Times Distance: 6 f

Jockey Wt..... Ø

	Track	Dist.	Split Times			Lengths Out			Wt.	SR	TV	
1	AQU	6 f	Ø:ØØ.Ø	Ø:ØØ.Ø	Ø:ØØ.Ø	Ø	Ø	Ø	Ø	Ø	Ø	Abil. Ø
2	AQU	6 f	Ø:ØØ.Ø	Ø:ØØ.Ø	Ø:ØØ.Ø	Ø	Ø	Ø	Ø	Ø	Ø	
3	AQU	6 f	Ø:ØØ.Ø	Ø:ØØ.Ø	Ø:ØØ.Ø	Ø	Ø	Ø	Ø	Ø	Ø	Pure Ø
4	AQU	6 f	Ø:ØØ.Ø	Ø:ØØ.Ø	Ø:ØØ.Ø	Ø	Ø	Ø	Ø	Ø	Ø	
5	AQU	6 f	Ø:ØØ.Ø	Ø:ØØ.Ø	Ø:ØØ.Ø	Ø	Ø	Ø	Ø	Ø	Ø	Early Ø
6	AQU	6 f	Ø:ØØ.Ø	Ø:ØØ.Ø	Ø:ØØ.Ø	Ø	Ø	Ø	Ø	Ø	Ø	
7	AQU	6 f	Ø:ØØ.Ø	Ø:ØØ.Ø	Ø:ØØ.Ø	Ø	Ø	Ø	Ø	Ø	Ø	Late Ø
8	AQU	6 f	Ø:ØØ.Ø	Ø:ØØ.Ø	Ø:ØØ.Ø	Ø	Ø	Ø	Ø	Ø	Ø	

The "split-times" cells are used for the leader's call-point times, as shown in the newspaper. In the "lengths-out" cells, type in the horse's "lengths behind the leader" for those same call-points. Round up or down if necessary (thus, 4¼ lengths out becomes 4 lengths out, and 4½ lengths out becomes 5). Disregard the horse's position at the top of the stretch.

Whatever data is entered on the first three lines of the History Worksheet will be calculated as the Ability Factor unless you change it. As indicated on pages 88-91, the Ability Factor is really a measure of current form. As far as the P/M Rating is concerned, the Ability Factor is a relatively minor contributor, but it should NEVER be ignored!

Once all the desired races have been entered into the History Worksheet, it is possible to change the selection of Ability Factor races by simply instructing the computer to use another combination. Go to the Ability Factor screen, hit "u" and make the change. To exit, simply hit "m" to call up the menu and exit.

In the situation shown below, you will, as a handicapper, have to decide whether **Royal Reviewer's** 7 furlong race on September 21 better represents his ability to run today vs. the shorter, higher-class race of October 14.

```
Royal Reviewer        B. c. 3(May), by Wavering Monarch—In Review, by Reviewer                Lifetime
                      $75,000 Br.—Glencrest Farm (Ky)                                   112     8 2 2 2
Own.—Big Tarpon Stable        Tr.—Barbara Robert                                                $37,880
 1Nov90- 5Aqu fst 6f   :22⅕ :45⅘ 1:10   3↑Alw 30000   5 2 36½ 33½ 34½ 33   Smith M E       115  2.00  87-15 Nymphist1152¾ Valid Vign.
20Oct90- 6Bel fst 7f   :22⅘ :46  1:22⅘ 3↑Alw 30000   1 4 51¾ 42  23  25   Antley C W      114 *1.30  86-12 SirMichelJmes1145Ro
14Oct90- 9Bel fst 6f   :22  :44⅘ 1:08⅘   Clm 70000   8 8 65  65  56½ 47¼  Smith M E       113  9.30  89-09 LuckyTent1174½Rousingr
21Sep90- 2Bel fst 7f   :22⅗ :45⅖ 1:22⅖   Clm 35000   1 6 44½ 52  1hd 11¾  Smith M E       117  8.60  92-14 RoylReviewer1171¾Mc
15Jly90- 6Bel fst 1 1/16 :45⅕ 1:10⅖ 1:43⅖ Clm c-50000 4 4 49½ 59½ 516 522½ Thibeau R J Jr 117  9.30  62-16 Pocket Streaker1062¼ To
 2Jly90- 6Bel gd 6f    :22⅘ :46  1:09⅘   Clm 35000   3 2 21½ 32  33½ 26¾  Santos J A      117  6.00  84-14 FinlDestintion1196¾Ro
18Jun90- 9Bel fst 6f   :22⅖ :46⅗ 1:11⅖   Clm 35000  10 9 64¾ 52½ 22  37½  Santos J A      119 20.70  74-16 ColonelPickrd1195Boundi
30May90- 9Bel gd 7f    :23⅕ :47  1:26⅖ 3↑Md 35000    3 1 2½  1½  1½  11¼  Santos J A      115 *3.10  72-19 RoyalReviewer1151½P
```

royal reviewer   1st Race Aqueduct (Main) NY   December 15, 199-

Distance: 6 f

{ HISTORY }   Jockey Wt..... 112

	Track	Dist.	Split Times			Lengths Out			Wt.	SR	TV	
												1 2 3
1	AQU	6 f	0:22.1	0:45.2	1:10.0	7	4	3	115	87	15	Abil. 476
2	BEL	7 f	0:22.4	0:46.0	1:22.3	2	2	5	114	86	12	3
3	BEL	6 f	0:22.0	0:44.3	1:08.3	5	5	7	113	89	9	Pure 100

After the first three lines are entered, complete the additional lines on the worksheet by typing in any other data that appears relevant. Normally, a horse's capability can be read by the computer by entering only four or five lines on the History Worksheet. Sometimes a horse will have one or two extremely poor races (i.e., it was many, many lengths behind the leaders from the moment the gate opened and was never in contention). Whenever it's quite obvious that the numbers from an exceptionally poor showing could never change the final P/M Table calculation, do not waste time entering such a race. Blank lines on the worksheet will not alter the final P/M Rating. However, be sure that the race was poor from beginning to end; and do not be misled by low numbers simply because the race had been run at a different track or at a different distance than today's race. With a little experience, the useless races will be easy to spot and the number of keystrokes needed to complete each worksheet can be reduced.

royal reviewer   1st Race Aqueduct (Main) NY   December 15, 199-

{ HISTORY }   Split Times   Distance: 6 f
Jockey Wt..... 112

	Track	Dist.	Split Times			Lengths Out			Wt.	SR	TV
1	AQU	6 f	0:22.1	0:45.2	1:10.0	7	4	3	115	87	15
2	BEL	7 f	0:22.4	0:46.0	1:22.3	2	2	5	114	86	12
3	BEL	6 f	0:22.0	0:44.3	1:08.3	5	5	7	113	89	9
4	BEL	7 f	0:22.3	0:45.2	1:22.2	5	2	0	117	92	14
5	BEL	6 f	0:22.4	0:46.0	1:09.3	2	2	7	117	84	14
6	BEL	7 f	0:23.1	0:47.0	1:26.2	1	0	0	115	72	19
7	AQU	6 f	0:00.0	0:00.0	0:00.0	0	0	0	0	0	0
8	AQU	6 f	0:00.0	0:00.0	0:00.0	0	0	0	0	0	0

1 2 3
Abil.
476

3
Pure
100

3 2 3
Early
288

4
Late
793

The final calculations for the Ability Factor, the Pure Speed, the Early Speed and the Late Speed are all sent automatically to the *Performance Method* Table.

Aqueduct (Main) NY December 15, 199-
1st Race 6 f

PP	HORSE	Notes	Morn. Line	Ability Factor	Pure Speed	Early Speed	Late Speed	Max. Form	P/M RATING
1	royal reviewer		0:0	476	100	288	793	1081	3146

How to Use the P/M Table

Once the worksheets for all the horses in the race have been completed and you are satisfied that the history of each horse is well represented by the figures you've entered, return to the P/M Table. All the numbers have been automatically transferred from the worksheet. Now the table is ready to be printed. The P/M Table (80 characters wide) will be reproduced on an 8½″ × 11″ sheet of paper.

As each race is completed, its table can be printed. Once all the races that you intend to play have been entered, the computer's selections for the entire day can be printed on a single sheet (the "Best 4" Handicap Summary). The Pole Speed Rankings and the Last Quarter Rankings can also be produced on two more sheets by hitting "Other Print." Armed with this valuable data, you can begin handicapping the races with confidence.

On the table, circle the best two or three totals in each category, as well as the best three or four P/M Ratings found in the last column. The exact number to be circled will depend on the size of the field in each race. Try to keep the table clean and easy to read. Use arrows to point out other statistics worth noting. Very quickly it will become obvious which horses in the race are the contenders and which are not.

Handicapping Suggestion

To rank the contenders, first select one of the three highest P/M-rated horses to be your "key horse." It will be among the best Ability, Pure Speed, and Late Speed horses on the P/M Table—and usually on the "Last Quarter" sheet, often near the top. Next, identify the "exacta horse." Frequently, this horse will be found when you ask the question "which horse(s) will set the pace and which horse is good enough to catch them?" If this closer isn't your "key horse," re-examine the race. Be alert to the possibility of only ONE early speed horse in the race. A wire-to-wire victory could mean that your "key horse" will run second.

Learning from Experience

This race is the first half of a daily double at Aqueduct. It is a $6\frac{1}{2}$ furlong race. All seven horses in the race have useful statistics with which to work.

AQUEDUCT

6½ FURLONGS. (1.15) CLAIMING. Purse $9,000. Fillies and Mares. 4-year-olds and upward. Weights, 122 lbs. Non-winners of two races since March 1, allowed 3 lbs. Of a race since then, 5 lbs. Claiming Price $8,500; for each $250 to $8,000, 2 lbs. (Races when entered to be claimed for $7,500 or less not considered).

Jo Hill

Own.—Russo B — $8,000 — Dk. b. or br. f. 4, by Nehoc's Bullet—Infer, by Determined Man — Br.—Karlinsky & Levin (NY) — Tr.—Russo Benjamin — **113** — Lifetime 12 1 0 1 $3,024 — 1983 4 0 0 0 — 1982 8 1 0 1 $3,024

18Mar83- 9Aqu sly 7f :23⅕ :47 1:26⅕ ⒻClm 8000 1 11 77 915 1121 1017 Smith D L 115 73.50 53-27 Lady Hussymor 115nk DancingSwan108⁵Deckernight113²½ Outrun 12
21Feb83- 1Aqu fst 6f ⊡:23⅗ :47⅖ 1:13⅗ ⒻClm 8500 4 11 86½ 1111 1218 1320 Pernice J W10 108 17.40f 56-22 Prize Moment 112⁴½ Rustique 117¹½ Lady Judith 112²½ Outrun 13
9Feb83- 2Aqu fst 6f ⊡:23⅕ :47⅖ 1:13⅘ ⒻClm 10000 1 11 1113 1117 1124 1122 Pernice J W10 108 55.80 53-20 Elevenses 110½ Fast Knock 113¾ Dancing Swan 113nk Far back 11
29Jan83- 5Aqu fst 1⅟₁₆ ⊡:48⅘ 1:14⅘ 1:48⅗ ⒻⓈAlw 27000 8 11 1220 — — — Pernice J W10 b 108 89.20 — — CatO'Luck119nkReserveDecision117⁵¾LittleMissG.117¹½ Distanced 12
7Sep82- 8FL fst 5½f :23 :47⅘ 1:08 ⒻⓈClm 7500 2 7 723 725 723 724 Whitley K b 118 8.20 58-25 Gold Toga 115³ Bambina 116²½ Jim Alice 112¹½ Outrun 7
1Sep82- 5FL fst 6f :23⅗ :48⅕ 1:15⅕ 3↑ⒻⓈMd 7500 8 9 83¾ 41½ 2hd 1½ Whitley K b 118 6.90e 73-24 Jo Hill 118½ Harvard Miss 111³ Early Arrival 122² Driving 10
29Aug82- 3FL fst 170 :48⅘ 1:14⅘ 1:47 3↑ⓈMd 7500 7 7 67 78½ 812 815 Whitley K b 110 15.00 51-18 The Seneca Bus 122⁸ Turn My Fancy115¾Sofargoz122³ No factor 10
21Aug82- 2FL fst 5½f :23⅖ :49⅕ 1:09⅘ 3↑ⒻⓈMd 7500 3 12 98½ 107½ 97½ 64 Donahue G W b 117 9.40 69-23 Clareric 122¹ Harvard Miss 110½ Hillbilly Jewel 117hd No factor 12
11Aug82- 1FL fst 6f :23⅖ :47⅗ 1:15⅕ 3↑ⒻⓈMd 7500 1 8 32½ 33½ 33½ 33 Donahue G W b 117 11.40e 70-21 Jutesa 117¹ Harvard Miss 110² Jo Hill 117no Evenly 9
4Aug82- 9FL fst 170 :48⅖ 1:14 1:46⅗ 3↑ⓈMd 7500 11 3 32 44½ 56 813 Whitley K b 110 19.60 55-21 Stagger In Joe 115no Baltic 115² Turn My Fancy 115²½ Tired 11

LATEST WORKOUTS Mar 24 Bel tr.t 4f fst :49 b

Jolly April

Own.—Tambascoi D D — $8,000 — B. f. 4, by Jollify—April Cathy, by Banderilla — Br.—Karutz W S (NY) — Tr.—Smith David — **106**[7] — Lifetime 14 1 2 2 $10,072 — 1982 14 1 2 2 $10,072 — 1981 0 M 0 0

15Nov82- 6Aqu fst 1⅛ :49⅕ 1:14⅘ 1:54⅕ 3↑ⒻⓈAlw 26000 5 8 86¾ 75¾ 815 821 MacBeth D 115 21.20 43-24 N. Y. Pin Up 110³ Cold Tepee 110³¾ Valid Gal 115² Outrun 8
7Nov82- 3FL fst 5½f :22⅘ :48 1:09 3↑ⓈClm 7500 4 9 104½ 76¾ 52½ 21½ Giraldo A J 117 6.10 75-28 Teepee Creeper 122¹½ Jolly April 117¹ Cloudy Gold 117² Gamely 12
2Nov82- 6FL gd 5½f :22⅗ :46⅘ 1:07⅕ 3↑ⒻClm 7500 5 7 33 33½ 33½ 2nk McChesney A EJr 120 13.70 86-15 Jilly's Bullet 116nk Jolly April 120¹½ Satin 'n Steel 114½ Rallied 8
17Oct82- 9FL gd 6f :23 :47⅘ 1:15⅘ 3↑ⓈMd Sp Wt 8 5 65½ 53½ 4¾ 1¾ McChesney A EJr 116 11.90 70-27 Jolly April 116¾ Wittleson 119hd K. O. Punch 119²½ Driving 8
1Oct82- 1FL fst 6f :22⅘ :47⅕ 1:14⅗ 3↑ⒻⓈMd Sp Wt 2 5 42½ 52¾ 95 76½ Giraldo A J 119 4.40e 69-17 Hot Card 119nk Super Jezzy 119¹½ Ever Higher 112¹½ Tired 9
24Sep82- 1FL fst 5½f :22⅘ :47⅕ 1:07⅕ 3↑ⒻⓈMd 15000 2 5 4¾ 44½ 46½ 39 Giraldo A J 118 3.10 77-16 Daddy's Doreen 118⁴ Harvard Miss 118⁵ Jolly April 118¹ Evenly 7
11Sep82- 2FL fst 6f :23⅕ :47⅖ 1:14⅖ 3↑ⒻⓈMd Sp Wt 10 2 33 22 23 34½ Giraldo A J 119 13.30 72-19 Tanglewood Hills 118³ Super Jezzy118¹½JollyApril119² Weakened 11
5Sep82- 2FL fst 5½f :22⅘ :47⅗ 1:07 3↑ⒻⓈMd 15000 4 7 32 45 42½ 411 Giraldo A J 118 8.20 76-17 Caribbinn 115¹ Cloudy Gold 118⁷ Teepee Creeper 115³ Weakened 9
1Aug82- 2Bel fst 6f :23 :46⅘ 1:13 3↑ⒻMd 14000 1 1 1hd 43 88½ 89½ Caraballo R b 117 34.40 67-25 Dethroned 114²½ Miscast 112½ Little Countess 106¹½ Tired 9
19Jly82- 4Bel fst 6f :23⅕ :47⅖ 1:12⅗ 3↑ⒻⓈMd Sp Wt 9 6 76½ 910 617 521 Montoya D 116 34.50 58-19 Prize Moment 116⁸½ Grand Old Flag116½SomeCase116¹⁰ Swerved 14

LATEST WORKOUTS Mar 29 Bel tr.t 5f gd 1:01⅗ b — Mar 21 Bel tr.t 4f fst :51⅘ b — Mar 14 Bel tr.t 3f fst :36⅗ h

Barbecue Sunday

Own.—Jay Cee Jay Stable — $8,250 — Dk. b. or br. f. 4, by Embassy Row—Tex's Sweetheart, by Priam's Joker — Br.—Hoffman H (Va) — Tr.—DeStefano John M Jr — **110**[5] — Lifetime 27 2 6 2 $23,143 — 1983 2 0 0 0 — 1982 18 1 3 2 $14,003 — Turf 2 0 0 1 $1,010

25Mar83- 1Aqu fst 1⅛ :50 1:17⅘ 1:57⅖ ⒻClm 9500 6 7 919 939 — — Melendez J D5 b 110 22.50 — — FoolishEmpress108¹½Deckrnight113²¾DoublDcqur112⁶½ Distanced 9
12Mar83- 2Aqu sly 6f ⊡:23⅗ :47⅖ 1:13⅗ ⒻClm 9000 5 8 88¾ 815 823 824 Gonzalez M A b 113 11.60 52-15 Lady Dike 112no Little Countess 112¹ Marshi 106²½ Outrun 8
6Oct82-10Medfst 6f :22⅗ :46⅗ 1:13⅗ ⒻClm 8000 3 11 810 79 47 43½ Lopez C C b 115 3.80 71-19 Say G'Nite Gracie 115½ Oops A Daisy 115hdJ.Sutton113³ Late bid 11
29Sep82- 5Medfst 6f :22⅘ :46⅗ 1:12⅕ ⒻClm 10000 9 9 57½ 56½ 56 55 Lopez C C b 115 8.70 77-17 Mary'sRulerae108hdLookingGap115hdATimetoDnce113⁴ No threat 9
3Sep82- 4Mth gd 1 :48⅗ 1:13⅗ 1:40⅘ ⒻClm 13000 4 10 1021 1023 1025 1023 Wacker D J b 115 6.10 46-24 Front TheColors112³RanaRose110nkWayofLove113¹½ Unruly start 10
26Aug82- 6Mth gd *1 Ⓣ:47⅘ 1:13⅖ 1:42 ⒻClm 12500 5 8 818 813 55 32½ Wacker D J b 115 2.90 77-18 HomemdeHppiness108¾SpiritAwy118¹½BrbcuSundy115¹ Bore out 8
23Jly82- 3Mth fst 6f :22⅘ :45⅗ 1:12⅕ ⒻClm 16000 4 6 610 613 59½ 511 Fann B b 115 6.60 68-22 Proudest Charlie 115⁴ BustAFew109⁴DancingAnn114² No menace 6
16Jly82- 7Mth fst 6f :22⅘ :45⅘ 1:12⅖ ⒻClm 20000 1 6 55½ 712 611 79 Wacker D J b 115 5.10 69-19 Reasonable Nun 110¹½LadyTia115²½Ifdadcouldsee112²½ No threat 7
8Jly82- 8Atl fm 1 Ⓣ:46⅖ 1:11 1:36⅖ ⒻClm 20000 7 9 810 811 68 55¾ Wacker D J b 116 7.20 83-06 Lovin' Letter116²DukesRobbin112¹RunChipperRun112² No factor 10
22Jun82- 2Bel fst 6f :23⅖ :46⅘ 1:12⅗ ⒻClm 14000 2 5 21½ 32 31½ 32¾ Wacker D J b 116 3.90 76-20 Quaker Ridge 118²¾ Billowy 114no Barbecue Sunday 116¾ Evenly 9

LATEST WORKOUTS Apr 2 Bel tr.t 3f fst :37⅘ b — Mar 8 Bel tr.t 4f my :51 b — Mar 3 Bel tr.t 5f fst 1:03 bg — Feb 26 Bel tr.t 5f fst 1:02⅗ hg

Jen's Doll

Own.—Sweet Meadow Farm — $8,500 — Ch. f. 4, by In A Trance—Cedric's Sister, by Edliss — Br.—Siebel T A (Md) — Tr.—Gullo Thomas J — **117** — Lifetime 22 4 4 1 $29,216 — 1983 8 1 0 0 $5,700 — 1982 14 3 4 1 $23,516

18Mar83- 9Aqu sly 7f :23⅕ :47 1:26⅕ ⒻClm 8000 4 5 97¾ 714 615 68¾ Thibeau R J 115 8.40 61-27 Lady Hussymor 115nkDancingSwan108⁵Deckernight113²½ No rally 12
10Mar83- 9Aqu sly 1⅟₁₆ ⊡:47⅘ 1:13⅗ 1:48⅖ ⒻClm 9500 1 8 715 614 614 718 Smith A Jr 115 *2.50 53-17 Ever Higher 117¾ Diamond Shamrock 113³ Quisqueya113¾ Outrun 10
28Feb83- 1Aqu fst 1⅟₁₆ ⊡:49⅘ 1:16 1:49⅗ ⒻClm 8000 4 6 44½ 2½ 1½ 13¾ Smith A Jr 113 3.60 65-25 Jen's Doll 113³¾ Ultimate Step 117⁸½ Lady Clown 118² Driving 8
21Feb83- 1Aqu fst 6f ⊡:23⅗ :47⅖ 1:13⅗ ⒻClm 8500 1 6 98½ 911 913 813 Antongeorgi W A7110 3.50 63-22 Prize Moment 112⁴½ Rustique 117¹½ Lady Judith 112²½ Outrun 13
9Feb83- 2Aqu fst 6f ⊡:23⅕ :47⅖ 1:13⅘ ⒻClm 10000 10 1 31½ 34½ 53 53½ Cordero A Jr 117 3.50 71-20 Elevenses 110½ Fast Knock 113¾ Dancing Swan 113nk Tired 11
3Feb83- 9Aqu gd 6f ⊡:23⅕ :47⅕ 1:13⅖ ⓈClm 12500 10 1 71¾ 86½ 78¾ 86 Antongeorgi W A7110 *5.10 71-18 Winged Shot 110no Canino Vera 117½ La Foresita 113¾ Outrun 12
22Jan83- 1Aqu fst 1⅛ ⊡:47 1:12⅗ 1:50⅗ ⒻClm 18000 10 4 46 76¾ 1013 919 Antongeorgi W A7106 25.00 74-07 Patti's Ace 108⁶¾ Klara Balint 110⁴½ Shofoose 117²½ Early foot 11
7Jan83- 5Aqu gd 1⅛ ⊡:48⅗ 1:13⅘ 1:54⅗ ⒻClm 14000 6 3 42½ 41½ 54 66 Davis R G5 108 5.20 67-16 Bright Sky 117nk Baby Bonnie 113² Beaverboard 112hd Tired 10
29Dec82- 1Aqu fst 6f ⊡:23⅗ :47 1:12⅗ 3↑ⒻClm c-10500 6 6 54 34 33 1nk Alvarado R Jr5 106 *1.70 77-24 Jen's Doll 106nk Reasonable Nun113²½Coosahatchee110hd Driving 7
6Dec82- 2Aqu my 6f ⊡:22⅘ :46 1:12⅗ 3↑ⒻClm 9000 7 8 45½ 47 33½ 2¾ Alvarado R Jr5 106 4.80e 80-15 Icy Pleasure 104¾ Jen's Doll 106¾ Baby Bonnie 117hd Rallied 12

LATEST WORKOUTS Mar 30 Bel tr.t 4f fst :49⅘ b — Mar 24 Bel tr.t 3f fst :35⅘ h

Caribbinn

Own.—Wildman Jody — $8,000 — Dk. b. or br. f. 4, by Cutlass—Heathers Delite, by Flag Raiser — Br.—Binn M (NY) — Tr.—Lake Robert P — **103**[10] — Lifetime 21 1 2 3 $13,230 — 1983 6 0 0 1 $2,250 — 1982 15 1 2 2 $10,980

12Mar83- 2Aqu sly 6f ⊡:23⅗ :47⅖ 1:13⅗ ⒻClm 9000 8 7 52¾ 68 715 718 Thibeau R J7 b 106 9.20 58-15 Lady Dike 112no Little Countess 112¹ Marshi 106²½ Tired 8
6Mar83- 1Aqu fst 6f ⊡:23⅕ :47 1:12⅘ ⒻClm 8000 6 6 41½ 32½ 34 44½ Thibeau R J7 b 106 7.60 76-19 Lady Judith 112⁴ LadyHussymor108nkMarshi108hd Lacked a rally 10
28Feb83- 1Aqu fst 1⅟₁₆ ⊡:49⅘ 1:16 1:49⅗ ⒻClm 8250 6 1 2hd 31½ 38½ 618 Powers T M5 b 110 5.00 47-25 Jen's Doll 113³¾ Ultimate Step 117⁸½ Lady Clown 118² Tired 8
18Feb83- 9Aqu fst 6f ⊡:23⅗ :48⅕ 1:14⅕ ⒻClm 9000 12 6 31½ 43½ 24 45¾ Powers T M5 b 108 19.30 67-27 Fast Knock 117² Amy's Puff112¾LaForesita117³ Well up, no rally 12
4Feb83- 9Aqu fst 6f ⊡:22⅘ :46⅗ 1:13⅖ ⒻClm 8250 8 3 35 34½ 34 33 Powers T M5 b 110 17.60 74-20 Elevenses 110nk Lady Judith 112²¾ Caribbinn 110³ Lacked rally 10
16Jan83- 1Aqu sly 6f ⊡:23⅗ :47⅘ 1:13⅘ ⒻClm 12500 4 5 45½ 58 615 819 Melendez J D5 b 112 25.10 56-20 Committ 110¹² Lum Behave 117¹½ Onyx Fox 117nk Tired 10
27Dec82- 9Aqu fst 6f ⊡:23⅗ :47⅗ 1:14 3↑ⒻClm 10000 5 7 55 54 64½ 65½ Molina V H b 115 10.70 69-22 La Foresita 112hd Baby Bonnie 117³½ Lady Hussymor 108¾ Wide 10
15Dec82- 9Aqu fst 6f ⊡:23⅗ :47⅗ 1:14 3↑ⒻClm 9000 3 5 54½ 87¾ 73¾ 33½ Molina V H b 111 47.10 71-25 Committ 110¹½ First Enterprise 117² Caribbinn 111² Rallied 11
6Dec82- 2Aqu my 6f ⊡:22⅘ :46 1:12⅗ 3↑ⒻClm 9000 6 4 23½ 35½ 79½ 88¾ Molina V H b 111 31.70 73-15 Icy Pleasure 104¾ Jen's Doll 106¾ Baby Bonnie 117hd Tired 12
21Nov82- 4Aqu fst 7f :23 :47 1:25⅗ 3↑ⒻClm 14000 1 5 12 3nk 820 828 Migliore R b 111 23.40 47-24 Lin Di Lar 117¹½ Party Lady 115⁴ Patti's Ace 108⁴ Gave way 8

LATEST WORKOUTS Mar 31 Aqu 4f fst :49 h — Mar 21 Aqu 4f fst :50⅖ b

Fast Knock

Own.—Jopi Stable — $8,500 — Gr. m. 6, by Leematt—Lassie's Kingdom, by Three Kingdoms — Br.—Chapel View Farm (Pa) — Tr.—Picariello Joseph — **112**[5] — Lifetime 56 13 9 9 $58,760 — 1983 5 2 1 0 $13,110 — 1982 5 1 0 1 $4,395 — Turf 2 0 0 0

29Mar83- 9Aqu fst 6f :23⅘ :48⅖ 1:13⅖ ⒻClm 10000 4 4 2hd 21 812 813 Gonzalez M A b 119 5.10 61-28 Rouge Galop 112¹½ Marshi 106¹½ Lady Judith 114¹½ Tired 9
11Mar83- 3Aqu sly 6f ⊡:23⅕ :46⅘ 1:12 ⒻClm 15000 11 3 3½ 33 47 1012 Murphy D J5 b 110 4.40 72-11 Icy Pleasure 108² Campilan 110¹½ Lady Christina 108½ Stopped 11
18Feb83- 9Aqu fst 6f ⊡:23⅗ :48⅕ 1:14⅕ ⒻClm 10000 11 1 1½ 13 14 12 Gonzalez M A b 117 7.20 73-27 Fast Knock 117² Amy's Puff 112¾ La Foresita 117³ Driving 12
9Feb83- 2Aqu fst 6f ⊡:23⅕ :47⅖ 1:13⅘ ⒻClm 9000 11 3 1½ 12½ 11½ 2½ Santagata N b 113 11.40 74-20 Elevenses 110½ Fast Knock 113¾ Dancing Swan 113nk Weakened 11
2Jan83- 4Key fst 6f :22⅘ :47⅕ 1:14⅗ ⒻⓈClm 5500 5 4 32½ 32 1½ 11¾ Raney L A10 b 109 7.00 68-29 Fast Knock 109¹¾ Rostraver Ruby 109³ GambitLady110hd Driving 11
20Dec82-10Medfst 6f :22⅘ :46 1:13⅗ 3↑ⒻClm 5000 2 3 14 16 15 1nk McKnight R E b 116 5.30 76-18 Fast Knock 116nk Money Ahead 116² Tuffoldgirl 111¹ Driving 9
29Nov82- 2Med gd 6f :22⅗ :46⅗ 1:13⅗ 3↑ⒻClm 7000 1 2 21 66½ 714 815 McKnight R E b 114 20.50 60-25 Friendly Manner 116¹½ChosenCoin109½BrazenBrass119nk Stopped 8
19Nov82- 8Medfst 6f :22⅗ :46⅖ 1:13 3↑ⒻClm 9000 1 6 22 57 712 717 McKnight R E b 114 6.60 61-19 Hasty Sarah 109no Desert Sail 114⁵½ Lady Hussymor 112¹½ Tired 7
6May82- 6Mth fst 6f :22⅘ :46⅖ 1:13⅕ ⒻClm 16000 6 3 21 22½ 26 36½ Santagata N b 116 3.60 68-27 Castles Gift 119⁵½ Choice of Power 116¾ Fast Knock116nk Evenly 6
26Apr82- 6Key sly 6f :22⅘ :46 1:12⅖ ⒻClm 22500 5 5 52 45½ 49½ 510 Gomez M A b 116 6.10 70-27 Morning Jan 116nk Celtic Queen 116½ Clandesun 116⁸½ Wide 6

LATEST WORKOUTS Mar 9 Bel tr.t 3f sly :35⅘ h

This Time Around — Dk. b. or br. f. 4, by Subpet—Intel's Girl, by Impel
Own.—Lane G E — $8,250 — Br.—Dodson B C (Fla) — Tr.—Sedlacek Michael C — 1105

Lifetime: 9 1 5 0 — $10,940
1983: 5 1 3 0 — $6,930
1982: 4 M 2 0 — $4,010

Date/Race	Cond	Dist	Fractions	Class	PP	St	1st	2nd	Str	Fin	Jockey	Wt	Odds	Fig	Company line	Comment	Field
29Mar83- 9Aqu	fst	6f	:23⅘ :48⅖ 1:13⅖	ⒻClm 10000	8	7	64¾	85	65½	65	Alvarado R Jr5	114	*2.90	69-28	Rouge Galop 1121½ Marshi 1061¼ Lady Judith 1141¼	No threat	9
17Feb83- 9Bow	fst	6f	:23⅖ :47⅗ 1:14⅕	Md c-11500	10	2	53¼	43½	2hd	1nk	Miller D A Jr	115	*2.10	69-29	ThisTimeAround115nkIndinCnoe1202½YoungAristocrt1154	Driving	10
1Feb83- 1Bow	fst	6f	:23 :47⅕ 1:13	ⒻMd 11500	1	2	86½	45	31½	2nk	Bracciale V Jr	120	*.90	75-29	Friendly Hill 120nk This Time Around 120½JessicaLynn1136	Sharp	10
19Jan83- 1Bow	fst	7f	:23⅕ :46⅕ 1:26⅕	ⒻMd 11500	1	6	52¾	42½	22	2nk	Bracciale V Jr	120	*1.30	74-29	NorthTexsDncer120nkThisTimeAround1206KrensLiz120no	Gaining	10
6Jan83- 1Bow	fst	6f	:23 :47⅘ 1:13⅘	ⒻMd 11500	2	6	54	42	24	210	Edwards J W	120	*1.30	61-31	Lady'sBaby11310ThisTimeAround1202¾JessicaLynn113no	Checked	12
23Dec82- 3Lrl	fst	6f	:23⅖ :48⅖ 1:14⅕	3↑ⒻMd 13000	1	9	83	54¼	23½	24½	Edwards J W	120	*3.30	67-23	MrshDncr1204½ThsTmArond1206MssTsh'sTdr1151	Best of others	11
1Jun82- 6Del	fst	6f	:22⅗ :46⅖ 1:11⅗	ⒻClm 30000	1	4	32	66½	610	615	Calderon F	114	21.00	68-17	ⒹGosh All Hemlock114½SongMyDear1052PocketPasser1141	Tired	6
12May82- 4Spt	fst	6½f	:23⅗ :47⅗ 1:19⅕	ⒻMd Sp Wt	7	6	31½	31	23	24	Patterson A	113	4.40	77-17	Clyda's Joy 1124 This Time Around 1133¼ Our Rainy Day 113¾		10
23Apr82- 2Spt	fst	6f	:23⅖ :48 1:15⅕	ⒻMd Sp Wt	1	6	33½	31	2hd	43¼	Patterson A	119	53.10	71-20	ⒹPopular Pet 1191¼ Catch Jenny119noCecilyCardew1192	In close	10

LATEST WORKOUTS Apr 2 Pim 3f fst :39⅖ b

Normally, this would be an easy race to call. However, one of our two top horses, **Jolly April,** has not run since November.

Under the circumstances, **This Time Around** is clearly the first choice, with the other challengers being **Jolly April, Jen's Doll,** and **Fast Knock. Caribbinn** has an outside chance to be in the money, but the numbers are not high enough to replace any of the other three.

It is not difficult to imagine how this race is going to be run. **Fast Knock** will probably set the early pace. If **Jolly April** tries to match her, the horse will be passed in the stretch by **This Time Around** and **Jen's Doll.** Otherwise, **Jolly April** should have enough to make it close, or perhaps win. However, will she be in shape? Judging by her workout schedule, including a good 5 furlong showing, there is evidence that the trainer is serious about bringing the horse back soon.

The four selections for this race are:

1. **This Time Around**
2. **Jolly April**
3. **Jen's Doll**
4. **Fast Knock**

Without an exacta or quinella, this race can only offer the daily double in which all four horses should be played. Given the possibility of **Jen's Doll** or **Fast Knock** pulling an upset, they are each worth an extra daily double bet with the first choice in the second race.

Aqueduct (Main) NY April 5, 198-
1st Race 6 1/2 f

PP	Horse Name	Morn. Line	Ability Factor	Pure Speed	Early Speed	Late Speed	Max. Form	P/M RATING
1	Jo Hill	20:1	434	85	272	669	941	2952
2	Jolly April 11/15	6:1	478	100	288	672	960	3086
3	Barbecue Sunday	15:1	433	89	272	660	932	2941
4	Jen's Doll	3:1	469	91	277	672	949	3030
5	Caribbinn	10:1	467	86	280	661	941	2979
6	Fast Knock	4:1	464	84	294	662	956	2982
7	This Time Around	2:1	477	97	288	689	977	3120

FIRST RACE
Aqueduct
APRIL 5

6 ½ FURLONGS. (1.15) CLAIMING. Purse $9,000. Fillies and Mares. 4-year-olds and upward. Weights, 122 lbs. Non-winners of two races since March 1, allowed 3 lbs. Of a race since then, 5 lbs. Claiming Price $8,500; for each $250 to $8,000, 2 lbs. (Races when entered to be claimed for $7,500 or less not considered). (18th Day. WEATHER CLEAR. TEMPERATURE 63 DEGREES).

Value of race $9,000, value to winner $5,400, second $1,980, third $1,080, fourth $540. Mutuel pool $74,845, OTB pool $137,230.

Last Raced	Horse	Eqt.A.Wt	PP	St	¼	½	Str	Fin	Jockey	Cl'g Pr	Odds $1
15Nov82 ^{6}Aqu^{8}	Jolly April	4 106	2	5	3^{1}	5^{8}	1^{hd}	$1^{3\frac{3}{4}}$	Thibeau R J^{7}	8000	6.90
29Mar83 ^{9}Aqu^{6}	This Time Around	4 110	7	2	5^{3}	$4^{1\frac{1}{2}}$	2^{1}	$2^{1\frac{1}{4}}$	Alvarado R Jr^{5}	8250	1.40
18Mar83 ^{9}Aqu^{6}	Jen's Doll	4 117	4	4	4^{1}	3^{2}	$4^{\frac{1}{2}}$	3^{4}	Smith A Jr	8500	3.20
12Mar83 ^{2}Aqu^{7}	Caribbinn	b 4 103	5	3	2^{3}	1^{hd}	5^{10}	$4^{1\frac{1}{4}}$	Klinke W S^{10}	8000	9.70
29Mar83 ^{9}Aqu^{8}	Fast Knock	b 6 112	6	1	1^{2}	$2^{1\frac{1}{2}}$	3^{hd}	$5^{6\frac{1}{2}}$	Clayton M D^{5}	8500	3.60
18Mar83 ^{9}Aqu^{10}	Jo Hill	4 113	1	6	6^{hd}	6^{4}	6^{10}	6^{13}	Rogers A	8000	27.10
25Mar83 ^{1}Aqu	Barbecue Sunday	b 4 110	3	7	7	7	7	7	Melendez J D^{5}	8250	15.30

OFF AT 1:00. Start good, Won ridden out. Time, :23⅕, :47⅖, 1:13, 1:19⅖ Track fast.

Official Program Numbers↘

$2 Mutuel Prices:			
2-(B)-JOLLY APRIL	**15.80**	**4.80**	**3.20**
7-(G)-THIS TIME AROUND		**3.00**	**2.40**
4-(D)-JEN'S DOLL			**3.00**

B. f, by Jollify—April Cathy, by Banderilla. Trainer Smith David. Bred by Karutz W S (NY).

JOLLY APRIL, reserved early while saving ground, swung out for the drive, caught the leaders with a rush and drew off. THIS TIME around loomed boldly along the inside after entering the stretch but was no match for the winner. JEN'S DOLL made a run between horses entering the stretch but weakened. CARIBINN caught FAST KNOCK approaching the stretch but gave way during the drive. FAST KNOCK showed speed to the stretch and tired. BARBECUE SUNDAY broke slowly.

Owners— 1, Tambascoi D D; 2, Lane G E; 3, Sweet Meadow Farm; 4, Wildman Jody; 5, Jopi Stable; 6, Russo B; 7, Jay Cee Jay Stable.

Trainers— 1, Smith David; 2, Sedlacek Michael C; 3, Gullo Thomas J; 4, Lake Robert P; 5, Picariello Joseph; 6, Russo Benjamin; 7, DeStefano John M Jr.

The result was a pleasant surprise. It's too bad Aqueduct didn't offer exacta or quinella wagering. Given the strong possibility of a decent daily double payoff, we now have a little room to "hedge bet" the race if we wish. See the chapter, "How to Bet."

This, the second half of the daily double, is a mile race with ten horses entered. Most of the horses have run this mile distance at least once and all have raced at Aqueduct recently. In addition to the daily double, a quinella is available.

AQUEDUCT

1 MILE. (1.33⅕) CLAIMING. Purse $11,000. 4-year-olds and upward. Weights, 122 lbs. Non-winners of two races at a mile or over since March 1, allowed 3 lbs. Of such a race since then, 5 lbs. Claiming Price $12,500; for each $1,000 to $10,500, 2 lbs. (Races when entered to be claimed for $8,500 or less not considered).

Two Too Many *

Ch. h. 6, by Bye and Near—Twice Shy, by Double Eclipse
$11,500 Br.—Smythe C (Ont-C)
Tr.—Sallusto Justin
Own.—Sallusto J
115 Lifetime 75 10 7 9 $84,188 | 1983 6 1 0 1 $7,260 | 1982 22 4 3 3 $43,940 | Turf 9 0 1 0 $3,754

31Mar83- 1Aqu fst 1⅛ :49⅗ 1:14⅘ 1:53⅗ Clm c-8500 5 2 2³ 1½ 1¹ 1³½ Velasquez J b 117 *1.40 68-21 Two Too Many117³½TogetherAgain117³½Cincelari108² Ridden out 8
24Mar83- 1Aqu fst 7f :23⅗ :47⅕ 1:25 Clm 16000 11 3 94½ 5⁴ 78½ 78¼ Miranda J b 117 13.20 68-26 PrgrinPowr113²CourtWs112hdSprtnMonk117¹ Lacked a response 11
18Feb83- 2Aqu fst 1¼ ⊡:47⅘ 1:41⅗ 2:08⅕ Clm c-15000 3 1 2½ 53½ 5⁶ 5⁸ Kaenel J L b 115 18.20 69-27 Mr. October 108¹½ Hail to Hardin 117¹½ Bright Current113² Tired 10
9Feb83- 6Aqu fst 1⅛ ⊡:47⅗ 1:12⅗ 1:52⅗ Clm 16000 4 6 65½ 6⁹ 5¹¹ 59½ Kaenel J L b 117 10.10 73-20 Axe The Fool 117½ Mr. October 108½ Prather's Image117³ Evenly 10
19Jan83- 9Aqu fst 1⅛ ⊡:47⅘ 1:13⅘ 1:53⅗ Clm 16000 8 7 7⁷ 4⁵ 3⁶ 3¹⁰ Kaenel J L b 117 12.40 68-24 Psychosis 112¹½ Delta Leader108⁸½TwoTooMany117⁵½ Evenly late 11
5Jan83- 9Aqu fst 170 ⊡:48⅖ 1:14 1:44⅘ Clm 20000 9 8 75½ 8⁹ 7¹³ 6¹² Antongeorgi W A7 110 16.00 69-24 CounselorGeorge112noSolidGoldSoul117⁴Interferenc112³½ Outrun 9
28Dec82- 9Aqu fst 1⅙ ⊡:48⅗ 1:14 2:00⅗ 3+ Clm 20000 5 5 5⁶ 54½10¹⁰10¹⁴ Beitia E 117 4.50 61-22 Gig's LittleTiger112²BraveTheReef117²½PerfectBidder108nk Tired 10
17Dec82- 6Aqu gd 1⅛ ⊡:48⅕ 1:14⅕ 1:54⅕ 3+ Clm 20000 12 5 43½ 2½ 5² 2½ Beitia E 117 27.50 74-25 Ultra Suede 117½ Two Too Many 117½ Psychosis 108no Gamely 12
11Dec82- 9Aqu fst 1⅛ ⊡:48⅘ 1:13⅘ 1:53⅕ 3+ Clm 25000 10 4 3³ 54½108½ 89½ Beitia E 117 24.00 70-20 Larking's Run 119⁴ Daring Bet 117hd Master Force 117no Tired 12
21Nov82- 5Aqu fst 1⅛ :48⅘ 1:13⅘ 1:52⅘ 3+ Clm 25000 5 6 5¹¹ 6⁹ 67½ 4⁸ Beitia E 117 9.40 63-24 Larking'sRun115²LetterFromLucy117⁵½KingBelgin117½ No threat 9
LATEST WORKOUTS Mar 20 Bel tr.t 5f my 1:01 h Mar 14 Bel tr.t 4f fst :48⅗ h Mar 6 Bel tr.t 4f fst :48⅘ h Feb 27 Bel tr.t 4f fst :48⅘ h

Quicksilver Luck

Gr. g. 4, by Silver Saber—Fast Luck, by Piet
$10,500 Br.—Onett G L (Fla)
Tr.—Bolton Amos E
Own.—Ginsberg Shirley K
108⁵ Lifetime 36 3 5 5 $43,010 | 1983 5 0 1 0 $3,380 | 1982 23 2 4 2 $30,960 | Turf 1 0 0 0 $140

21Mar83- 1Aqu sly 1⅛ :49⅕ 1:15 1:54⅗ Clm 10000 3 4 3⁴ 3² 2hd 32½ Alvarado R Jr5 b 112 5.80 60-26 Alcor117²½ⒹComeUpPence119nkQuicksilverLuck112¹½ Weakened 8
21Mar83-Placed second through disqualification
16Mar83- 1Aqu fst 1 :47⅗ 1:13⅘ 1:39⅘ Clm 12500 10 9 7⁵ 138½12¹⁰12¹⁰ Alvarado R Jr5 b 112 6.20f 57-27 Sealed Conquest 117¹½ Flatbush 110nk Singh Boldly 113¹½ Outrun 14
17Feb83- 2Aqu fst 1⅛ ⊡:48⅕ 1:13⅘ 1:53⅘ Clm 20000 1 6 915111511171114 Gonzalez M A b 117 30.00 64-17 Argonaftis 113nk Creme De LaFete117nkPsychosis108⁵½ Fell back 11
30Jan83- 9Aqu fst 1⅙ ⊡:47⅗ 1:13⅖ 1:46 Clm c-16000 3 7 8¹¹ 81110171021 AntongorgiWA7 b 110 4.30 62-20 Delta Leader 108⁵½ Prather's Image 117³½ Atop It All110½ Outrun 11
3Jan83- 2Aqu fst 170 ⊡:48⅕ 1:13⅘ 1:43⅘ Clm 25000 3 3 2² 2⁵ 3¹¹ 4¹⁵ Skinner K b 117 4.30 68-25 No Heir 117⁶½ Red HotandCole106⁷½Mr.Nicefield115hd Weakened 9
16Dec82- 9Aqu sly 170 ⊡:48⅗ 1:14⅕ 1:44⅘ Clm 25000 1 2 3¹ 2½ 2hd 1½ Schoeller C F7 b 110 6.10Ⓓ 78-23 ⒹQuicksilver Luck 110½ CastleGem117⁴ShoreLeave117³ Bore Out 10
16Dec82-Disqualified and placed second
9Dec82- 5Aqu fst 1⅙ ⊡:48⅘ 1:14⅗ 1:48⅘ Clm c-19000 3 3 45½ 34½ 2⁵ 24½ Alvarado R Jr5 b 110 *1.70 67-30 RighteousAnger117⁴½QuicksilverLuck110⁶ArdntBid117½ Game try 8
1Dec82- 5Aqu fst 1¼ ⊡:48⅘ 1:40⅗ 2:07⅗ Clm 15000 1 5 4¹⁴ 2½ 1²½ 13½ Alvarado R Jr5 b 110 *1.00 80-17 QuicksilverLuck110³½CommncheBrve107hdCllProudly106½ Driving 7
21Nov82- 2Aqu fst 1 :47⅗ 1:12⅘ 1:38⅘ Clm 19000 8 5 3½ 43½ 43½ 31½ Velasquez J b 115 5.30 71-24 Fire Away 110hdTullie'sSlugger115¹½QuicksilverLuck115nk Rallied 9
5Nov82- 9Aqu gd 1⅛ :49⅕ 1:13⅘ 1:53⅘ Clm 19000 2 3 3½ 3nk 2³ 4² LizarzburuPM5 b 110 13.90 64-24 Years Away 117½ Tribal Prince 117noUpMySleeve117¹½ Weakened 9
LATEST WORKOUTS Mar 6 Bel tr.t 5f fst 1:05⅖ b

Flatbush

Ch. h. 5, by Wig Out—Angel Aid, by Gentle Art
$12,500 Br.—Koones R (Ky)
Tr.—Acerno John
Own.—Acerno Sharlene
110⁷ Lifetime 55 2 7 8 $44,660 | 1983 5 0 2 0 $5,420 | 1982 17 0 0 3 $5,130 | Turf 2 0 0 0

24Mar83- 1Aqu fst 7f :23⅗ :47⅕ 1:25 Clm 15000 9 1 73¾ 64½ 65½ 4³ Thibeau R J5 b 108 7.20 73-26 PeregrinePower113²CourtWise112hdSpartanMonk117¹ No excuse 11
16Mar83- 1Aqu fst 1 :47⅗ 1:13⅘ 1:39⅘ Clm 12500 14 10 95½ 96½ 32½ 21½ Thibeau R J7 b 110 9.00 66-27 Sealed Conquest 117¹½ Flatbush110nkSinghBoidly113¹½ Game try 14
21Feb83- 2Aqu fst 6f ⊡:23 :46⅗ 1:12⅘ Clm 11500 9 9 119½ 98¾ 54½ 21½ Thibeau R J7 b 108 22.80f 80-22 Pokie Joe 117¹½ Flatbush 108½ Big Beau Ridge 117¹½ Rallied 13
20Jan83- 9Aqu fst 6f ⊡:23⅗ :47⅗ 1:12⅕ Clm 11500 6 7 74¾ 76½ 6⁷ 69¾ Garramone A b 115 13.90 74-24 Prther'sImge113⁴½Michl'sEdg107nkBigBuRidg112½ Lacked a rally 10
10Jan83- 1Aqu fst 6f ⊡:23 :46⅘ 1:12⅘ Clm 12500 10 10 109½10¹² 8¹⁰ 66½ Garramone A b 117 39.00 76-23 Ted Brown 114¹ Delta Leader 113³½ Spanish Beat 117¹ Outrun 11
15Dec82- 3Aqu fst 1⅛ ⊡:48⅕ 1:14⅖ 1:55⅘ 3+ Clm 12500 2 8 9¹² 87¾ 86¾ 85½ Clayton M D7 b 110 8.60 61-25 Personal Beau 115nk Going Orange 117¹½ IndigoStar115nk Outrun 12
3Dec82- 1Aqu my 1⅛ ⊡:48⅗ 1:13⅘ 1:52⅗ 3+ Clm 15000 6 5 5⁵ — 64¾ 6⁵ Clayton M D7 b 108 6.10 78-13 Atop It All 110¹½ Atractivo 113hd Port On 117²½ Fog, no factor 6
22Nov82- 2Aqu fst 7f :23⅗ :46⅗ 1:25⅕ 3+ Clm 12500 8 1 67½ 5⁶ 65½ 42¾ Clayton M D7 b 110 4.20 72-23 Pokie Joe 117nk Untamed 117no Sir Sizzling Nehoc 115²½ Rallied 8
4Nov82- 9Aqu fst 7f :23⅕ :46⅖ 1:25⅖ 3+ Clm 12500 3 8 9¹² 89½ 54½ 31½ Clayton M D7 b 110 9.30 73-24 Big Beau Ridge 110¾ Port On 112½ Flatbush 110hd Lost whip 11
24Oct82- 9Aqu fst 7f :23 :46⅗ 1:25⅕ 3+ Clm 16000 5 10 118¾ 98¹ 63½ 72½ Clayton M D7 b 110 16.20 72-25 Charlie'sStr112noKingofClssics112¹½NeedAPenny117no No factor 12
LATEST WORKOUTS Mar 13 Bel tr.t 4f my :49⅖ h (d) Mar 5 Bel tr.t 4f fst :53 b Feb 18 Bel tr.t 4f gd :49⅖ h

Axe The Fool

B. g. 5, by Hatchet Man—Time To Turn, by Turn-To
$12,500 Br.—Lin-Drake Farm (Fla)
Tr.—Cunningham Bill W
Own.—McGraw R
117 Lifetime 32 8 6 4 $128,960 | 1983 7 1 0 1 $9,660 | 1981 14 4 4 3 $78,260 | Turf 3 0 0 0

26Mar83- 9Aqu fst 1⅛ :48⅗ 1:13⅗ 1:52⅗ Clm 12500 7 8 87½ 85½ 86½ 7⁹ Gonzalez M A b 117 9.40 64-19 Atop It All 117² Read Me The Names112⁴SinghBoldly113nk Wide 11
20Mar83- 3Aqu fst 1⅛ :49 1:14 1:52⅘ Clm 16000 3 6 75½ 64¾ 8¹¹ 9¹⁸ Graell A b 117 6.40 53-27 Christy's Ridge 117no Recidian 110¾ Hopehard 108¹½ Tired 9
27Feb83- 3Aqu fst 1¼ ⊡:48⅖ 1:40⅗ 2:07⅖ Hcp 12500s 4 8 9¹⁵ 99½ 6⁵ 45¾ Graell A b 112 19.80 75-20 Imaromeo 122½ Soudan 116⁴½ Recidian 112½ Rallied 9
17Feb83- 2Aqu fst 1⅛ ⊡:48⅕ 1:13⅘ 1:53⅘ Clm 20000 10 9 7¹² 9¹⁰ 89½10¹⁰ Kaenel J L b 117 7.40 68-17 Argonaftis 113nk Creme De La Fete 117nk Psychosis 108⁵½ Wide 11
9Feb83- 6Aqu fst 1⅛ ⊡:47⅗ 1:12⅗ 1:52⅗ Clm c-16000 9 3 21½ 21½ 2hd 1½ Cordero A Jr b 117 *2.00 83-20 Axe The Fool 117½ Mr. October 108½ Prather's Image117³ Driving 10
30Jan83- 5Aqu fst 1⅛ ⊡:48⅘ 1:13⅗ 1:52⅕ Clm 12500 9 2 2hd 2hd 2⁴ 39¾ Smith A Jr b 117 2.80e 75-20 Imaromeo 117⁵½ Indigo Star 108⁴ Axe The Fool 117⁷ Weakened 9
23Jan83- 9Aqu sly 6f ⊡:23 :47⅗ 1:12⅘ Clm 16000 3 — — — — 9²⁷ Miranda J b 117 *1.50 53-26 Duck Key Taurian 117⁹ In the Process 108³SixthCavalry108² Fog 9
29Dec81- 8Lrl fst 7f :23⅗ :47 1:26⅕ 3+ Alw 11500 4 1 32½ 43½ 42¾ 36½ Krone J A5 b 109 *1.00 73-34 El Punchero 114¹½ Majestic Song 109⁵ AxeTheFool109³ Ret. sore 6
10Dec81- 8Lrl fst 1⅙ :47⅕ 1:12⅘ 1:44⅗ 3+ Alw 12000 1 1 1½ 1hd 22½ 23½ Daniels W H b 113 *1.20 93-25 Issue Joined 116³½ Axe The Fool 113¹¾ El Punchero109⁵ 2nd best 10
26Nov81- 2Aqu fst 1 :46⅘ 1:12⅘ 1:37⅗ Clm 45000 8 9 9⁵ 4² 1½ 14¾ Avalon W AIII5 b 112 *1.50 79-21 AxeTheFool112⁴¾NativeGroogle113²½KingBelgin114²¾ Ridden out 13
LATEST WORKOUTS Mar 31 Bel tr.t 4f fst :49⅕ b Feb 6 Bel tr.t 3f fst :38 b

Christopher Star

Dk. b. or br. c. 4, by Christopher R—Shining Darkly, by Dark Star
$12,500 Br.—Soule C I Jr (Md)
Tr.—Puentes Gilbert
Own.—Garren M M
106⁷ Lifetime 44 4 5 3 $47,800 | 1983 10 1 0 1 $6,690 | 1982 28 3 3 1 $35,440 | Turf 2 0 0 0

28Mar83- 9Aqu my 6f :22⅗ :45⅘ 1:11⅘ Clm 10000 5 7 21½ 3³ 33½ 43½ Thibeau R J7 b 110 18.80 81-14 Richness 119hd Joan's Poker 108² BigBeauRidge109¹½ Weakened 12
23Mar83- 9Aqu fst 6f :22⅗ :46⅘ 1:13 Clm 12500 1 3 1² 2½ 4³ 108½ Thibeau R J5 b 112 16.50 68-28 A ManShort112nkMoonGlider108noPassTheLeader112hd Gave way 10
13Mar83- 1Aqu fst 6f ⊡:22⅘ :46⅘ 1:11⅘ Clm 12500 8 3 32½ 5⁴ 86½ 8¹⁰ Vergara O b 117 9.80 78-08 King of Classics 119½ Another Rodger 117³Whambang109¹½ Tired 8
10Mar83- 3Aqu sly 1⅙ ⊡:47⅕ 1:12⅘ 1:46⅗ Clm 14000 12 2 1hd 4³ 111411¹⁸ Lovato F Jr 113 20.40 63-17 On The Charles 106¹½ Ben Marino 117½ Rout 113¾ Speed 1/2 mile 12
10Mar83-Placed tenth through disqualification
6Mar83- 2Aqu fst 6f ⊡:22⅘ :45⅘ 1:11⅘ Clm 16000 12 11 118½11¹³ 8¹⁰ 66½ Powers T M5 112 17.50f 82-19 Rapido'sRepet112¹½InfiniteSg112¹½RulerComeBck117½ No threat 14
17Feb83- 2Aqu fst 1⅛ ⊡:48⅕ 1:13⅘ 1:53⅘ Clm 18000 2 1 1¹ 1½ 41½ 56½ Davis R G5 108 14.70 71-17 Argonaftis 113nk CremeDeLaFete117nkPsychosis108⁵½ Weakened 11
31Jan83- 9Aqu fst 6f ⊡:22⅘ :46⅖ 1:12 Clm 10500 11 2 31½ 3nk 1hd 3² Davis R G5 b 108 14.70 82-15 Alturas 119½ Extradite 113¹½ Christopher Star 108¹¾ Weakened 12
23Jan83- 9Aqu sly 6f ⊡:23 :47⅗ 1:12⅘ Clm 14000 6 — — — — 5¹⁵ Belmonte J E10 b 103 11.40 65-26 Duck Key Taurian 117⁹ In the Process 108³SixthCavalry108² Fog 9
13Jan83- 3Aqu fst 6f ⊡:23⅗ :48⅗ 1:14 Clm 7500 7 4 21½ 21½ 1² 12¾ Belmonte J E10 b 107 5.40 74-26 ChristopherStr107²½PinkMonk117³SouthrnPrinc112²½ Drew clear 14
6Jan83- 3Aqu sly 6f ⊡:23⅕ :46⅗ 1:11⅘ Clm 18000 6 3 3² 43½ 56½ 77½ Graell A b 117 6.50 77-17 Poker At Nan's 117¹½TedBrown110²DeltaLeader117hd Wide, tired 9
LATEST WORKOUTS ●Mar 20 Bel tr.t 3f my :35 h Mar 3 Bel tr.t 4f fst :47⅘ h Feb 15 Bel tr.t 4f fst :47⅕ h Feb 6 Bel tr.t 4f fst :48 h

American Royalty

Dk. b. or br. g. 9, by Native Royalty—Gusellie, by One-Eyed King
$12,500 Br.—Harbor View Farm (Fla)
Tr.—Nieminski Richard
Own.—Kerr Mrs D
117 Lifetime 97 7 9 12 $121,470 | 1983 4 0 0 1 $2,100 | 1982 2 0 0 0 | Turf 41 5 3 6 $72,700

26Mar83- 9Aqu fst 1⅛ :48⅗ 1:13⅗ 1:52⅗ Clm 12500 8 9 98½11⁹ 10¹² 9¹⁴ Samyn J L 117 18.20 59-19 Atop It All 117² Read MeTheNames112⁴SinghBoldly113nk Outrun 11
16Mar83- 1Aqu fst 1 :47⅗ 1:13⅘ 1:39⅘ Clm 12500 3 8 64¾ 85¾ 85½ 95½ Hernandez R 117 12.60 62-27 Sealed Conquest 117¹½ Flatbush 110nk Singh Boldly 113¹½ Outrun 14
11Feb83- 3Aqu fst 170 ⊡:47⅘ 1:14⅖ 1:44⅖ Clm 10000 9 10 1017109¾ 4⁷ 36¾ Skinner K 117 13.60 74-24 GoingOrnge117¹½CornishConquror112⁵AmricnRoylty117nk Rallied 10
19Jan83- 9Aqu fst 1⅛ ⊡:47⅘ 1:13⅘ 1:53⅗ Clm 16000 3 9 8¹³ 87½ 59½ 4¹⁶ Asmussen S M5 112 18.70 62-24 Psychosis 112¹½ Delta Leader 108¾ TwoTooMany117⁵½ No factor 11
13Dec82- 5Aqu fst 6f ⊡:23⅕ :47⅕ 1:12⅕ 3+ Clm 25000 4 3 8¹¹ 8¹⁰ 8¹¹ 8¹¹ Santiago A 117 33.20 72-22 Riva's Magic114²½CatchMatthew110hdBusyHilarious116hd Outrun 8
3Dec82- 9Aqu my 6f ⊡:22⅘ :45⅘ 1:11⅘ 3+ Clm 25000 10 10 10¹⁴ 8²¹ 7¹³ 7¹³ Santiago A 117 35.40 75-13 Riva's Magic 114²½ Rapido'sRepeat117³WorthyPiper119¹½ Outrun 10
7Nov81- 1Aqu fst 1⅛ :48⅗ 1:13⅗ 1:51⅘ 3+ Clm 35000 1 6 6⁹ 69½ 6¹⁶ 6²⁰ Santiago A 114 6.90 59-22 Delta Leader 112⁵½ Spartan Knight 115²½ Steelwood 114¾ Outrun 7
7Oct81- 6Bel gd 1 Ⓣ:47⅘ 1:12 1:37⅘ 3+ Clm 35000 4 8 84½ 6⁹ 57½ 35½ Santiago A 115 8.30 72-22 Deedee's Deal 114⁴½ Caraqueno115¹½AmericanRoyalty115hd Wide 9
30Oct81- 1Bel fm 1⅛ Ⓣ:50⅕ 1:40⅗ 2:17⅘ 3+ Clm 35000 7 6 7¹⁴ 7¹³ 6¹¹ 6¹³ Santiago A 113 8.50 57-19 No Neck 122no Greenwich Village 114³½SirViolet114³ Never close 7
13Sep81- 9Bel fm 1⅙ Ⓣ:45⅘ 1:10 1:42⅕ 3+ Clm 35000 4 10 10¹¹ 8¹⁰ 4² 1no Santiago A 113 9.20 85-15 AmericanRoylty113noPrincelyHeir113¹½SprtnKnight113³½ Driving 10
LATEST WORKOUTS Mar 6 Bel tr.t 4f fst :48⅗ h Feb 6 Bel tr.t 4f fst :48⅘ h

Prince of Sport — Ch. g. 4, by Prince Dantan—First Pitch, by Hitting Away — $12,500 — Br.—Sedlacek Mrs W (Fla) — Tr.—Sedlacek Woodrow — 117
Lifetime 16 1 0 2 $10,620 — 1983 3 0 0 0 — 1982 8 1 0 2 $10,020
Own.—Heller W B
Entered 4Apr83- 2 AQU
23Mar83- 9Aqu fst 6f :22⅗ :46⅘ 1:13 Clm 11500 2 5 66 44 32½ 51¼ McCarron G b 115 11.80 75-28 A Man Short 112nk Moon Glider 108no PassTheLeader112hd Hung 10
13Mar83- 1Aqu fst 6f ⊡:22⅘ :46⅘ 1:11⅕ Clm 12500 4 5 52¾ 32 53½ 66 McCarron G b 117 8.80 82-08 King of Classics 119½ Another Rodger 1173Whambang1091¾ Tired 8
27Jan83- 5Aqu fst 6f ⊡:22⅘ :46⅕ 1:11⅘ Clm 18000 12 9 118¼ 1212 1313 1313 McCarron G b 113 38.50 72-19 SirSizzlingNhoc113noBusyHlrous1141¾SwssConncton117hd Outrun 14
30Dec82- 9Aqu fst 6f ⊡:23 :47⅖ 1:14⅖ Clm 15000 2 7 42½ 43¼ 4¾ 1hd Cole A K5 b 110 10.30Ⓓ 72-24 ⒹPrncfSprt110hdFrskRgrs113nkUndrthnflnc117no Bore out, drvng 12
30Dec82-Disqualified and placed fourth
1Nov82- 2Aqu fst 7f :22⅘ :45⅘ 1:24⅗ Clm 15000 11 1 42 2½ 1hd 3½ McCarron G b 115 5.80e 77-23 FriskyRgorous113½BrghtCurrnt109noPrncofSport1151¼ Weakened 11
18Oct82- 3Aqu fst 6f :22⅗ :46⅖ 1:12⅕ Clm 16000 2 8 2hd 32 46 66¾ McCarron G b 117 8.80 73-23 Mesnge'sMystir1091¼HrsAnthony1151¼Blu'sChoic1132¾ Early foot 10
19Sep82- 2Bel fst 6½f :23⅕ :46⅘ 1:18⅘ Clm 19000 6 9 85 65½ 46 68 McCarron G b 115 18.70 74-20 CastleGem1173¼ChristopherStr1073¼Blue'sChoice1081¼ No threat 11
12Jun82- 1Bel fst 1 :46⅘ 1:11⅘ 1:38⅖ Clm 22500 4 5 21½ 1hd 3½ 45¾ McCarron G b 115 3.40 68-14 OilCanHarry1174¾HangoverYnk117½BrndiedSunset115½ Weakened 7
29May82- 4Bel gd 1 :46⅕ 1:11⅖ 1:37⅘ Clm 19000 2 1 11 12 12 32¼ McCarron G b 115 16.50 75-13 Sir Joseph 117½ Flamingo Two1081¾PrinceofSport1157 Weakened 9
14May82- 2Aqu fst 6f :24 :48 1:12⅖ 3↑Md 15000 4 6 11 12½ 13 1¾ McCarron G b 113 2.40 79-19 Prince of Sport 113¾ Pink Party 1137½ WeatherHelm1063 Driving 6
LATEST WORKOUTS ●Feb 24 Aqu ⊡ 5f fst 1:00⅗ h

Singh Boldly — Ch. g. 4, by Singh—Maxi Skirt, by Bagdad — $10,500 — Br.—Allen Joe (Ky) — Tr.—Schaeffer Stephen — 113
Lifetime 33 3 7 10 $42,739 — 1983 7 0 0 3 $4,710 — 1982 16 2 4 5 $26,975 — Turf 1 0 1 0 $2,000
Own.—Spiegel R
26Mar83- 9Aqu fst 1⅛ :48⅗ 1:13⅗ 1:52⅖ Clm 10500 6 6 65¼ 52½ 43 36 Migliore R b 113 5.70 67-19 Atop It All1172ReadMeTheNames1124SinghBoldly113nk Wide str. 11
16Mar83- 1Aqu fst 1 :47⅗ 1:13⅘ 1:39⅘ Clm 10500 12 12 1110 75½ 42½ 31¼ Graell A b 113 10.80 65-27 Sealed Conquest 1171¼ Flatbush 110nk Singh Boldly 1131¼ Rallied 14
6Mar83- 9Aqu fst 1⅛ ⊡:48⅗ 1:13⅖ 1:52 Clm 10500 8 11 117 75¼ 58¼ 510 Santiago A b 113 5.40 76-19 Hopehard 1152¾ Castle Gem 1171¼ Sonny Booth 1122¼ No threat 12
25Feb83- 3Aqu fst 1 1/16 ⊡:49⅕ 1:15⅗ 1:49⅕ Clm 10500 10 6 66½ 43½ 32½ 31 Santiago A b 113 31.70 66-27 On The Charles 108½ ElevatorShoes115½SinghBoldly1136½ Rallied 11
11Feb83- 3Aqu fst 170 ⊡:47⅘ 1:14⅖ 1:44⅕ Clm 10000 7 6 67½ 63½ 68 611 Santagata N b 117 *2.70 70-24 GoingOrnge1171¾CornishConquror1125AmricnRoylty117nk Outrun 10
30Jan83- 9Aqu fst 1 1/16 ⊡:47⅗ 1:13⅖ 1:46 Clm 16000 2 5 67½ 56 47½ 49½ Cordero A Jr b 117 5.00 73-20 DeltLeder1085¼Prther'sImg1173¾AtopItAll110½ Lacked a response 11
5Jan83- 3Aqu fst 170 ⊡:49⅕ 1:14⅗ 1:44⅕ Clm 20000 9 6 44½ 57 613 614 Milo R7 b 110 12.20 67-24 Golden Crest 1164 Oscar My Love 117¾ Soudan 1142 Tired 10
23Dec82- 2Aqu fst 1⅛ ⊡:49 1:14⅘ 1:55 Clm c-16000 2 2 23 23 35½ 36¾ Cole A K5 b 112 4.50 64-27 Sonny Booth 1081IntheProcess1175¾SinghBoldly1122¼ Weakened 11
8Dec82- 8Med fst 1 :48 1:12⅗ 1:39⅕ Clm 20000 4 2 31 4¾ 33 34 McCauley W H b 118 *1.30 82-21 HndsomeJoeAl1082Tullie'sSlugger1152SinghBoldly1182¾ Steadied 5
26Nov82- 1Med fst 1 :46⅘ 1:13 1:40⅗ Clm 20000 1 4 45½ 42½ 21 2½ McCauley W H b 118 3.30 78-21 On the Helm 115½ Singh Boldly1182¼CountOfBagdad1152 Gaining 6
LATEST WORKOUTS ●Apr 3 Bel tr.t 3f sly :38⅖ b Mar 24 Bel tr.t 3f fst :37⅕ b Mar 4 Bel tr.t 3f fst :37⅖ b Feb 22 Bel tr.t 4f fst :50⅖ b

Kenny J. — Dk. b. or br. g. 5, by Droll Role—Jennie Murphy, by Royal Serenade — $11,500 — Br.—Carter Donald W (Ky) — Tr.—Barrera Oscar S — 110[5]
Lifetime 63 6 12 6 $85,463 — 1983 3 0 1 0 $1,870 — 1982 28 2 4 4 $20,103 — Turf 2 0 0 0
Own.—Barrera Oscar S
29Mar83- 3Aqu gd 1 :47⅕ 1:12⅖ 1:38⅖ Clm c-7500 10 1 1½ 1½ 22 21½ Miranda J b 117 5.70 72-28 Delta Leader 1121½ Kenny J. 1179 Irish Poplar 1121¼ Bumped 12
19Mar83- 1Aqu my 1¼ :47⅕ 1:38⅖ 2:04⅗ Hcp 10000s 2 1 2½ 714 829 835 Graell A b 109 16.50 38-21 Count Advocate 1136 Imaromeo 124¾ Ardent Bid 1115 Used early 9
26Feb83- 9Aqu fst 6f ⊡:23⅕ :47⅘ 1:13⅕ Clm c-10000 2 5 21½ 32 56½ 68 Rogers K L b 117 4.50 70-25 Foxmoor Flight 117½ Rapido's Repeat 1122¾AManShort1124 Tired 12
28Dec82- 9Haw sly 6½f :22⅗ :45⅖ 1:18⅗ 3↑Clm 15000 8 3 41½ 42 42¼ 811 Strauss R b 115 4.70 69-26 Mr. Cleve T. 117½ Marty's First 1143 Thebian Ruler 1171¼ Tired 9
21Dec82- 9Haw fst 6½f :22⅕ :45⅗ 1:18⅕ 3↑Clm 15000 12 1 78 45 32½ 31¾ Strauss R b 116 7.60 80-26 Superstep 1171¼ King Sid 115½ Kenny J. 116nk Rallied 12
14Dec82- 9Haw fst 6f :22⅕ :46⅕ 1:12⅕ 3↑Clm 12500 5 5 74 75½ 31½ 2no Louviere G P b 116 5.60 80-25 Conestoga Eagle 116no Kenny J. 116nk Jims Lt. 1131½ Sharp 9
6Dec82- 5Haw gd 6½f :22⅘ :45⅖ 1:17 3↑Clm 10000 3 1 2hd 1½ 11 11¾ Strauss R b 116 22.00 88-16 Kenny J. 1161¾ Bold Plea 1171¼ Rep's Streak 117nk Driving 11
23Nov82- 9Haw fst 6f :22⅕ :46⅖ 1:13 3↑Clm 12500 11 1 4¾ 43¼ 77¼ 77¾ Medina N R b 116 24.20 68-24 Dreamer Boy 109no William Bos 1161¼ Bold Plea 1182 11
1Nov82- 9Haw sly 6½f :22⅗ :46⅕ 1:19⅕ 3↑Clm 15000 5 3 47 513 512 714 Hirdes R J Jr b 115 5.70 63-31 Superstep 1154¼ Tenshua's Bid 1151½ Vuelo's Tester 1134¼ 8
26Oct82- 4Haw fst 6f :22⅗ :45⅗ 1:10 3↑Clm 12500 7 1 1hd 1hd 23 47½ Hirdes R J Jr b 116 17.80 83-17 Amphitrion 1166 Thebian Ruler 1161½ Needle Nice 111hd 12
LATEST WORKOUTS Mar 9 Bel tr.t 3f sly :38⅖ b

Atop It All — B. h. 5, by Best Turn—Pom Pom, by Fleet Nasrullah — $12,500 — Br.—Calumet Farm (Ky) — Tr.—Lake Robert P — 119
Lifetime 50 5 5 8 $73,760 — 1983 8 1 0 2 $10,320 — 1982 31 4 3 4 $51,340 — Turf 3 0 .0 0
Own.—Gir-Sto Stable
26Mar83- 9Aqu fst 1⅛ :48⅗ 1:13⅗ 1:52⅖ Clm 12500 10 5 43½ 41½ 2½ 12 Fell J 117 20.00 73-19 Atop It All 1172 Read MeTheNames1124SinghBoldly113nk Driving 11
16Mar83- 1Aqu fst 1 :47⅗ 1:13⅘ 1:39⅘ Clm 12500 9 14 1411 107¾ 95¾ 105½ Rogers K L 117 22.70 61-27 Sealed Conquest 1171¼ Flatbush 110nk Singh Boldly 1131¼ Outrun 14
2Mar83- 9Aqu fst 1⅛ ⊡:47⅖ 1:12⅘ 1:52⅖ Clm c-10000 10 6 67 65 65 66¼ Melendez J D5 112 14.10 78-12 ComeUpPence117hdGoingOrange119hdIndigoStr108nk No menace 11
2Mar83-Placed fifth through disqualification
25Feb83- 3Aqu fst 1 1/16 ⊡:49⅕ 1:15⅗ 1:49⅕ Clm 12500 6 8 78 78¾ 69½ 47½ Alvarado R Jr5 b 112 5.30 59-27 OnThChrls108½ElvtorShos115½SinghBoldly1136½ Lacked late rally 11
18Feb83- 2Aqu fst 1¼ ⊡:47⅘ 1:41⅖ 2:08⅕ Clm 14000 2 8 815 710 79½ 68½ Venezia M 113 11.20 68-27 Mr. October 1081¾HailtoHardin1171¼BrightCurrent1132 No factor 10
30Jan83- 9Aqu fst 1 1/16 ⊡:47⅗ 1:13⅖ 1:46 Clm 15000 8 10 915 914 79½ 39 Davis R G5 110 8.50 74-20 Delta Leader 1085¼ Prather's Image1173¾AtopItAll110½ Mild rally 11
19Jan83- 5Aqu fst 1⅛ ⊡:47⅗ 1:13⅕ 1:53 Clm 15000 1 6 87¼ 77¼ 67½ 59½ Cordero A Jr 115 *2.20 71-24 Recidian 112½ Sir Sizzling Nehoc 1136 Tantivy 115¾ No factor 11
9Jan83- 3Aqu fst 1¼ ⊡:49⅘ 1:41⅘ 2:07⅘ Clm 16000 5 5 49½ 32 32 32 Cordero A Jr 119 2.80 77-17 Sonny Booth 114hd Perfect Bidder 1102 Atop It All 1192 Evenly 8
31Dec82- 2Aqu fst 170 ⊡:48 1:14⅕ 1:44⅘ 3↑Clm 15000 2 6 910 55 43 32¼ Cordero A Jr 117 6.50 76-25 Golden Crest 1172 Sonny Booth 112nk Atop It All 1175¾ Rallied 10
22Dec82- 2Aqu fst 1 1/16 ⊡:48⅘ 1:14⅖ 1:47⅖ 3↑Clm 16000 9 9 109¼ 912 811 67¾ Cordero A Jr 119 8.60 68-22 Charlie's Star 1124 Recidian 117¾ Soudan 1172 Slow early 12
LATEST WORKOUTS Feb 24 Bel tr.t 3f fst :38⅕ b

By a wide margin, **Kenny J.** is the top choice in this race. But the question is: which horse should be second? If we accept the computer figures blindly, **Axe the Fool** becomes our second selection. However, do not set anything in cement immediately.

2nd Race 1 Mile	Odds	Rating
9 - Kenny J.	3:1	3346
4 - Axe the Fool	12:1	3240
10 - Atop It All	6:1	3161
2 - Quicksilver Luck	20:1	3127

By comparing **Axe the Fool** with the others, it is clear he has done nothing since being claimed in early February, and is not in his best form. In fact, **Atop It All** beat him easily last time out. Does **Axe the Fool** really deserve to be #2?

Another computer choice, **Prince of Sport**, should be eliminated. He has not run more than six panels in almost 6 months. A mile race is tough, the longest of the sprints. The horse must be ready! **Quicksilver Luck** appears on neither the Pole Speed Ranking list nor on the Last Quarter Ranking list. Usually, the best two horses will appear on at least one list or the other.

Pole Speed

2nd Race 1 Mile		Odds	Rating
9 - Kenny J.		3:1	80
7 - Prince of Sport	6f	10:1	78
5 - Christopher Star		15:1	74
4 - Axe the Fool		12:1	70

Last Quarter

2nd Race 1 Mile	Odds	Rating
10 - Atop It All	6:1	190
9 - Kenny J.	3:1	189
3 - Flatbush	5:1	188
4 - Axe the Fool	12:1	188

Christopher Star will probably show early speed again today, but his figures show he is not a contender. This leaves us with two horses, **Atop It All**—normally not a sprinter—and **Flatbush.** Each has beaten the other at least once. **Atop It All** has the better numbers and seems to be improving from the March 16 race when **Flatbush** finished stronger. It should be noted that, aside from the low Early Speed figures (he has run only one sprint race), **Atop It All** could be ranked much higher in the totals. A low Early Speed number is sometimes misleading, as it was in this case. It pays to be alert.

Our selections in this race are:

1. **Kenny J.**
2. **Atop It All**
3. **Flatbush**
4. **Axe the Fool**

This race offers quinella wagering and all four selections should be played in the double, with an emphasis on **Kenny J.**. Since our second and third choices appear equal, additional quinella tickets with **Flatbush** would probably be worth the risk.

Aqueduct (Main) NY April 5, 198–
2nd Race 1 Mile

PP	Horse Name	Morn. Line	Ability Factor	Pure Speed	Early Speed	Late Speed	Max. Form	P/M RATING
1	Two Too Many	5:1	461	84	246	725	971	3116
2	Quicksilver Luck	20:1	456	83	248	732	980	3127
3	Flatbush	5:1	452	85	257	723	980	3112
4	Axe the Fool	12:1	460	98	262	745	1007	3240
5	Christopher Star	15:1	423	87	275	719	994	3089
6	American Royalty	20:1	440	78	244	723	967	3060
7	Prince of Sport 6f	10:1	430	87	279	726	1005	3120
8	Singh Boldly	10:1	453	84	255	722	977	3105
9	Kenny J.	3:1	478	100	291	764	1055	3346
10	Atop It All	6:1	463	88	244	735	979	3161

SECOND RACE
Aqueduct
APRIL 5

1 MILE. (1.33⅕) CLAIMING. Purse $11,000. 4-year-olds and upward. Weights, 122 lbs. Non-winners of two races at a mile or over since March 1, allowed 3 lbs. Of such a race since then, 5 lbs. Claiming Price $12,500; for each $1,000 to $10,500, 2 lbs. (Races when entered to be claimed for $8,500 or less not considered).

Value of race $11,000, value to winner $6,600, second $2,420, third $1,320, fourth $660. Mutuel pool $91,483, OTB pool $167,487. Quinella Pool $132,075. OTB Quinella Pool $236,074.

Last Raced	Horse	Eqt.	A.	Wt	PP	St	¼	½	¾	Str	Fin	Jockey	Cl'g Pr	Odds $1
29Mar83 ^{3}Aqu^{2}	Kenny J.	b	5	110	9	1	2^{2}	1^{hd}	1^{6}	1^{6}	1^{3}	Davis R G^{5}	11500	2.60
26Mar83 ^{9}Aqu^{1}	Atop It All		5	119	10	2	$3^{\frac{1}{2}}$	3^{1}	$2^{1\frac{1}{2}}$	2^{4}	$2^{6\frac{1}{2}}$	Fell J	12500	5.40
31Mar83 ^{1}Aqu^{1}	Two Too Many	b	6	115	1	7	4^{4}	4^{4}	4^{2}	3^{1}	3^{2}	Velasquez J	11500	4.40
26Mar83 ^{9}Aqu^{9}	American Royalty		9	117	6	8	$6^{\frac{1}{2}}$	6^{2}	6^{3}	4^{2}	$4^{2\frac{3}{4}}$	Maple E	12500	26.70
26Mar83 ^{9}Aqu^{3}	Singh Boldly	b	4	113	8	3	$9^{\frac{1}{2}}$	$8^{1\frac{1}{2}}$	$7^{1\frac{1}{2}}$	6^{2}	5no	Migliore R	10500	9.90
23Mar83 ^{9}Aqu^{5}	Prince of Sport	b	4	117	7	4	5^{2}	5^{1}	$5^{\frac{1}{2}}$	5^{2}	6^{nk}	McCarron G	12500	10.20
24Mar83 ^{1}Aqu^{4}	Flatbush	b	5	110	3	9	10	10	9^{2}	$7^{\frac{1}{2}}$	7^{6}	Thibeau R J^{7}	12500	4.20
26Mar83 ^{9}Aqu^{7}	Axe The Fool	b	5	117	4	10	7^{hd}	7^{hd}	$8^{1\frac{1}{2}}$	$8^{\frac{1}{2}}$	$8^{4\frac{1}{4}}$	Graell A	12500	14.60
21Mar83 ^{1}Aqu^{2}	Quicksilver Luck	b	4	108	2	6	8^{hd}	9^{hd}	10	10	9no	Alvarado R Jr^{5}	10500	21.20
28Mar83 ^{9}Aqu^{4}	Christopher Star	b	4	106	5	5	1^{2}	2^{3}	3^{1}	9^{4}	10	AntongorgWA^{7}	12500	17.30

OFF AT 1:28; Start good, Won ridden out. Time, :23⅖, :46⅗, 1:11⅗, 1:37⅕ Track fast.

$2 Mutuel Prices:

9–(K)–KENNY J.	7.20	4.60	3.40
1–(L)–ATOP IT ALL		6.80	4.00
1–(A)–TWO TOO MANY			3.40

$2 QUINELLA 9–10 PAID $22.20.

Dk. b. or br. g, by Droll Role—Jennie Murphy, by Royal Serenade. Trainer Barrera Oscar S. Bred by Carter Donald W (Ky).

KENNY J. took over racing into the turn,quickly drew off and held sway under good handling. ATOP IT ALL finished well to best the others. TWO TOO MANY rallied from the outside approaching the stretch but lacked a further response. AMERICAN ROYALTY failed to be a serious factor. PRINCE OF SPORT tired. FLATBUSH was always outrun. CHRISTOPHER STAR tired badly.

Owners— 1, Barrera Oscar S; 2, Gir-Sto Stable; 3, Sallusto J; 4, Kerr Mrs D; 5, Spiegel R; 6, Heller W B; 7, Acerno Sharlene; 8, McGraw R; 9, Ginsberg Shirley K; 10, Garren M M.

Trainers— 1, Barrera Oscar S; 2, Lake Robert P; 3, Sallusto Justin; 4, Nieminski Richard; 5, Schaeffer Stephen; 6, Sedlacek Woodrow; 7, Acerno John; 8, Cunningham Bill W; 9, Bolton Amos E; 10, Puentes Gilbert.

Atop It All was claimed by King Sea Stable; trainer, Martin Jose; Two Too Many was claimed by Sommer Viola; trainer, Martin Frank.

Scratched—Richness (28Mar83 ^{9}Aqu^{1}); Etito (16Mar83 ^{1}Aqu^{14}).

$2 Daily Double 2–9 Paid $107.40. Daily Double Pool $207,149. OTB Daily Double Pool $548,568.

$2 Quinella Wagering	
Bet	$20.00
Return	$88.00
Profit	$68.80

$2 Daily Double Bets	
Bet	$ 46.00
Return	$322.20
Profit	$276.20

The double proved to be quite profitable and the quinella was worth the time spent to analyze it. Had that effort not been made, the quinella profit would have been only a little better than breakeven.

Pace Handicapping

"The Pace Makes the Race"

Today, handicapping is LIGHT YEARS ahead of what it was, even a few years ago. Racegoers are more knowledgeable about the trainers, the jockeys, and the talents of each horse than at any time in the history of this sport. The introduction of computers, of course, has been important in this regard. And most observers agree: those who go to the cashier's window more often today are usually able to identify the pacesetter(s) of the race and can explain how the contest is likely to unfold. Some have a natural "feel" for what can be expected, while others are much more precise in their analysis.

About fifteen or twenty years ago, Huey Mahl, the author of *The Race is Pace*, outlined an approach that involved the measurement of each horse's capability in "feet-per-second." Although the book is now outdated, the concept has been adopted by many in recent years, proclaiming that new secrets have been found. Hardly. It is only another way of looking at the same picture.

Pace is becoming less of an esoteric subject. Pace is actually easy to interpret and apply with a little practice – but with the right tools. Danny Holmes' book *Ten Steps to Winning* is one excellent way to do it and, of course, *The Pace Analyst* (see page 84) is another. Yet, even with the right tool, common sense will still always be an important ingredient.

There is an old saying: "The Pace Makes the Race," and it is true for almost every contest that we see at the race track. In fact, nearly every race can be analyzed in this manner. Broadly speaking, a pace handicapper initially expects a race to be one of three types:

1. One Dominant Pacesetter

   There is one pacesetter alone that determines the pace of the race. This horse is capable of opening up daylight on the field and winning gate to wire. Usually, this horse's lead amounts to several lengths ("loose on the lead"), it becomes brave, and continues on to the wire. Also, sometimes the horse can be rated and is usually victorious even if it runs head-to-head with a slower competitor.

2. Two Pacesetters, One Stronger Than the Other

   When one of two evenly-matched Early Speed horses has a better ability to finish, a speed duel typically ends in total defeat for one, and possible victory for the other. The survivor is usually first, second, or third at the wire, depending upon the extent of early lead attained by the two pacesetters over the rest of the field. The winner is frequently an off-the-pace runner or, sometimes, a "closer" from further back.

3. Two Pacesetters, Equal in Talent

   If there are two pacesetters and both are equal in overall ability, a speed duel can set the race up for the closers. Usually the two Early Speed horses "cook each other" and neither finishes in the money. The first two horses to cross the wire are usually horses that like to run just off-the-pace or closers that come from far behind.

Experienced pace handicappers also classify each horse in the race according to its running style, and each normally fits into the patterns noted above. Although some horses are more versatile and can run a race with more than one style, most are creatures of habit and tend to run or favor one distinct pattern.

The *Winning at the Track* program shows the talents of each horse based on the computer's reading of all the figures entered for each contestant. *The Pace Analyst* module, a separate program, works (only) with *Winning at the Track*, reads its file, and ranks the three best races for each horse, thus showing a "depth of talent." It indicates the likely pacesetters and the horses capable of running with the pace.

Using the earlier example from page 58, the illustrations to follow show how a pace handicapper can see a race unfolding by applying the *Winning at the Track* software, along with *The Pace Analyst*. Also, it is easy to imagine how the race might have been different had **Cucuchuchu** not been scratched.

As *The Pace Analyst* numbers clearly indicate, John Mobberley, the trainer of **Rest**, would want the horse loose on the lead by at least six or seven lengths. If not, **Out of Wedlock and Ineffable Affair** would be capable of making up the difference.

Pimlico Race Course April 5, 198-
3rd Race 6 f

PP	HORSE	Notes	Morn. Line	Ability Factor	Pure Speed	Early Speed	Late Speed	Max. Form	P/M RATING
1	rest	89/83	8:5	461	94	292	769	1061	3043
2	out of wedlock	86/82	4:1	481	88	280	771	1051	3007
3	ancient image	87/79	10:1	478	83	284	764	1048	2960
4	inffble affair	89/79	5:1	479	90	293	773	1066	3035
5	cucuchuchu	SCR	0:0	0	0	0	0	0	0
6	transporter	83/87	2:1	473	87	274	764	1038	2975

Race: 3 PIM 6 f

PP	Horse		Morn. Line	Pole Speed
1	rest	89/83	8:5	87
4	inffble affair	89/79	5:1	83
6	transporter	83/87	2:1	83
2	out of wedlock	86/82	4:1	81

PP	Horse		Morn. Line	Pole Speed
1	rest	89/83	8:5	89
4	inffble affair	89/79	5:1	82
6	transporter	83/87	2:1	82
2	out of wedlock	86/82	4:1	77

PP	Horse		Morn. Line	Pole Speed
4	inffble affair	89/79	5:1	89
3	ancient image	87/79	10:1	87
1	rest	89/83	8:5	85
6	transporter	83/87	2:1	78

```
* PACE ANALYST *
Expected Pole Speed..... 88 - 0:46.2
Pure Speed Estimate..... 90 - 1:13.1
Required Last Quarter...180   L/S  759

CAPABLE OF RUNNING WITH THIS PACE:
---------------------------------------
 4-inffble affair 89/79    83/183    773
 2-out of wedlock 86/82    81/184    771
 1-rest           89/83    87/185    769
 3-ancient image  87/79    81/183    764
 6-transporter    83/87    83/182    764

 2-out of wedlock 86/82    77/189    768
 4-inffble affair 89/79    82/180    765
 1-rest           89/83    89/178    765
00-                        00/000   0000

 4-inffble affair 89/79    89/180    764
 2-out of wedlock 86/82    72/190    763
 1-rest           89/83    85/181    763
00-                        00/000   0000

     Current Race File: 4-5-8-.pim
     Likely Pacesetters:  #  1  #    4
```

The actual running time to the second call point (the Pole Speed) proved to be :46.1 seconds, equal to Rest's best 89 Pole Speed rating. This was still not enough to steal the race and both Late Speed horses were ready. **Out of Wedlock** passed the leader at the top of the stretch, and **Ineffable Affair** was also able to beat the discouraged horse before the wire.

The handicappers of "class" at Pimlico that day discounted the chances of **Ineffable Affair** and carelessly let the horse go to the post at 5 to 1. After all, they reasoned, the horse never won a race other than its maiden contest. But this simple example shows why "The Pace Makes the Race."

Long Shot Surprises

Here is a classic example of how pace handicapping can pay off handsomely with a little racing luck. This Breeders Cup sprint at Gulfstream Park was won by **Dancing Spree**, just up in time to catch **Safely Kept** at the wire. The exacta paid a whopping $383!

Race: 4 GP 6 f

PP	Horse		Morn. Line	Pole Speed
11	safely kpt-3yf	04/00	8:1	104
10	sam who	00/05	10:1	100
5	on the line	00/04	4:1	100
3	olym prspct-jl	02/93	15:1	100

PP	Horse		Morn. Line	Pole Speed
3	olym prspct-jl	02/93	15:1	102
10	sam who	00/05	10:1	100
5	on the line	00/04	4:1	99
9	mr.nickrsn-3y	97/97	12:1	97

PP	Horse		Morn. Line	Pole Speed
11	safely kpt-3yf	04/00	8:1	98
10	sam who	00/05	10:1	98
3	olym prspct-jl	02/93	15:1	98
1	sewickley	97/07	9:2	97

```
* PACE ANALYST *
Expected Pole Speed.....100 - 0:44.0
Pure Speed Estimate.....104 - 1:10.0
Required Last Quarter...182   L/S  793

CAPABLE OF RUNNING WITH THIS PACE:
----------------------------------------
 9-mr.nickrsn-3y   97/97    96/194   813
 1-sewickley       97/07    92/196   810
 2-dancing spree   94/92    89/195   809
10-sam who         00/05   100/190   809
 7-once wild       96/97    94/191   805

 9-mr.nickrsn-3y   97/97    97/189   809
10-sam who        00/05   100/187   804
 2-dancing spree   94/92    83/198   803
 7-once wild       96/97    96/187   802

 9-mr.nickrsn-3y   97/97    96/190   807
 1-sewickley       97/07    97/190   798
 2-dancing spree   94/92    86/196   797
11-safely kpt-3yf  04/00    98/185   794

     Current Race File: 11-4-89.gp
     Likely Pacesetters:  #  3  #  11
```

Handicapping this race clearly shows that the two expected pacesetters, **Safely Kept** and **Olympic Prospect**, have an equal ability to set the pace, but an unequal ability to maintain it. **Olympic Prospect**, returning from a 3-month layoff, could never hope to be more than the "cheap speed" of this contest, pushing the pace, making **Safely Kept** "the horse to beat." Below are the *Winning at the Track* Late Speed screens for the two pacesetters. Note the Last Quarter figures for each:

798...LATE SPEED safely kpt-3yf 04/00

	Track	Dist.	Time	Out	Time	Out	TV	Pole Speed	Last Qtr.	Late Speed
1	PIM	6 f	0:46.1	0	1:11.1	0	18	89 –	189	790
2	PIM	6 f	0:45.0	0	1:10.0	0	9	95 –	189	794
3	SAR	7 f	0:44.2	0	1:21.0	0	14	98 –	185	794
4	BEL	6 f	0:45.0	0	1:11.3	0	22	95 –	178	774
5	MTH	6 f	0:43.1	0	1:08.3	0	13	104 –	182	798
6								–		
7								–		
8								–		

Selection: 5 Computer Selected

795...LATE SPEED olym prspct-jl 02/93

	Track	Dist.	Time	Out	Time	Out	TV	Pole Speed	Last Qtr.	Late Speed
1	DMR	6 f	0:43.4	0	1:08.0	12	10	101 –	175	767
2	LAD	6 f	0:44.0	0	1:09.4	0	19	100 –	182	795
3	HOL	6 f	0:44.2	0	1:09.3	0	12	98 –	184	789
4	CD	6 f	0:44.1	0	1:10.2	4	21	99 –	177	780
5	SA	6 f	0:43.3	0	1:09.0	0	16	102 –	180	791
6								–		
7								–		
8								–		

Selection: 2 Computer Selected

Four competitors have an obvious ability to close on the pace. **Sam Who** is a horse with good Early Speed capability but with weaker Last Quarter figures; while **Sewickley** and **Dancing Spree** should be considered the Late Speed "closers" of the contest. **Mr. Nickerson** also has an impressive ability to finish well after running a decent pace. However, it should be noted that in all of his successes to date, he has been one of the pacesetters (with Pole Speed figures at least 3-5 lengths slower than he will see in this race). He could be out of it if he runs a pole speed slower than :45.

813...LATE SPEED mr.nickrsn-3y 97/97

	Track	Dist.	Time	Out	Time	Out	TV	Pole Speed		Last Qtr.	Late Speed
1	BEL	7 f	0:44.4	1	1:23.0	1	18	95	–	183	785
2	BEL	6 f	0:44.4	0	1:08.1	0	10	96	–	194	813
3	SAR	6 f	0:44.4	0	1:08.4	0	12	96	–	189	800
4	PHA	5 f	0:44.3	0	0:56.3	0	19	97	–	189	809
5	FL	6 f	0:44.3	1	1:09.2	3	16	96	–	190	807
6									–		
7									–		
8									–		

Selection: 2 Computer Selected

Dancing Spree was ignored by the crowd for three reasons: 1) His best races failed to show any impressive Early Speed figures; 2) The horse was assigned the second post position, a very poor spot for a closer in a fourteen-horse field; and, 3) He had been beaten by **Sewickley** and **Mr. Nickerson** on prior occasions.

The crowd decided against **Safely Kept** because this horse was the only filly in the race.

After the gate opened, and exactly 44 seconds later, most of the spectators were watching in disbelief: **Safely Kept** was 1/2-length in front of a tiring **Olympic Prospect**, while the remainder of the field was six lengths further back. The rest is history!

How to Bet

To make money with the *Performance Method*, you must concentrate your efforts on the daily doubles and exactas (also called perfectas at some tracks) and quinellas. An exacta (or perfecta) will pay if you correctly call the exact order of finish for win and place. A quinella will pay you to correctly predict the finish of the first two horses, regardless of their order. It is not necessary to bet every race. Be selective. Many times I've gone to the track, played the daily double, or only two or three exactas, collected my money and left.

In exacta wagering, the term "box" refers to betting more than one horse in its different combination possibilities. For example, if you expect #2 to win and #6 to place, a straight 2-6 exacta ticket can be cashed if the #2 horse wins and #6 crosses the wire in second place. A 2-6 exacta "box" will pay if the finish is either 2-6 or 6-2. At tracks that offer $2 exacta wagering, the straight exacta ticket would cost $2. A two-horse exacta "box" would cost $4 (i.e., $2 for each combination). If a three-horse exacta box were purchased, there would be six combination possibilities and, at the same track, the cost becomes $12. If four horses were boxed, there would be 12 possible combinations and the ticket would cost $24.

With each successive step, the probability of going to the cashier's window increases but the profits are reduced. For each race there is an optimum betting stance. Not only is your wager against all other people betting on the same race, but by betting two horses in an exacta box, you are also betting against yourself. Except for the unlikely event of a "dead heat," if one bet is successful, the other is automatically a loser. If three horses are played in an exacta box, one combination can win and five will lose. The greater the number of different combinations played, the less net profit to be enjoyed, regardless of which handicapping method is used.

You can see how it is possible to reach a "point of no return" . . .

> Assume that your #1 choice wins and your #2 choice runs second 10% of the time. This means that your winning ex-

acta tickets must average more than $20.00 or no profit will be realized. If the same two horses are played in an exacta box, regardless of the order, the chance of both horses constituting the exacta must be *twice* as great to enjoy the same average of $20.00. Otherwise, if the two top horses produce an exacta only 15% of the time, to profit, your winning tickets must be more than $26.66. And so it goes; the more combinations made, the larger the average payoff must be to make a profit.

Using the handicapping method outlined in this book, the recommended procedure for betting would be as follows:

1. List the four horses of your choice in the precise order in which they are expected to finish;

2. "Box" your two top choices with your third choice;

3. If necessary, "box" your two top choices with your fourth choice;

4. "Box" your two top choices alone (or, if it's a quinella, buy a ticket for these choices);

5. When your first choice is a strong selection and appears to be the likely winner, play the exacta (or perfecta) straight with your second choice.

The betting scheme outlined above may be referred to as a "three-horse multiple box." No more than three horses are boxed at any one time, and each ticket always contains the top two horses.

As an example, suppose the exact order for your first four selections are: #2, #6, #1, #7 in a race with $2 exacta wagering. The bets would be as follows, with a total $30 investment required:

"Box"	#1, #2, #6	($12 ticket)
"Box"	#2, #6, #7	($12 ticket)
"Box"	#2, #6	($ 4 ticket)
2-6	Exacta	($ 2 ticket)

The decision to include the fourth horse rather than betting only three rests with your confidence in the first three choices and/or the strength of the third vs. the fourth choice. Needless to say, the larger number of horses that are bet, the greater your chance of going to the cashier's window. But, again, the objective here is to make a profit, not to satisfy your ego. If possible, bet *three* horses rather than four. Unfortunately, much of the time, it is necessary to go with four. Do not play a fifth horse with your top two unless it is a long shot with a valid chance to win or place. (If this horse is such a good possibility, perhaps it should be your third or fourth choice.) Or, maybe the race should be avoided altogether. Over the long term, the profitability of playing five horses in a single race is poor.

If you bet four horses with a three-horse multiple box and you are correct, with the #2 horse winning and the #6 horse running second, you will be handing the cashier four winning exacta tickets. If either the third or fourth choice wins or places, along with either of your first two selections, the single winning exacta ticket will most likely return more than the total $30 investment. Based on my experience with the *Performance Method*, there is a high probability that at least one of your two top selections will be in the exacta.

Experience will be an important ingredient as you learn to bet with this method. For instance, if you conclude that the above #1 and/or #7 horses have a fairly strong chance to win, it is often profitable to also box your third and fourth choices at least once or box all four together rather than play the three-horse multiple box. Although once in a while I am burned, the three-horse multiple box will produce, over time, higher profits than will the four-horse box. The third and fourth choices, together, constitute an exacta less than 10% of the time.

National statistics point to the fact that the public favorite will win about 3 times out of 10, and be in the money (first, second, or third) 6 times out of 10. This can be somewhat discouraging for handicappers using the *Performance Method* because the favorites seem to pop up more frequently than we'd like them to. However, remember: BET THE HORSES YOU LIKE AND NOT THE HORSES THE CROWD LIKES. With this method, you will be right more often than they will!

As a general rule, the horses' odds should not influence the way you bet. However, this is not *always* the case. If the race has a small field of less than seven horses, the payoff for two of your top horses could be smaller than the total investment. This problem can be overcome to some extent by adding another exacta box, or two, for this low-payoff combination. If all four of your choices offer little profit, no matter what the outcome, do not bet the race; there will be others. Depending on the circumstances, sometimes it is best to bet only three horses, even if you like four, or bet the fourth choice with only the first pick. Again, experience is the key.

Even with this method, it is usually not profitable to bet individual horses unless one stands out and is not a "prohibitive" favorite of, say, less than 1-to-1 on the tote board. As a rule of thumb, betting an individual horse is not worthwhile unless it is a clear #1 pick and a meaningful return can be made with a place ticket (i.e., a return of more than 2 to 1).

To cash a winning daily double ticket, you must pick the winners of two consecutive races, often the first and second races of the day. (Sometimes a track will offer more than one double.) To bet with this method, select two or three horses in the first race and wheel each with your best two or three selections in the second race. In other words, if your choices in the first race are #2, #6, and #1 (in that order), and your top three picks in the second race are, in order, #3, #8, and #5, your daily double tickets (usually costing $2 each) will be 2/3, 2/8, 2/5; 6/3, 6/8, 6/5 and 1/3, 1/8, 1/5. In addition, the two top picks in each race should be played in the same manner: 2/3, 2/8 and 6/3, 6/8.

Playing the top choice in the first race with the top choice in the second race is, again, a matter of judgment. If three horses in each race are played in full combination, a total of 14 tickets are possible. At $2 each, the total investment would be $28.

Making money with the daily double can become an art (and a profitable one at that!) if you successfully call the winner of the first race and use potential payoff odds to your advantage with "hedge betting." Here is a real-life example:

Assume that your #1 choice, **Battle Crown,** won the first race and you are holding the following potential payoff tickets for the double . . .

1st choice: **So So Sorry** (5 to 1), 3 tickets @ $81 each;

2nd choice: **Homestead Boy** (3 to 1), 2 tickets @ $52 each;

3rd choice: **Gatogay** (8 to 1), 1 ticket @ $95.

There are seven other horses in the race. Of these, only three are given a remote chance of beating your three choices to the finish line. Two are "long-shots," plus **Suedburg Express,** 4 to 1, and also fourth choice in your exacta betting. You did not play this horse in the double. The other two horses are **Au Fait** (10 to 1) and **Cultured Blade** (10 to 1). Knowing the chances are very good that one of your top two choices will finish first or second, what is the best way to bet this race and thus be reasonably sure that you walk away with a nice profit in the daily double?

The answer is to hedge by betting straight exactas with the two long-shot horses on top of each of your best two, plus four straight exacta tickets, two with **Suedburg Express** on top of **So So Sorry** and two on top of **Homestead Boy.** By spending another $16, you can be reasonably sure that you will make money with the double.

The results of this race:

1st	**So So Sorry**
2nd	**Homestead Boy**
3rd	**Cultured Blade**
4th	**Suedburg Express**

Exacta paid $39.60
Daily Double paid $81.80

One additional advantage that computer handicappers have over those applying the "shortcut" version is the greater ease of finding a "key horse" in each race. When the bettor has ONE horse in which he or she has great confidence running first or second, it helps significantly when playing an exotic wager. Write or call Liberty Publishing Company for more information on this subject.

Now a few words of caution are in order . . .

When using the *Performance Method*, it is important to realize that you cannot win *every* time you go to the track. It works best over time. And never take to the track more money than you can afford to lose. For most of us, this is an enjoyable hobby. Be carefree (note: care*free*, not care*less*) with this game. Money should only be a means of keeping score. Do not let it become more than just an enjoyable hobby—unless you plan to become a professional handicapper.

Finally, never bet "everything" on what seems to be a certainty. More than once I've been on my way to the pay window only to have my winner disqualified. There is no such thing as a sure thing.

In Search of the "Dark Horse"

It happens once in a while. Expect it. Your bets are down, the horses are now approaching the finish line and out of the clear blue sky, a mystery horse emerges to win or place upsetting your chance of going to the cashier's window. "Where the hell did he come from?" is your immediate reaction.

For every one hundred races that you bet, there will be no fewer than fifteen that can be called a complete surprise. It's simply the nature of this sport. However, many of the mystery horses that come out of the blue can be anticipated, even when they do not figure in your calculations initially. What are some of their common characteristics? Can the surprises be kept to a minimum? If so, how?

By reviewing many past races in which a "dark horse" upset my exacta or quinella, one or more of these "warning signs" seemed to be present in most cases. In the order of their importance, they are:

1. Within the last 60 days, the mystery horse had run a faster split (4 furlongs for sprints, or 6 furlongs for route races) than had either my #1 or #2 choice in its last race.

2. In either of its last two races, the mystery horse gained at least two lengths in the last quarter mile, or in the stretch, vs. the competition in that particular race.

3. In the past, the mystery horse had, at least once, beaten either my #1 or #2 choice in another race of a similar, or nearly similar, distance to today's race.

4. The mystery horse has earned more money in its lifetime, or has been in as many exactas in the past year or two than either the #1 or #2 choice.

5. Within the past two months, the mystery horse has been given an active schedule of at least three or four workouts, often including one of five or more furlongs, disregarding the times.

As a general rule, *very few* of the mystery horses had records so poor they had to be completely overlooked. In fact, it can be said they were simply good enough to win and, most importantly, fit and ready to run. The majority of these mystery horses had run at least within four lengths of the leader, or no worse than fourth place at some point during one or both of its last two races. (Read this sentence once again, along with #1 and #2 on the preceding page.)

Please note, these are just "warning signs" and not meant to be more than just that. They are merely indications that any horse that possesses one or more of these signs should be given a second look before the final three or four horses are bet. Perhaps this new horse should be added to the betting scheme. Remember, the selections made by the *Performance Method* are not set in stone, but simply a guide for better handicapping. Shuffle them around according to your best judgment, keeping in mind that one of the two best totals stands a good chance of being in the exacta.

If you are using the *Winning at the Track* computer program, also be sure to check the Speed Ranking table (for sprints) and Last Quarter Ranking table (for routes) to uncover any potential surprise. They are extremely valuable tools when making your final selections.

Users of *The Pace Analyst* software should also learn to apply its "depth of talent" feature. It is possible for a horse's *third-best* race to be better than the *best* race of a competing animal. When this situation presents itself, an overlay is not uncommon.

APPENDIX A

How to calculate an average purse:

HORSE	TOTAL RACES	WINS	PLACE	SHOW
Mt. Excellor	24	2	6	4

TOTAL WINNINGS
$30,000

	Normal % Share of Any Purse		No. of Purses
2 wins	x .65	=	1.3
6 place	x .20	=	1.2
4 show	x .10	=	0.4
	TOTAL		2.9

$30,000 Total Winnings ÷ 2.9 = $10,345 average purse

Appendix B

Here is a list of track records for more than 50 of the most important dirt tracks in North America. Included are the best times recorded for 6 furlongs, 7 furlongs, 1 mile, 1 mile-70 yards, 1 1/16 miles, and 1 1/8 miles. The records for additional distances and tracks may be found in the *American Racing Manual* in most libraries. New records are made from time to time. Therefore, some care should be taken when these figures are used to compute your Adjustment Tables.

	6F	7F	1 mi	1.70	1 1/16	1 1/8
Ak-Sar-Ben (Aks) Omaha, NE	107 2/5	–	138 2/5	139 2/5	140 3/5	147 2/5
Albuquerque (Alb) Albuquerque, NM	108 3/5	121	136	141 3/5	142 1/5	149 4/5
Aqua Caliente (AC) Tijuana, Mexico	107 4/5	123 3/5	134	138 2/5	141	147 4/5
Aqueduct Jamaica, NY						
Inner Track (AQI)	108 4/5	–	140 2/5	140	141 4/5	148 2/5
Outer Track (AQU)	108	120 1/5	132 2/5	–	–	147
Arlington (AP) Arlington Heights, IL	108	120 2/5	132 1/5	142 4/5	141 2/5	146 1/5
Atlantic City (Atl) Atlantic City, NJ	108 1/5	120 2/5	–	–	141	146 3/5
Bay Meadows (BM) San Mateo, CA	107 4/5	–	133 3/5	141 3/5	138 2/5	146 1/5
Belmont (Bel) Jamaica, NY	107 4/5	120 2/5	133	–	140 2/5	145 2/5
Bowie (Bow) Bowie, MD (closed)	108	120 2/5	139	143	140 1/5	148 4/5
Calder (Crc) Opa-Locka, FL	110	123	137 3/5	142	143 4/5	150

	6F	7F	1 mi	1.70	1 1/16	1 1/8
Charles Town (CT) Charles Town, WV	111 4/5	124	–	–	144	150 1/5
Churchill Downs (CD) Louisville, KY	108 3/5	121 1/5	133 4/5	141 3/5	141 3/5	148 2/5
Delaware Park (Del) Wilmington, DE	108 1/5	–	135 1/5	139 2/5	141 3/5	147 2/5
Del Mar (Dmr) Del Mar, CA	107 3/5	120 2/5	133 3/5	–	140	146
Detroit Race Course (Det) Livonia, MI	108	–	135 4/5	139 2/5	140 3/5	147 2/5
Exhibition Park (EP) Vancouver, B.C.	110 2/5	–	–	140 2/5	142 1/5	148 2/5
Fair Grounds (FG) New Orleans, LA	109	–	138 3/5 (1 mi. 40 yds.)	–	142 2/5	148 4/5
Fairplex Park (Fpx) Pomona, CA	109 2/5	123 3/5	–	–	142 1/5	148 3/5
Finger Lakes (FL) Canandaigua, NY	109 1/5	126 4/5	136 4/5	140 1/5	143 1/5	151
Fresno (Fno) Fresno, CA	108	–	133 4/5	–	139 4/5	146 2/5
Golden Gate Fields (GG) Albany, CA	107 4/5	–	133	–	139 4/5	145
Gulfstream Park (GP) Hallandale, FL	107 4/5	120 4/5	–	139 3/5	140 1/5	146 2/5
Hawthorne (Haw) Cicero, IL	108 1/5	–	–	140 2/5	139 3/5	146 3/5
Hazel Park (HP) Hazel Park, MI	110 2/5	–	136 3/5	139 1/5	139 3/5	146 3/5
Hialeah Park (Hia) Hialeah, FL	108	120 3/5	136 3/5	–	140 2/5	146 1/5

	6F	7F	1 mi	1.70	1 1/16	1 1/8
Hollywood Park (Hol) Inglewood, CA	108 1/5	120 4/5	132 3/5	–	140	147 2/5
Keeneland (Kee) Lexington, KY	108 2/5	121 1/5	–	–	141 1/5	146 4/5
Laurel Race Course (Lrl) Laurel, MD	108 3/5	122 1/5	134 2/5	–	141 4/5	148 1/5
Longacres (Lga) Renton, WA	107 1/5	–	133 4/5	–	139 4/5	146 3/5
Los Alamitos (LA) Los Alamitos, CA	108 3/5	121 3/5	–	–	141	146 3/5
Louisiana Downs (LaD)	108 2/5	121 3/5	–	139 2/5	140 4/5	149
The Meadowlands (Med) East Rutherford, NJ	108 2/5	–	135	139 1/5	140 3/5	146 3/5
Monmouth Park (Mth) Oceanport, NJ	108	–	133 4/5	139 1/5	141	146 4/5
Oaklawn Park (OP) Hot Springs, AK	108	–	134 2/5	138 2/5	140 1/5	146 3/5
Penn National (Pen) Grantville, PA	108 4/5	–	136 1/5	140	141 1/5	149 4/5
Philadelphia Park (Pha) Bensalem, PA	108 1/5	121 2/5	134 4/5	139	140 4/5	147
Pimlico Race Course (Pim) Baltimore, MD	109 1/5	126	137 3/5	141 2/5	140 4/5	148 2/5
Pleasanton (Pln) Pleasanton, CA	108 2/5	–	136 1/5	138 4/5	140 4/5	147
Portland Meadows (PM) Portland, OR	109 2/5	–	136 1/5	144 1/5	143 1/5	148 4/5
River Downs (RD) Cincinnati, OH	108 3/5	128 4/5	136 1/5	140	141 4/5	149
Sacramento (Sac) Sacramento, CA	107 4/5	–	134 4/5	–	140 3/5	146 1/5

	6F	7F	1 mi	1.70	1 1/16	1 1/8
Santa Anita Park (SA) Arcadia, CA	107 3/5	120	133 3/5	–	140 1/5	145 4/5
Santa Rosa (SR) Santa Rosa, CA	108	–	134 2/5	–	139 4/5	147 2/5
Saratoga (Sar) Saratoga Springs, NY	108	120 2/5	134 4/5	–	–	147
Solano (Sol) Vallejo, CA	108 1/5	124 4/5	134 4/5	–	139 4/5	148 2/5
Sportsman's Park (Spt) Cicero, IL	110	–	136	–	142 4/5	149
Stockton (Stk) Stockton, CA	109 2/5	–	135 3/5	–	140 3/5	149 4/5
Suffolk Downs (Suf) East Boston, MA	108 1/5	–	135 1/5	140	141 4/5	147 3/5
Tampa Bay Downs (Tam) Oldsmar, FL	109	124	142 3/5	141 4/5	143 4/5	151
Thistledown (Tdn) Cleveland, OH	108 2/5	–	135 4/5	141	141 4/5	147 2/5
Turf Paradise (TuP) Phoenix, AZ	106 4/5	126 1/5	133 4/5	–	139 1/5	148 1/5
Woodbine (Wo) Rexdale, Ontario	108 3/5	121 4/5	–	140 3/5	141 4/5	148

Below are several more North American tracks contained in the computer program. There are others. Check the program's HELP menu for a more complete listing.

Assiniboia Downs (ASD)
Atokad Park (Ato)
Balmoral Park (Bml)
Canterbury Downs (CBY)
Columbus (Cls)
Ellis Park (Elp)
Fairmount Park (FP)
Ferndale (Fer)
Fonner Park (Fon)
Garden State (GS)
Jefferson Downs (JnD)

La Mesa Park (LaM)
Lincoln State Fair (LnN)
Northampton (Nmp)
Playfair (Pla)
Remington Park (RP)
Rockingham Park (Rkm)
Santa Fe (SFe)
Stampede Park (Stp)
Sunland Park (Sun)
Turfway Park (TP)
Yakima Meadows (YM)

Every few issues, the *Daily Racing Form* prints a list of times on which their Speed Ratings are based. This list shows the best times recorded over the three preceding years for each distance at each race track. These racing times are most likely different from the historic track records appearing in the tables on pages 144-147. In fact, because the *DRF* figures change as often as they do, this book could never be published frequently enough to keep the list current. The computer program calculates most of the necessary figures internally and is, of course, improved and updated regularly.

Index

Acknowledgments

The author and the publisher express gratitude to the Daily Racing Form, Inc. for the use of their copyrighted materials and to the Maryland Jockey Club at Pimlico Race Course for their assistance.

Additional information about the *Daily Racing Form* newspaper may be obtained by contacting:

Daily Racing Form
10 Lake Drive
P.O. Box 1015
Hightstown, N.J. 08520

or

Daily Racing Form
170 South Bimini Place
Los Angeles, CA 90004

Winning at the Track Software will run on any IBM PC or IBM-compatible using MS- or PC-DOS (including Tandy models 1000, 1200 and 3000) with a minimum memory of 256k.

The software, written in pascal, automatically corrects to more than 140 track surfaces, dirt or turf, and features a parallel speed table to adjust 14 different distances.

The package includes a 5¼″ floppy disc and a copy of this book. If you own this book and do not need another copy, please indicate this when ordering. The price of the complete package is $49.95 ($39.95 without the book) plus $3.00 for shipping. Please add $20.00 if you require a 3½″ disc. The package does not include **The Pace Analyst.**

(305) 360-9000

SOFTWARE ORDER FORM

To: **Liberty Publishing Company, Inc.**
440 South Federal Highway
Deerfield Beach, Florida 33441

Gentlemen:

Please rush my **Winning at the Track** software program. I expect the package to be shipped to me UPS. The prices below include shipping costs.

______ Enclosed is $52.95 ($72.95 for 3½″ format) for another book and diskette.

______ I do not need another book. Enclosed is $42.95 ($62.95 for 3½″ format) for a diskette only.

______ Yes, I would like to learn more about **The Pace Analyst** software.

Ship to:

____
(Name)

____
(Street)

____
(City and Zip)

To: **Liberty Publishing Company, Inc.**
440 South Federal Highway
Deerfield Beach, Florida 33441

Gentlemen:

Please rush forty (40) 8½″ × 11″ blank *Performance Method* Tables. Enclosed is my check or money order for $6.95 plus $1.00 for shipping and handling.

Ship to:

____
(Name)

____
(Street)

____
(City and Zip)

To: **Liberty Publishing Company, Inc.**
440 South Federal Highway
Deerfield Beach, Florida 33441

Gentlemen:

Please rush forty (40) 8½″ × 11″ blank *Performance Method* Tables. Enclosed is my check or money order for $6.95 plus $1.00 for shipping and handling.

Ship to:

____
(Name)

____
(Street)

____
(City and Zip)

To: **Liberty Publishing Company, Inc.**
440 South Federal Highway
Deerfield Beach, Florida 33441

Gentlemen:

Please rush forty (40) 8½″ × 11″ blank *Performance Method* Tables. Enclosed is my check or money order for $6.95 plus $1.00 for shipping and handling.

Ship to:

____
(Name)

____
(Street)

____
(City and Zip)